POETRY OF THE NINETIES

Poetry of the Nineties

With an Introductory Essay
by C. E. Andrews and
M. O. Percival

New York
Harcourt, Brace and Company

COPYRIGHT, 1926, BY

HARCOURT, BRACE AND COMPANY, INC.

PRINTED IN THE U·S·A

To

JOSEPH VILLIERS DENNEY

CONTENTS

Contents

Contents

POETRY OF THE NINETIES

INTRODUCTION

A NEW poetry was inevitable in the eighteen-nineties, for a spirit of change was abroad, recreating everything. Those were the days of bicycles and bridge, of ladies' clubs and comic operas, of the yellow press and the *Yellow Book*, the short story and the problem play. The Victorian extinguisher, which had descended upon the extravagances of the Romantic Movement, was removed, and the fire rekindled. The age surrendered to the younger generation, who were determined not to walk in the ways of Queen Victoria and Mrs. Grundy. Those potentates had been challenged, in the plenitude of their power, by Swinburne; but he had winced under their disapproval, and he was, in his rebellion, a rather lonely, though brilliant figure. Thirty years were to be required before such figures could arise on every hand and captivate a generation. In the nineties youth behaved with an audacity that bewildered their Victorian elders. Press and periodical solemnly discussed the menace of " revolting daughters." The indictment reads oddly enough today. They were dismissing chaperons; they were riding bicycles, even in knickerbockers; they were invading the tennis courts and the golf links; they were brightening the color of their cheeks with rouge; they were writing plays, and demanding votes and university degrees; they were using slang and smoking cigarettes; they went slumming in the East End and served in rescue homes; they were establishing clubs and clubhouses, where they discussed literature or politics, and sometimes played at cards for money. A few of them mentioned their own latchkey. " Their mothers," it was urged against them, " did none of these things! " The revolting sons had fewer opportunities for exploitation; but they turned Bohemian not only with the readiness that youth

3

always grants to fashion, but with the joyousness of school-
boys entering upon a holiday. Paris became the literary
capital of England. The astonishing success of *Trilby* must
have been largely due to the allurement of the Latin Quarter; a Parisian setting and a few French phrases gave
piquancy to many a short story; while in the actual life of
men of letters, Paris and Dieppe seemed hardly more than
remote suburbs of London. Those who had to remain at
home, if they belonged to the world of fashion, adopted the
Parisian custom of dining out. After dinner the dice
rattled in the box, cards were flung upon the table, and
money changed hands rapidly. The man who broke the
bank at Monte Carlo was a hero. England was becoming
merry. It could even dally with imbecility. No popular
song had ever enjoyed such vogue as Ta-ra-ra-boom-de-ay.
Introduced by Lottie Collins at a popular music hall, it
soon became a country-wide continuous performance. The
judicious grieved in vain. They discussed the odium of its
origin as carefully as we have canvassed the origin of jazz,
but the song raged on. Max Beerbohm did not boast, but
wrote the sober truth of history when he declared, in the
Yellow Book: " The Victorian era comes to its end, and the
day of sancta simplicitas is quite ended."

If the manners and fashions of the Victorian age had
ended, it was but natural that Victorian literature should
also come to an end. And so it did. The literature which
followed was extremely conscious of the Victorian past and
the French present; these might be called the negative and
positive poles of its inspiration. It saw in Victorian literature mainly things to challenge or avoid; it saw in French
literature models for imitation — the realistic novel and the
poetry of the Parnassians. Victorian writers had not gone
further in faithful portrayal of life than realistic scenes and
characters; the warp and woof of their literary tapestries
were always woven within the moral law. Poetic justice
ruled even prose. The wicked are not successful in the
end; the good do not perish utterly; love does not prosper

apart from marriage. The nineties admitted the ideal appropriateness of such conclusions, but did not always find them in their observation of the facts of life — nor in their favorite French novels, nor in Ibsen's plays. Certain authors undertook, in all high seriousness, to represent life with increased sincerity. Others were gay and irreverent, rather than highly serious, and were not so much concerned with the tree of Victorian morality as with the twin cherubs of decorum and respectability, which had so jealously guarded it. To *épater le bourgeois* became literary sport. And there was much in the Victorian tradition to urge a Beardsley or a Shaw, or any spirited young fellow, to the attack. For it had been an age when the Reviews could say that *Jane Eyre* could not have been written by a respectable woman; and that *Enoch Arden* was of doubtful morality — it extenuated concubinage! This latter charge was indignantly refuted by the *Quarterly,* which proclaimed the poet "one of the chosen few who have held the proud honour of never uttering one single line which an English mother once would wish unwritten, or an English girl would wish unread." The Victorians accomplished great work in spite of reticence. But at last the bars were drawn, and the time had come to do new things, among them the very thing that had been forbidden the Victorians, and even because it had been forbidden them.

The new spirit showed itself in poetry as well as in novel and drama. Tennyson fell into disrepute on account of his Victorianism. The *Quarterly* reviewer alluded to above had hoped that the fitness of Tennyson's poetry for mothers and daughters would, in the poet's old age, be his dearest memory. It became his besetting sin with the younger generation. Tennyson's muse is very feminine and very decorous. He could create an Elaine for the *Idylls of the King* but not an Arthur; and he provided Elaine with a chaperon, lest her tendance upon the wounded Lancelot be called in question. The *Idylls* alienated Tennyson from the younger poets, who thought that the wild flowers of medieval romance had withered in their trim Victorian garden; but they brought him into still closer association with the Queen. Her portrait, which commonly adorned the homes of the middle class, may be said to have commonly looked down upon the works of her poet laureate; and there is something sinister in the coincidence — something that tends to justify Mr. Chesterton's pitiless remark, that Tennyson " really did hold a great many of the same views as Queen Victoria, though he was gifted with a more fortunate literary style." The poets of the nineties repudiated such ideas, no matter what their style. Most of them would have cared as little for Elaine as Lancelot did; and would not have wished to wear, or to make their heroes wear, with Arthur, the white flower of a blameless life. Their heroine is often Vivien; not, however, a romantic medieval Vivien, but the common one of street and music hall. And their hero is — not Tomlinson.

As the field of poetry expanded in one direction it contracted in another. The Victorians were deeply interested in the new science, and the challenge that it made to previous interpretations of life. Science is in continual hostility to poetry because it is continually reducing to a level of rationalistic explanation facts and experiences which hitherto have been subject to the degree of emotion which is a necessary element of poetry. Thus Keats decried science because it had destroyed the poetry of the rainbow, and enrolled it in the dull catalogue of common things. This complaint, which poets often make, is not entirely just; for if science removes one veil of mystery it is only to reveal deeper and deeper depths; and so, in theory, the field of poetry should be enlarged. But these new areas cannot be immediately entered; they may be difficult for a poet, not scientifically trained, to understand; they may make demands on his imagination which he cannot fulfill. This is the situation in which the Victorian poets found themselves. Their whole theory of life had been shaken by the new evolutionary science. The problem could not be ignored; it was too new and interesting and terrible. The Victorian poets were notably concerned with it, sounding all the notes, from glad acceptance to despair. But their efforts did not commend them to the generation of the nineties. The poets of that decade were weary of the problem. Some of them seem to be as ignorant of science as Queen Victoria herself; others seem to know it and wish sadly to forget. Some believe that subjects of that sort are not true themes for poetry; others hold that reason cannot solve the problem. The common element in these various attitudes is that none of the poets undertake discussion. They give no reason for their position. In the poetry of this volume one has to look beneath the surface to find any evidence of the profound disturbance of life that science had created.

The new spirit of the nineties expressed itself characteristically in the Rhymers' Club and the *Yellow Book*. Both undertakings reflect the eagerness and confidence of youth that has faith in itself and in its time. The Rhymers' Club consisted of about a dozen members [1] who, for several years, gathered regularly at the Cheshire Cheese, where they smoked long clay pipes, drank a little wine, and talked of poetry. John Davidson thought the club wanted " blood and guts " ; and certainly it did want the vigor and spontaneity that we associate with the gatherings at the Mermaid Tavern, or the social and intellectual qualities that made the meetings at Mallarmé's house so influential. The Rhymers were deeply influenced by French poetry, and the younger members had adopted from France the belief that poetry should not concern itself with public interests, or with theories and generalizations of any kind. This faith

---

[1] The members of the Rhymers' Club were: John Davidson, Ernest Dowson, Edwin J. Ellis, G. A. Greene, Lionel Johnson, A. C. Hillier, Richard Le Gallienne, Victor Plarr, Ernest Radford, Ernest Rhys, T. W. Rolleston, Arthur Symons, John Todhunter, W. B. Yeats. (John Davidson did not contribute to either of the Rhymers' volumes.) The Club often met at the residence of one or another of its members.

they carried not only into their poetry but into their meetings also. One of the members, fresh from Paris, would say, " We are concerned with nothing but impressions "; but that itself was a generalization, and was received with stony silence. Under such a taboo, conversation languished. Any departure from conventionality of dress was frowned upon. " One should be quite unnoticeable," Lionel Johnson explained to Yeats, who had erred in this respect. Certainly the Cheshire Cheese, under the Rhymers' influence, stands in strange contrast with the Mermaid Tavern. The Mermaid stood at the center of national life, and roared with activity and mirth. The Cheshire Cheese, when possessed by the Rhymers' Club, had the remoteness and something of the silence of a convent. And yet we must not be misled into a harsh judgment by Yeats's rather gloomy recollections. One thing is undeniable — that some of the best poetry of the decade was first read at those meetings, and first published in the two volumes of the Rhymers' Club.

The *Yellow Book*, excelling in prose, rather than in poetry, also saw the first publication of some distinguished work. As one looks over the early numbers, mindful of the excitement they aroused, one is at first somewhat puzzled to account for it. It is true that the size and color, and sometimes the contents, suggested a French novel. It is almost incredible, and yet it is a fact, that the merry essays of Max Beerbohm were caviled at; and if this be so, what misgiving and apprehension must have been aroused by the gay and satirical irreverence of Aubrey Beardsley? Oscar Wilde did not contribute to the *Yellow Book*, and was, indeed, thoroughly disliked by its publisher, John Lane; but at his trial he had the impudence to carry a copy of it to the witness stand. It was felt in certain quarters that the *Yellow Book* would have to declare its principles. Mrs. Humphry Ward urged William Watson to the challenge. Watson had contributed to the earlier numbers, and his work expressed the Victorian tradition, as Beardsley's expressed the spirit of the nineties. It presently became noised about that Watson had assumed his task and was prepared to make the last sacrifice. Just what, if anything, this grandiloquent phrase meant cannot be stated; but it indicates the nervousness of the time. What William Watson did was to write to the editor of the *Yellow Book* and impose upon him the necessity of choosing between his own work and Beardsley's. In this dilemma the editor, in a fit of excitement, chose Watson. Beardsley was abruptly dismissed; the designs that he had made for the forthcoming number were canceled; and volume five opened with Watson's *Hymn to the Sea,* a piece of surging rhetoric that easily submerged all anxiety about the *Yellow Book.*

Thus chastened, the *Yellow Book* continued its career through thirteen numbers. But some of the younger-spirited contributors withdrew, and at the beginning of the following year (1896) founded the *Savoy.* Arthur Symons was editor and Aubrey Beardsley art editor of the new periodical. The first number contained drawings by Aubrey Beardsley, Max Beerbohm, and Joseph Pennell; and prose and verse by Arthur Symons, Ernest Dowson, W. B. Yeats, Havelock Ellis, and Bernard Shaw. Seldom does a periodical make such an offering, and the *Savoy* was prepared to maintain those standards. But the British public was indifferent and the new venture died at the conclusion of the year.

❖

The men of the nineties in their attitude to life and in their theory of the relation of poetry to life differed widely among themselves, but in two things they were evidently in agreement. Poetry should free itself as far as possible from ideas and should discard an excess of sentiment. It might express life directly or it might escape from life in a dream of some imagined beauty; it might find its source in human action, or in some visual impression, or in a mood.

But these things should not be reasoned about or explained; it was sufficient merely to present an action, a personality, a picture, or a mood. The significance or point, if there were any, was to be left to the mind of the reader. At one extreme is the obvious poetry of action in Kipling's songs and ballads, which may be appreciated by readers who do not think about the world at all, but just enjoy it; and at the other extreme there are the subtle mystical moods of A. E. and Yeats, which may suggest to another type of reader musings and reflections which take him beyond the flaming ramparts of the world. But in neither of these kinds of poetry does the poet tell or explain; he merely presents his picture or suggests his mood. When Verlaine tried to translate *In Memoriam* he gave up the task, saying: " Tennyson is too noble, too *anglais;* when he should have been broken-hearted, he has many reminiscences." This might also be taken to express the feeling that the poets of the nineties felt for the seer who ruled Victorian poetry. They hated his attempt to reason himself into an acceptance of orthodox views of life and death, and they hated the sentimental haze through which he looked at life in *Enoch Arden* and *Maud*. There was a lack of sincerity in these things; this was a poetry which represented life as conforming to an accepted theory. The eighteen-nineties believed in frankly admitting that life did not conform to theories. Mr. Yeats in a conversation once remarked, " Sentimentality is deceiving one's self, and rhetoric is deceiving other people." The contemporaries of Mr. Yeats were trying to eliminate sentimentality and rhetoric, as well as argument and explanation from poetry.

There was, of course, much Victorian poetry that was not sentimental and much that was not thoughtful. In the *Northern Farmer* Tennyson looked straight at life and told the truth, and there are many great lyrics in *In Memoriam* that are as utterly broken-hearted as Verlaine could have wished them. And there are Browning's monologues and Morris's ballads. But the Browning and Tennyson which we read today is only about a quarter of their work; the other three quarters loomed larger to the eighties and nineties, for time had not made the selection. And the members of the younger generation were more conscious of the faults of their predecessors than of their virtues.

Stevenson in his novels and essays was one of the first to react from the Victorian literature that was written with a theory of life behind it, and presented as his philosophy: " Do not have any philosophy. Do not think about life, but live it and enjoy it." And the poets Kipling and Henley, both great forces in the nineties, wrote from the same point of view. If either of them had any interest in the apparently discrepant conclusions of science and religion about the world their poetry does not show it. And far from feeling the ugliness of an industrial world which drove the Pre-Raphaelites to the refuge of dreams, they gloried in everyday life and saw it as poetry.

Kipling is interested in the external life of men, their appearance, their actions, their speech. He cares little for their thoughts and nothing for their theories. There is no room in heaven or hell for Tomlinson with his secondhand philosophies and his secondhand experiences and his book-read sins:

" Ye have read, ye have heard, ye have thought," he said, " and
  the tale is yet to run:
By the worth of the body that once ye had, give answer
  —what ha' ye done? "

Kipling finds inspiration not in the ruling classes or the thinking classes, but in the people who are in the thick of life, the workers, fighters, explorers, or tramps. He dislikes conventional people, conventional actions and conventional language — and above all, hypocrisy. The world of people who do not conform, the Victorians ignored or sentimentalized, or else excused by placing them back in those wicked old unenlightened times when people did such things, for time whitewashes the blackness of evil. But

Kipling wrote of the British soldier, sailor, and tramp as he knew them, without apology for their swearing or their sinning. He did not sentimentalize about them; the sentiment in *Mandalay* is the sentiment in the British soldier himself.

To Kipling the poetry of life is in action. He loves people who do difficult things, who show courage in struggling with obstacles. He admires the engineer, the border-thief, Tommy Atkins, and the explorer, for their stout-hearted fighting qualities, and for their sincerity and manliness. And he admires these qualities anywhere in the world, under brown skins or white, in enemies and lawbreakers as well as in friends.

And a part of his acceptance of life is his love of the great industrial and commercial civilization of which he is a part. Nothing in the world is ugly to him. The railway trestle, the hold of a cattle boat, the frontiersman's shack, the engine room of a liner, a drunken soldier's guard-house cell, Hotchkiss guns, lobster-pots, or whackin' white cheroots may be the material out of which poetry is made. Kipling sees all these things and finds them good. He shows us modern life and does not want it made over; it is already to his heart's desire.

Another poet with the same spirit of acceptance of life as it is, is William Ernest Henley. He accepts it with a Whitman-like exultation, a joyous love of living itself. He takes the crosses and troubles and the blunders with a stoical fortitude, for there are also love and work and friendship and dreaming and art and drink — all of them part of the fullness and the goodness of life. And he looks forward to death with the calm of Rabbi ben Ezra. But Henley's optimism, like Kipling's, is emotional rather than philosophic. They *feel* that the world is good, but they do not try to prove that it is. Browning's optimism was also a part of his temperament — as optimism always is — but, being a Victorian, he liked to speculate upon it, to find a cause for it, and he tried to base it upon a philosophy.

And this attempt to be logical about an attitude which can only be emotional led him to some strange judgments and some paradoxical positions. Primitive Italian art is superior to perfect Greek art merely because of its imperfection, and life is good not merely in spite of its failures, but because of them! Failures are a proof of the existence of heaven! Henley never falls into these pitfalls of logic, because he has no logic. He does not feel an intellectual necessity of proving that life is good; he accepts his own intuition about it and goes on living it in its fullness and shouts in the face of the world that he is the master of his fate and the captain of his soul.

This famous battle cry is altogether un-Victorian. Neither the orthodox Christian nor the scientist can feel that he is the master of his fate. But it is the man who will not rationalize about either point of view who can feel this, and who substitutes for thought his own moods and emotions.

But in the moods of Henley there are many admissions of the glooms and shadows of life, for he is not an optimist as the result of experience but by the force of temperament and will. He does not, as Browning did in *La Saisiaz*, admit that life would be unbearable but for his certainty of personal immortality, for Henley's immortality is but an eternal peace:

> Life — give me life until the end,
> That at the very top of being,
> The battle-spirit shouting in my blood,
> Out of the reddest hell of the fight
> I may be snatched and flung
> Into the everlasting lull,
> The immortal, uncommunicable dream.

No one could doubt the sincerity of Henley, but in these poems that rejoice in life even at its very darkest — especially at its darkest — there is something of the spirit of Mark Tapley, who always " came out strong " under adverse circumstances. He seems to be whistling in the dark to keep up his courage. He has the optimism of an invalid determined to be cheerful.

And his invalidism too, is perhaps responsible for a love of activity that sometimes actually becomes a love of ferocity. He praises war and holds to a politic dependent upon it. Not only is life in general good, but English life and English civilization. It is so good that it must be spread over the world. He has no conflicts and doubts about commercialism and imperialism, like the young man in *Locksley Hall*. Henley is so sure of his civilization that he sings the *Song of the Sword*, the glorious instrument of its propagation. Neither Henley nor Kipling questions the values of English standards. These are so good that we must take up the white man's burden and spread them over the earth. This means the shedding of blood, but that in itself is a fine, manly thing.

But the best of Henley is neither in his fierce imperialism and his love of strength nor in his shrill optimism. It is in his pictures of London life. He loves London, its streets, its traffic, its workers, its cold fogs, its warm autumn sunsets, its lights at night, and its fleeting contacts of human millions. Kipling knows human character better than Henley, but Henley feels the significance of the lights, colors, lines, and movement that make up a painter's world. And he groups these impressions so that they create moods. The *London Voluntaries* are the work of a poet who puts into words the great glorifying dream that the surging life of London may inspire in a painter and a musician. It is the cosmic emotion of Whitman's mind expressed by a nature with finer senses and a more subtle perception of values. Henley's joyous acceptance of life transfigures the commonplace multitude of city impressions in which no Victorian poet could find poetry, and makes of them the romantic vision of a newly discovered modern world.

A. E. Housman is another poet who faces the visible world with stoical acceptance and refuses either to reflect about life or to dream. He finds no ultimate good in life and is cynical about the hope of immortality, but like the old cynic who wrote *Ecclesiastes* and found nothing but vanity in life, he perceives that " there is nothing better than that a man should rejoice in his own works: for that is his portion: for who shall bring him to see what shall be after him? " The lyrics that make up the *Shropshire Lad* have the pagan view of the world, that life has no final meaning, but that there is love and beauty in it to be enjoyed, and suffering and trouble in it to be accepted manfully. He loves the fleeting things of life as Horace does, and bears the wrong of the universe with Marcus Aurelius. And like the Latin poets, Housman finds symbols of this view of the world in the peaceful bucolic life. He finds pleasure in the wild green hills of Shropshire, the sighing poplars, the sky-lit water, the lady-smocks, the crocuses and daffodils; in country fairs and athletic bouts, and in the sight of handsome girls and lads and red-coated soldiers.

These things in life are lovely, but the beauty of the death-stricken year cannot last, and heaven and earth ail from the prime foundation. There is a note of sadness in almost every one of the lyrics. Housman is preoccupied with the thought of death, which is the end of the pleasantness of life; the lovers lie two and two in the graveyard, and the steeple clock strikes the hour and tells the time to none. And this dwelling on the thought of death has its macabre touch in recurring allusions to hangings and to suicides.

Housman with his beautiful sadness and his pessimistic way of looking at life does not seem to have anything in common with the two poets just considered. But, though his vision is different, he is, like them, facing life and not trying to escape it. And like them he does not believe in thinking about it.

> Think no more, lad; laugh, be jolly,

sings Housman, the pessimist — a line which Stevenson, the optimist, might have written.

> Think no more; 't is only thinking
> Lays lads underground.

And this is the point of view of the poetical generation of the nineties. It is also the point of view of the *Rubaiyat* — a poem that only attained its full popularity in the decade that felt,

> Oh, 't is jesting, dancing, drinking,
> Spins the heavy world around.

And in these lines from another lyric, Housman has again approached the old Persian hedonist:

> And malt does more than Milton can
> To justify God's ways to man.
> Ale, man, ale's the stuff to drink
> For fellows whom it hurts to think.

There was another point of view besides that of accepting life without thinking about it. The Esthetic Movement, which belongs to the eighties, continued to be a strong force until its spectacular collapse at the time of the Wilde trial. This movement which had its origin in the Pre-Raphaelites, and before them in the poetry of Keats, was a reaction against the ugliness of modern life which has sacrificed beauty to utility, and against the democratic standardization of art and conduct, and the suppression of the individuality of the artist. Walter Pater, to whom the young esthetes of Oxford looked as their prophet, taught them to live intensely in a world of intellect and emotions. His estheticism was a withdrawal into the ivory tower, not to dream, but to make every moment count for its fullest in a life of feeling and appreciation. The thought and emotion which the love of the beautiful may inspire was not to be merely a relaxation from the life of getting and spending; it was to be life itself. No moment should be wasted; every pulse-beat should have its part in a life which was made up of an intense appreciation of values.

The followers of Pater, the prophet, came down from the

ivory tower and brought their estheticism into everyday life. But they left behind the intellectual side of Pater, and the gemlike flame was fed purely by emotions. The esthetes' search for beauty became a search for sensations. They did not face the whole of life as did Stevenson, Kipling, and Henley, and they did not seek the remote and unreal beauty of the Pre-Raphaelite painters, but they selected from life its strange colors and its strange experiences. They loved to see in the real world glimpses that *seemed* exotic and remote.

The " incomparable " Max Beerbohm wrote a joyfully amusing picture of the esthetes in his essay " 1880," which appeared in the *Yellow Book.* It has the superiority of 1894, now almost recovered from estheticism, looking back with amused scorn at the preceding decade:

Beauty had existed long before 1880. It was Mr. Oscar Wilde who managed her début. To study the period is to admit that to him was due no small part of the social vogue that Beauty began to enjoy. Fired by his fervid words, men and women hurled their mahogany into the streets and ransacked the curio-shops for the furniture of Annish days. Dadoes arose upon every wall, sunflowers and the feathers of peacocks curved in every corner, tea grew quite cold while the guests were praising the Willow Pattern of its cup. A few fashionable women even dressed themselves in sinuous draperies and unheard-of greens. Into whatsoever ballroom you went, you would surely find, among the women in tiaras and the fops and the distinguished foreigners, half a score of comely ragamuffins in velveteen, murmuring sonnets, posturing, waving their hands. Beauty was sought in the most unlikely places. Young painters found her robed in the fogs, and bank clerks, versed in the writings of Mr. Hamerton, were heard to declare, as they sped home from the City, that the underground railway was beautiful from London Bridge to Westminster, but not from Sloane Square to Notting Hill Gate.

By 1883 Oscar Wilde found himself the acknowledged leader of the esthetes. He had published a volume of poems, he had been ridiculed in *Punch,* had been satirized in *Patience,* and had preached the gospel of beauty in innocent and unbeautiful America. His work in the eighteen-nineties is chiefly prose. In fact, the esthetic movement in literature expressed itself almost wholly in prose. His prose is subtle in style, rich with every kind of fine ornament. He has a love of words for their sound and for their suggestiveness. Max Beerbohm has said of all these prose men, followers of Pater and the modern French stylists, that the *mot juste* was the Holy Grail of the period. They went in for paradox, or archaisms, or a languorous manner, or a love of strange and exotic words, a sheer delight in style for its own sake.

The poetry of Wilde is a poetry that seeks escape from the world in an Endymion-like pursuit of sensuous beauty. It is overrich with ornamental diction and outdoes Keats in love of colors and odors. The *Garden of Eros* expresses the creed of the esthetes, the worship of what they conceived to be the spirit of things Greek:

> Spirit of Beauty! tarry still awhile,
>   They are not dead, thine ancient votaries,
> Some few there are to whom thy radiant smile
>   Is better than a thousand victories,
> Though all the nobly slain of Waterloo
> Rise up in wrath against them! tarry still,
>   There are a few,
> Who for thy sake would give their manlihood
>   And consecrate their being, I at least
> Have done so, made thy lips my daily food,
>   And in thy temples found a goodlier feast
> Than this starved age can give me, spite of all
> Its new-found creeds so sceptical and so dogmatical.

There are only two of Wilde's poems that belong to the nineties, *The Sphinx* and *The Ballad of Reading Gaol*. *The Sphinx* is a long poem on the cat as a symbol of the esoteric, exotic mysteries of the past. It has the love of strangeness, the fearful joy in unusual terror that gives to *Salome* an almost unique fascination in English literature. In such pieces, the esthete in his search for beauty has gone beyond the visible world of the Greeks, and sought a thrill in creating strange imaginings, and in a wonder at exotic forbidden things. But in the other poem, *The Ballad of Reading Gaol,* Wilde, with the terrible memory of his prison experience freshly before him, dropped his search for remote beauty and his interest in the masks which life wore for him, and looked at reality. The man who preached insincerity as a means of multiplying the artist's personalities dropped all his pose and expressed a genuine reaction instead of an attitude. But the poem is overlong and the fearfulness of its impression Wilde has tried to intensify by rhetoric. When Wilde ceased to be an esthete he reverted to Victorianism. One has but to turn from *The Ballad* to *On moonlit heath and lonesome bank* in the *Shropshire Lad* to feel that Wilde at his best is not so true a poet as A. E. Housman. And it is significant of the value of Wilde's estheticism that the one poem in which he turned his back upon it and touched reality is today the most read of all his verse.

The true disciple of Walter Pater is the poet Arthur Symons. He has the scholarly, intellectual side of the great esthete, as well as the sensitiveness to beauty, color, and emotion. Much of the early part of his career was spent in Paris, where he fell in with groups of French men of letters who held views of life and art most congenial to his own temper and to his own theories. He too is an esthete not content to dwell in an ivory tower. He loves reality, but a reality carefully selected for the value of the vivid sensations and vivid emotions it may evoke. As he said of Verlaine, who, next to Pater, had the greatest influence on him, he is " a man who gave its full value to every moment, who got out of every moment all that that moment had to give him. It was not always, not often, perhaps, pleasure. . . . To Verlaine every corner of the world was alive with tempting and consoling and terrifying beauty." Symons loves to look at life for the sheer delight the impression gives his eyes — for, as he was fond of saying, the visible world exists for him; and he loves to experiment with life not

merely for the sake of new emotions themselves, but for the
sake of the intellectual pleasure of trying to understand
them. In his *Credo* he places the highest value on this
desire of the individual for experience:

> If he has any valiancy within,
> If he has made his life his very own,
> If he has loved or labored, and has known
> A strenuous virtue, or a strenuous sin;
> Then, being dead, his life was not all vain.

This is Symons's development of Pater's philosophy of
life and art. From Verlaine and perhaps from Mallarmé,
to whose Tuesday evenings in the rue de Rome he had the
entrée, he caught " that wise and subtle unconsciousness "
in verse, that art of suggesting poetry rather than falling
into explicit eloquence. " Take eloquence and wring its
neck," advised Verlaine, whom he admired for his " art of
painting the fine shades of landscape, of evoking atmosphere
which can be compared only with the art of Whistler."
Symons looks at the world through the eyes of an impressionist. He loves blurred London fogs, moments and half-
seen flashes, yellow lamplight, the faces in a Paris omnibus,
intoxicating eyes across the footlights and the body's
melody of a beautiful dancer, a kiss from lips wet with
Benedictine, or the memory called up by a handkerchief
scented with white heliotrope, or the breath of orchids,
which has power to move the curiosity in his blood.

The poems of Symons written toward the end of the
decade have the sadness of the hedonist's recollections of
lovely moments. The old, weary desire of life, the un-
quenchable flame of desire, still urges him to seek the
beauty of the world, but he finds it now in the memory of
beauty rather than in the joy of immediate moments.
There is still the esthete's love of exquisite glimpses and
rare emotions, but there is also the fear of exhausting the
possibilities of life, that its flame may not burn with the
same intensity. There are gray hours when he drinks of
indifference. There are moments when the world exists

only in his dream, and life becomes a beautiful illusion woven by a lonely god.

Ernest Dowson is another poet who sought to fling the roses of life riotously with the throng. Without the keen intellectual side of Arthur Symons, which produced brilliant and scholarly criticism, Dowson tried to make life purely pleasurable experience. But life to him was " temptation and defeat." He found disillusionment; and a delicate sadness of regret is the mood of his poetry. His themes are the sadness and insufficiency of life, or the refuge of an esthetic mysticism. For his religion he wavered between heaping garlands upon the altars of Aphrodite and Dionysus and lighting candles to the Blessed Virgin.

His poetry is simple and exquisite, direct and sincere in phrase. His range is very narrow and the body of his work is small, but in the moods that he has chosen to express he is a true poet, perhaps the greatest artist of his group. His poem to Cynara — *Non sum qualis eram* — has been praised often as the greatest poem written in the decade of the nineties. It is certainly a poem of the period. At no other time in the nineteenth century could it have been written. Its amazing sincerity belongs to the decade that felt that there is nothing in the emotional life of a poet which he needs to conceal. The Cavalier poets, with a perfection of classic grace, had charmingly idealized their light loves, and romantic and Victorian poetry is filled with perfect expressions of pure devotion. But Dowson in Cynara has dared to be frank about his libertine life in order to make more emphatic his devotion to his pure ideal.

And then there are the religious poems of Dowson, in which, turning from the love and beauty of the world that has become ashes at his touch, he looks with admiration at men who have found lasting beauty in the joy of loving God. Like many others in the generation that tried to live life intensely he sought a final refuge from his defeat in accepting the rites and doctrines of the Roman Church.

At no period in the history of English poetry has the

Catholic Church claimed so many singers of real distinction as in the eighteen-nineties. Of those born in the faith were Francis Thompson, John Gray, Katharine Tynan Hinkson, and Dora Sigerson Shorter. Of the notable converts there were Oscar Wilde, who died in the Church, Ernest Dowson, Lionel Johnson, Alice Meynell, and the still living Laurence Housman, who felt and wrote from the intense experience of their conversion. And to the list must be added the great artist of the period, Aubrey Beardsley. And there are two or three poems in which Arthur Symons, though not a convert, contemplates religious mysticism as one more esthetic emotion. The reasons for this very marked Catholic movement may be found for certain poets in the esthetic appeal and for others in a sense of failure of the Victorian attempt to understand life intellectually.

The esthete who sought pleasure in beauty and in emotions found one more satisfaction in the sheer effect of line and color and composition in the gorgeous ceremonial, the feel of the steady candle flame, the taste of strong, thick, stupefying incense-smoke, the rich associations of age-old symbols in signs and vestments, the echo of the ancient language of the ritual and the astounding daily miracle of the Mass. The lover of emotion found in Catholicism the final experience of transcending all emotion in one great moment of supreme wonder. For those who wished to live intensely, the beauty of religion could not be left out. If there had been a temple to Apollo in London, where beautiful youths and maidens moved in choric processions scattering flowers and incense before pagan ideals, the esthetes would have flocked there, and found a religion that more nearly expressed their attitude; but, that failing them, they adopted the only modern religion with an appeal of beauty.

The Catholic Church thus stood as a refuge of beauty and devotion from a world of pleasure and ugliness and sin. The poets of the preceding group sought the Church only on occasion, or at the end of a worldly life. But the world may be rejected utterly, and life be passed in dream or contemplation. That is the mystic way, and we now come to a group of poets, some of whom within and some without the Church, set foot upon that path.

Lionel Johnson was by nature a student and a recluse. His poetry has the mood of cloistral silences and solitudes. He loves to recall the scholarly atmosphere of Winchester and Oxford; he praises with the enthusiasm of a young B.A. with honors, some score of classics, and writes poems in fluent Latin. His rooms in London were choked with books, scholarly ancient books. It was his custom, says his friend W. B. Yeats, to sleep all day and read or work all night, for actual contact with the world meant nothing to him. " In my library," he said, " I have all the knowledge of the world that I need."

Even before his conversion his mind dwelt on medieval Christianity. Through his historic imagination he came to accept the doctrines of St. Thomas and the faith of St. Francis. " Historic Catholicism, with all its counsels and its dogmas, stirred his passion like the beauty of a mistress." He loved to think of long vigils in austere sanctuaries in the gray peace of Lent. And his heart wished to fear the dark anger of God. It was perhaps because of the very repression of his severe nature that he sought an escape in a poetry that glisters with fires and stars. His cold soul yearned for the ardors of the infinite. He writes with joy of the " sweet white fires of purgatory." He sings of the golden vestures of old saints, of armed angels and white horses, and the flashing swords of the chivalry of God.

But he writes of all these symbols and images of an ancient ideal as of echoes from books in which he believes, rather than remembrances of visions seen. He sings but he does not soar.

Francis Thompson had an excess of the qualities that Johnson lacked. His first ambition was to be a priest, but he was rejected at his college as unfit and this frustration

of purpose is a symbol of his life.   Endowed by nature with
" slow foot " and " swift desire," his life was harried by this
discordance, the swift desire lifting him up to mystic
heights, the slow foot dragging him back to earth.   Traces
of the discord can be discovered in his poetry.   For although his deepest kinship was with the flaming heart of
Crashaw and the ethereal soul of Shelley, he drank in his
youth fairly to intoxication (if we may believe him) of the
sensuous beauty of the world.   Recalling those days, he
says (in his *Anthem of Earth*)

> I broke through thy doors of sunset,
> Ran before the hooves of sunrise,
> Shook thy matron tresses down in fancies
> Wild and wilful
> As a poet's hand could twine them.

The rapture of the early poems frequently breaks out in
fancies of this sort —

> Mark yonder, how the long laburnum drops
> Its jocund spilth of fire, its honey of wild flame;

or this, again, with a touch of Browning's grotesqueness:

> I know in the lane, by the hedgerow tracks
>   The long, broad grasses underneath
> Are warted with rain like a toad's knobbed back.

These are from the Sister Songs — poems that rejoice in
flowers and stars and sky, music and dancing.   The beauty
of women had also thrilled him, as he recalls in *Her
Portrait:*

> My hand hath shook at gentle hands' access
> And trembled at the waving of a tress;
> My blood known panic fear, and fled dismayed,
> Where ladies' eyes have set their ambuscade.

The very excess of emotion might be regarded as fore-
shadowing the inability of such a weakly organized nature
as Francis Thompson's to follow in Love's train or worship

at the shrine of Nature. At any rate, it was not long before he felt Nature's foot upon his neck and cried:

> She is not as we dreamed,
> Ah me! we are beguiled!

The recovery from that collapse is recorded in *The Hound of
Heaven*. The title alludes to Aeschylus's hound, which pur-
sues its prey even under the earth, but the dominant con-
ception is from the Psalms:

> Whither shall I go from thy spirit?
> Or whither shall I flee from thy presence?
> If I ascend up into heaven, thou art there:
> If I make my bed in Sheol, behold, thou art there.
> If I take the wings of the morning,
> And dwell in the uttermost parts of the sea;
> Even there shall thy hand lead me.
> And thy right hand shall hold me.

Something of Job is in it also — in the broken poet's
lamentation, and the Voice that answers him, not from the
whirlwind, but " like a bursting sea," and brings reconciliation.

To one who can look back over Francis Thompson's life,
it is clear that he would be rescued from any attempt to
worship long at pagan altars. For the worldly element in
him was minor — the " slow foot " a slighter thing, after
all, than the " swift desire." Mystics have delighted in
magnifying the wickedness from which they have been
saved. Those laburnums of a previous page came acci-
dentally into his life one spring morning, not far from his
dismal lodgings in Paddington; and those fair ladies who
set him trembling — did they come nearer than Beatrice
to Dante? He walked through the London streets ab-
stractedly, or transformed them in imagination into fairy
places. He could write of grapes against the sun, but could
not tell one vintage from another. He paid no attention
to his fellow passengers in an omnibus, and never recog-
nized an acquaintance in the streets. But sleeping all

night on the Embankment, his spirit could thread the labyrinth of stars with ease. He was not an observer but a dreamer. He had the kind of imagination that can easily abandon the thing for the symbol, and lose the Many in the One. Of such stuff are mystics made.

The culmination of mystical experience is to bring the human soul into such close and harmonious relationship with God that soul and oversoul respond to one another as tone and overtone. The saint reaches this height only after a long and arduous climb such as Francis Thompson never undertook; but he had glimpses of it, being lifted thither by his " swift spirit." *Contemplation* describes a condition of trance, or ecstasy, such as could be paralleled in the lives of most mystics, and which surpasses the attempts of Blake and Wordsworth to report similar experiences. The poet gradually sinks into oblivion of his natural surroundings, these surroundings, at the same time, seeming to assume a similar passivity, and then, with heart and breathing hushed, and his body sharing " the immobility of rocks," the whole universe streams through him, while his mind, in turn, explores the universe, and hears the stars singing together. Those are the heights, but he is ever dragged down thence by his " slow foot," and he suffers what mystics call the " dark night of the soul," when the beatific vision fades, and leaves them in despair. The *Dread of Height* is a cry from the depths into which the poet has fallen, after having made

> Of the deific peaks dim escalade.

Such cries are heard again in the poems of the *Dead Cardinal of Westminster,* and *Any Saint.* Cardinal and saint have reached a height from which the poet feels debarred, and he is tortured with the fear lest, at the final judgment, he shall be condemned to

> tryst
> With the sensualist.

These alternations of rapture and despair were in part the result of his poverty-stricken, opium-harassed life. Worn out with the passion of successive height and depth, the poet envies those who walk steadily on their chosen elevation:

> Ah for a heart less native to high Heaven,
> A hooded eye, for jesses and restraint
> Or for a will accipitrine to pursue!

In theory the contradiction between height and depth, between Seen and Unseen, can be resolved into a harmony which includes them both. Not all mystics can make this reconciliation; some of them can only approach the Unseen over the path of negation; but Francis Thompson made it at least in theory. His *Mistress of Vision* says:

> When to the new eyes of thee
> All things by immortal power,
> Near or far
> Hiddenly
> To each other linkèd are,
> That thou canst not stir a flower
> Without trembling of a star . . .
> Pass the gates of Luthany, tread the region Elenore.

With such a vision one would not need to climb the dizzy heights to catch some glimpse of the Unseen; the doors of perception have been opened, and the Infinite streams in everywhere.

> Not where the wheeling systems darken
> And our benumbed conceiving soars! —
> The drift of pinions, would we hearken,
> Beats at our own clay-shuttered doors.

But the doors were not always opened wide; commonly they swung about halfway, and his poetry is then on the level of devout Catholicism rather than of Catholic mysticism. On this half-height are *An Anthem of Earth* and *Of Nature, Laud and Plaint*. These poems are parallels of Wordsworth's *Ode on Immortality,* in that they recall an ecstasy now gone forever, but find it replaced by a profounder insight. The poet now finds Nature in herself careless of mankind. Though " beautiful of ways," she is " barren of heart," and has " no hands to bless." The gate of Nature is closed, but the portals of the church are open.

This Lady is God's daughter and she lends
Her hand but to His friends.
But to her Father's friends the hands which thou wouldst win.

In the majority of the later poems Nature is seen through the doorway of the church. The imagery of the poet's church and creed governed his seeing, as its dogma governed his thinking. He had laid mind, heart, and imagination upon the altar, and the church repaid him with a wealth of imagery and symbol. If, as a boy, he had been frustrated in his ambition to be a priest, he may be said to have fulfilled it as a priestly poet.

In passing from Francis Thompson to A. E., we pass from Catholic mysticism to what we might call pagan mysticism. The Protestant faith in which A. E. had been brought up he very early cast aside; but at the age of sixteen or seventeen he was awakened, with religious solemnity, by a voice, or rather by visions, from nature. The hills around Dublin soon became his mystic shrine where at dawn or twilight he would be visited by strange and beautiful visions, some of which seemed to come from centuries past, and so to revive past phases of his soul's existence. Thus for the moment the poet's mind seemed to be caught in an influx of eternity — and this, in one form or another, is the basic mystical experience.

Casting about for some interpretation of these experiences, A. E. soon came in contact with several other young men of a temperament similar to his own, and with them dipped into all kinds of mystic lore, from the Upanishads of the ancient East to Emerson and Whitman of the modern West. The creed that A. E. formulated in the end was based on the Hindu pantheism of the Upanishads. Earth became, to the poet's new apprehension, a " mighty mother," communion with whom brings joys and peace, strength of soul for the daily battle, and alleviation from pain. The great game that the pantheistic spirit is playing throughout the universe is a happy one; stars and children dance to the selfsame tune. Not to find this joyous, redeeming force in nature — to suppose, as Francis Thompson did in his later verse, that she is " barren of heart," a " fair and brute-brained beast," is a sign of man's fall from his primitive high estate. In the ancient Celtic days, which share the honors in A. E.'s mind with ancient eastern times, the heroes of the Red Branch were not thus degraded. " I cannot think," he says, in his poem of *The Earth,*

> I cannot think the hearts that beat so high
> Had not a lordlier palace roof of sky,
> And that the earth on which the heroes trod
> Seemed not to live beneath them like a god
> Who loved them and could answer to their cry.

So it was in the days of the Upanishads and Celtic legends, and A. E.'s hope for the world is in the recovery of that lost vision.

The mysticism of W. B. Yeats is more complex than that of Francis Thompson and A. E. It was nourished by European as well as by English and Irish influences. Yeats's ambition was nothing less than to found a new poetry which should avoid the pitfalls into which, as he thought, Victorian poetry had fallen — those curiosities about politics, science, history, morality, and religion which wrap it round with a husk of externality. No more should poetry concern itself with outward things for their own sake; it would be the pure gold, without alloy. The retreat which Rossetti had made from a world too ugly and complex for him to love or understand was a move which had its counterpart and completion in France, where the symbolists, reacting against the externality of the Parnassians, went to extreme lengths in their renunciation of outward things. In that literature Yeats found the land of his heart's desire. Only his own glowing words can express the thrill of that spiritual home-coming. " Count Villiers de l'Isle Adam," he has written, " swept together, by what seemed a sudden energy, words behind which glimmered a spiritual and passionate mood, as the flame glimmers behind the dusky blue and red glass in an Eastern lamp; and created persons from whom has fallen all even of personal characteristic except a thirst for that hour when all things shall pass away like a cloud, and pride like that of the Magi following their star over many mountains; while Maeterlinck has plucked away even this thirst and this pride and set before us faint souls, naked and pathetic shadows already half vapour and sighing to one another upon the border of the last abyss." It appeared to Yeats that a European movement had set in toward the goal that he had chosen, and that the Irish were the people of Europe best fitted to bring such a movement to perfection.

The decisive question, among the French symbolists and their followers in England, was whether, for a given person, the visible world existed. For Yeats and the French symbolists it did not exist. What did exist was the poet's moods. These, Yeats thought, were the true subject matter — the soul — of poetry. The moods, he thought, are eternal, ever new and ever ancient; whereas argument, theory, erudition, observation, are " illusions of our visible passing life," and must be made to serve the moods, or they can have no part in eternity. Of course, poetry has always given utterance to moods, but it has also given utterance to argument, theory, erudition, and observation; and from these eminently Victorian alliances Yeats wished to rescue it. His own poetry is entirely free of such entanglements. It renders one or another of the " fire-born moods," as it leaps up in tongues of flame or fades away in dying embers. The imagery is never merely decorative; it is always fused with the emotion. And the music of the poem is equally essential and always exquisite, so that the mood may seem to be dissolved in music rather than revealed in imagery. Poetry like this, that has no outward props on which to lean, demands a kindred emotion in the reader. It cannot be read listlessly, as one may read the *Idylls of the King,* or glance over a gallery of pictures. Mood must answer mood, as, in rationalistic poetry, reason answers reason; and a subtlety of mood may be as difficult to solve as a subtlety of argument.

But the subjectivity of Yeats is not that kind in which the soul is a lonely prisoner within the body, and seeks its lonely realization in the face of a hostile world; on the contrary, it seeks to lose itself in the contemplation of a transcendental world, and this, in turn, is ever seeking to redeem the soul from its mortal bondage. The " sweet everlasting voices " are never still; the fairies lure to the land of heart's desire; the shee come rushing by, and call —

> Away, come away:
> Empty your heart of its mortal dream.

Thus, if the world of fact is ugly and restraining, the call comes from a free and lovely world of imagination. This is the core of mysticism, and it is enwrapped, in the poetry and prose of Yeats, with all sorts of magical and mystical envelopment. The poet believes that the borders of our minds and memories are ever shifting, and may recede, at favorable moments, before the flow of the great Mind and the great Memory; that our purposes and emotions are often not really ours, but incursions from that other Mind and Memory; that the imagination is always seeking to remake the world according to the great Mind and the great Memory; that the world as imagination sees it is the durable world; that the imagination has some way of lighting on the truth that the reason has not, and that its commandments, delivered when the body is still and the reason silent, are the most binding we can ever know. These articles of faith, which have been garnered in from Yeats's essays, and make no pretense to completeness, are familiar mystic doctrines, the world over; and they are the shaping forces of Yeats's poetry.

The mystic begins by rejecting the world of fact, though he may find it again with the light of imagination. His rejection of the world of fact arises from the failure of this finite world to satisfy his infinite desires. He has drunk the cup, say, of earthly beauty, and his heart is fired with passion for heavenly beauty; and so with love or goodness or whatever principle he may pursue; for it is seldom given a man to follow more than one path toward infinite perfection. The way of Yeats, like that of Shelley, was Love and Beauty, the two being scarce dissociable. These were his passions, and he found them continually thwarted by the wrong of unshapely things.

The wrong of unshapely things is a wrong too great to be told, I hunger to build them anew —

And he does so build them in his poetry. It is in his capacity to build anew that Yeats is poet as well as mystic — in the opinion of some readers, more of a poet than a mystic. It must be admitted that his glimpses of eternity seem more like romantic dreaming and less like sheer vision, than, for instance, Blake's. We stand in awe of those remote, mysterious personages who people Blake's Prophetic Books — Los, Vala, Luva, and the rest; compared with these the legendary heroes and the dreamy sensuous heroines who adorn the poetry of Yeats are relatively familiar. But if our poet's vision sometimes fades to dream, we should at least be thankful that he reveals to us, in lovely language, a habitable world; for the seers are likely to be vague and incoherent. Yeats's world is chiefly built of Celtic myth, in which he found the spontaneous delight that Keats found in the mythology of Greece. It has the beauty of the romantic past, and the heroic love of ancient days. The leaves of the mystic rose enfold the mighty heroes of the past, who staked everything for love. The women are fair counterparts to such men — pale, dreamy, and

passionate, with long heavy hair, pearl-pale hands, passion-
dimmed eyes; clearly the young art student had drunk
deep of Rossetti's portraits. The service of such women
would be, ideally, to lay " the heaven's embroidered cloths "
under their feet; this being impossible, the poet offers
them his " passionate rhyme " and his " numberless
dreams." Though passion remains, it is the " autumn of
the body "; for one might say of Yeats's characters what
Yeats said of Maeterlinck's, that they have " so little self,
that they are like shadows sighing at the edge of the
world." The natural background of this world is appro-
priately dim and unsubstantial. We catch glimpses of pale
waters in their wintry race, of dim tides and long gray
ships, of a curd pale moon and a shadowy hazel grove, of
white moths and shadowy pools and drifting smoke.
Nature is never felt to be there substantially; there are
only hints and sketches which symbolize the moods of those
sighing, passionate, disembodied lovers. Over all, in solitary intensity of color, rests, in impassioned serenity, the
mystic rose.

It is obvious that the world in which we find ourselves
when we read such poems as *The Wind Among the Reeds,*
is one of dream, or, as the mystic would prefer to say, of
vision. It has floated into the poet's consciousness out of
the great Mind and the great Memory. Yeats found that
he could induce such visions through the agency of symbols.
A symbol, as he defined it, is " whatever the passions of
men have gathered about "; and if such an object — the
rose, let us say, or the moon, or the ebbing tide — be subjected, in quietude of spirit, to one's own mind and
imagination, the great Mind and the great Memory may be
evoked. Yeats has described an instance of such contemplation in its two stages, the first being merely emotional,
the second rising to the intellectual. " If," he says, " I
watch a rushy pool in the moonlight, my emotion at its
beauty is mixed with memories of the man that I have seen
ploughing by its margin, or of the lovers I saw there a

night ago; but if I look at the moon herself and remember any of her ancient names and meanings, I move among divine people and things that have shaken off our mortality, the tower of ivory, the queen of waters, the shining stag among enchanted woods, the white hare sitting upon the hilltop, the fool of faëry with his shining cupful of dreams, and it may be ' make a friend of one of these images of wonder,' and ' meet the Lord in the air.' " In some such reverie we may fancy many of the poems taking shape. Are such visions " eternal realities " or " a momentary dream " ? Yeats stated these alternatives in an essay, and said that " to answer is to take sides in the only controversy in which it is greatly worth taking sides, and in the only controversy which may never be decided." It is the controversy between the rationalist and the mystic.

To obtain a vision of eternal reality, and then again to lose it, are the height and depth of mystical experience. Poetry can be made of both extremes, as we find in Francis Thompson and in Shelley. Yeats never reaches the height of their ecstasy, nor the depth of their despair. He seems never to have entertained Shelley's eager hope of finding the heavenly love and beauty incarnated in a Harriet or a Mary or an Emilia; and nursing no such rapturous expectation, he is not, on the other hand, left

> naked to laughter
> When leaves fall and cold winds come.

His passion is resignation; his themes are weariness and defeat; his verse echoes with " earth's old and weary cry." But if Yeats's estrangement from our common lot enables him to avoid Shelley's tragedy, it also withholds him from the reconciliation which Francis Thompson made partially, and Wordsworth wholly. He seldom finds in earthly imperfection some saving degree of heavenly perfection. He desired such insight; he feared lest his preoccupation with things afar would alienate him from common things — from

> The weak worm hiding down in its small cave,
> The field mouse running by me in the grass,
> And heavy mortal hopes that toil and pass;

and he prayed to his rose upon the rood of time to enable him to find

> In all poor foolish things that live a day
> Eternal beauty wandering on her way.

The prayer was not answered. For him the daisy and the celandine might have symbolized some inward passion; they could never have come into his life, as comrades, to solace it. Nor could he have entered into comradeship with Michael or Matthew, though he would have listened to their stories of the shee, had they been Celtic peasants. No, his solace was not from round about him, but from afar.

> When the flaming lute-thronged angelic door is wide,
> When an immortal passion breathes in mortal clay,

— in these circumstances, he says, we can endure life's travail. He was smitten with the passion for perfect beauty, and condemned to live in a world of unshapely things. He suffered, with Browning's hero,

> Infinite passion, and the pain
> Of finite hearts that yearn.

❖

The change in point of view which gave the men of the nineties their sense of newness and sense of difference from their Victorian predecessors naturally expressed itself in a new technique. Certain elements of this technique came as a reaction from Victorian poetic style, and other qualities derived from the strong French influence which all the new men felt in their desire for experiment and their search for new effect.

One of the most marked differences between the work of

Kipling, Henley, Yeats, and Symons, and their Victorian predecessors is their elimination of poetic diction and their attempt to approach as closely as possible to a direct prose order of words. In these matters they are at one with their successors, the poets of the present day. Wordsworth, in reacting against the poetic style of the eighteenth century, had stated his theory that poetry should be written in the real language of men, and he said that he took as much pains to avoid poetic diction as others commonly did to achieve it. But he was only partly successful; his poetry, judged by his own principle, shows many awkward inversions of phrase and many " poetic " words. And the other great romantics evidently felt that there was a separation between poetic and prose style. Tennyson in the *Idylls* developed a grand style of his own, filled with strange words, rich archaisms, and quaint inversions of phrase; but in the great lyric *Break! Break! Break!* he is flawlessly simple and direct, and not a word is out of its natural speech order. In a number of pieces, however, in which Tennyson attempts to be realistic he falls into unfortunate compromises and ridiculous contrasts. In *Aylmer's Field,* an Indian kinsman's tanned complexion " sear'd by the close ecliptic was not fair "; he tells a story by dashing " into the chronicle of a deedful day," while my lady listens " with her fingers interlock'd, and rotatory thumbs on silken knees." In *Enoch Arden,* we are so close to the language of men in the phrase

" Take your own time, Annie, take your own time,"

that the rhythmical pattern is lost; and yet in the same poem occurs the famous description of a basket of fish as " ocean-spoil in ocean-smelling osier! " The occasional lapses into a perfect colloquialism make the usual ornate Tennysonian diction seem the more glaringly artificial. And it was against artificiality and convention that the men of the nineties were reacting. To them, King Arthur's Victorian whiskers were not beautified by being called " the knightly

growth that fringed his lips." Except for an occasional
light or playful poem of Stevenson or Dobson, the poets of
the seventies and eighties were as much inclined as Tennyson was to fall into a poetic diction which allowed *ruth,
forsooth, doth aspire, did enfold, fillèd, lo! ah! haply,* and
why comes he not?

Browning was the only Victorian who affected a colloquial style in poetry. There is a different feel to his phrase
when one turns to him from reading the ornate Laureate.
Browning's poetry sounds like some one talking. For
example, read a passage from Pompilia's speech when
printed as prose — a good way of making this point clear:
" All these few things I know are true, — will you remember them? Because time flies. The surgeon cared for
me, to count my wounds — twenty-two dagger wounds,
five deadly, but I do not suffer much — or too much pain,
— and am to die to-night." This, of course, is dramatic
verse, as so much of Browning's is, but you find the same
feeling of speech-tune in passages in which the poet himself is speaking, for example: " Oh, to be in England now
that April's there, and whoever wakes in England sees, some
morning, unaware, that the lowest boughs and the brush-
wood sheaf round the elm-tree bole are in tiny leaf while
the chaffinch sings on the orchard bough." But Browning's themes often require archaisms for atmosphere, and
his colloquial manner, full of abrupt jumps, is a thing of
Browning's own. And his love of the grotesque led him
to invent such a twisted phrase as " turned your eyes' tail
up " to rhyme with " ran the chromatic scale up." But,
if we except a few of Burns's poems in dialect, Browning's
work, when all is said, is nearer the language of men than
that of any other poet since John Donne.

Back in the seventies, when Henley wrote *In Hospital,* he
had caught the lilt of natural speech and fitted it into
poetry. The following, for example, makes excellent prose:
" Her little face is like a walnut shell with wrinkling lines;
her soft white hair adorns her withered brows in quaint,

straight curls like horns; and all about her clings an old, sweet smell." And yet this passage is the first four lines of a sonnet. It is significant that Henley could find no publisher for his poetry until 1888 and was not a prominent force in poetry until the nineties, the period which fully accepted Browning as a poet of the first rank. And from the same source Kipling may have caught his colloquial manner, his straightforward word order, and his love of plain words and plain things which made him the poet of unpoetical readers — and of others too.

The Bohemians of the Rhymers' Club were interested in other phases of life than those that inspired Henley and Kipling, but they wrote of them with the same directness that eschewed all purely decorative phrases and special licenses of diction and inversion of order. Here is a description from Arthur Symons: " Gently a little breeze begins to creep into the valley, and the sleeping trees are stirred, and breathe a little in their sleep, and nod, half-awakened, to the breeze." It makes excellent prose, but it also perfectly fits the pattern of a quatrain. And one may try the same trick with Yeats's poetry almost at random. Compare the inverted word and phrase order of Rossetti's

> Her robe, ungirt from clasp to hem,
> No wrought flowers did adorn,
> But a white rose of Mary's gift,
> For service meetly worn,

with the directness of word order in Yeats's

> When my arms wrap you round I press
> My heart upon the loveliness
> That has long faded from the world;
> The jewelled crowns that kings have hurled
> In shadowy pools, when armies fled. . . .

The influence toward directness in the case of these Rhymers does not seem to be Browning, but rather Arthur Rimbaud and Paul Verlaine, who had started French poetry toward this aim. These brilliant and eccentric French

Bohemians fascinated not merely their own groups of younger poets, but also the younger English esthetic coterie, most of whom had played about Paris and had become interested in modern French literary movements. Poems of Rimbaud and Verlaine were translated by Symons, Dowson, John Gray, and others. Verlaine was the great enemy of poetic rhetoric; he expressed direct and sincere emotion in simple musical language without embellishment.

This direct manner, which has been further developed, within the last ten years by our American poets, came then from the double influence of Browning and the French schools, as a reaction from Tennyson's style. The poets of the nineties did not always succeed completely in their aim in this respect, but they first made fashionable the simplicity which is a marked trait in the manner of the great majority of modern poets. A reading over of Wordsworth's *Michael* and of Robert Frost's *Death of the Hired Man* will show that it has taken a hundred years for a poet to catch the last lilt of local speech rhythms, and really to carry out Wordsworth's own theory — " to adopt the very language of men " — to its complete conclusion.

In a few poets of the nineties, however, the love of Tennysonian diction survived. There was the voluble William Watson for one, and the richly sensuous Wilde for another. The old-fashioned ring of Wilde's

> The tired birds had stayed their amorous tune

may be forgiven because it was written in the early eighties, but Stephen Phillips's over-precious

> The summer day was at her blue deep hour
> Of lilies musical with busy bliss

shows a very conscious imitation of Tennyson as late as 1897. And the reactionary Francis Thompson deliberately prefers the inverted phrase and revels in ecstasies of strange, glamorous words.

Another point of technique which marks the nineties as

the beginning of our modern poetry is the impressionistic method, which with some modification has developed into Imagism. Henley, William Sharp, and Arthur Symons wrote many poems that aim merely to present a visual impression without sentiment or reflection, merely suggesting details of form, color, or sound, so chosen that they will convey a unified effect and evoke a mood in the reader. Henley's glimpses of types and scenes in the *Old Infirmary*, and of the barmaid, cabby, and the fishwife of London are like the sketches in an etcher's notebook, and his *London Voluntaries* are a painter's impressions of the color, light and shadow, and moods of the city in chosen moments, revealed in glimpses and gleams and flashes of lives and things. Arthur Symons gives us colorful and charming pastiches in his world of the music hall, the stage-door, and the café, or else a picture of the warm, pale color of a French summer holiday town. And William Sharp's *Sospiri di Roma* are pure color impressions of the quiet exquisite beauty of old Roman sunshine and warm Italian twilights. His *Susurro* is so purely without any intrusion of the author's thought or feeling that its impressionism is as absolute as a painting of Monet. Sharp belongs with the twentieth century Imagists. Here is the poem:

> Breath o' the grass,
> Ripple of wandering wind,
> Murmur of tremulous leaves.
> A moonbeam moving white
> Like a ghost across the plain.
> A shadow on the road:
> And high up, high,
> From the cypress-bough,
> A long sweet melancholy note.
> Silence.
> And the topmost spray
> Of the cypress-bough is still
> As a wavelet in a pool:
> The road lies duskily bare:
> The plain is a misty gloom:
> Still are the tremulous leaves;
> Scarce a last ripple of wind,

> Scarce a breath i' the grass.
> Hush: the tired wind sleeps.
> Is it the wind's breath, or
> Breath o' the grass.

This kind of poem does not try to show all the significance there may be in the scene or the object or the personality presented; it is merely a glimpse, a momentary
visual impression. Description, when used in poetry before,
had been more fully and formally composed, like the work
of the earlier landscape and genre painters, with their
tangible sense of solidity and perspective. It had now
become suggestive, and the mood or meaning of the thing
was left to the reader. Of course, descriptive impressions
are not new in poetry. Coleridge's *Kubla Khan* and William Morris's *Blue Closet* are impressions without idea or
story, and Poe's *Ulalume* is of the same type of poetry,
merely suggesting a mood, but these poems present the
unreal world of dreams, not the actual visual world of the
realist. Tennyson's *Lotus Eaters* has stanzas of absolutely
unified nature description, but they do not stand alone.
They give sympathetic atmosphere to a poem that aims
primarily at presenting a definite attitude to life. True
impressionism — significant details of actual life, sketchy
suggestions of character, or the lines, colors, and shadows
of nature, felt as sufficiently significant to stand alone as
a poem — this does not appear before Oscar Wilde's volume
of 1881 which contained such poems, with titles *In the
Gold Room: A Harmony, Les Silhouettes, Fuite de la Lune,
By the Arno,* and *Impression du Matin.* Here, for example,
is the last-mentioned poem:

> The Thames a nocturne of blue and gold
>   Changed to a harmony in grey:
>   A barge with ochre-coloured hay
> Dropt from the wharf: and chill and cold
>
> The yellow fog came creeping down
>   The bridges, till the houses' walls
>   Seemed changed to shadows, and St. Paul's
> Loomed like a bubble o'er the town.

Then suddenly arose the clang
Of waking life; the streets were stirred
With country wagons: and a bird
Flew to the glistening roofs and sang.

But one pale woman all alone,
The daylight kissing her wan hair,
Loitered beneath the gas lamp's flare,
With lips of flame and heart of stone.

The phrases " nocturne of blue and gold " and " a harmony in grey " suggest the origin of this kind of thing in poetry. It is a Whistler picture. Wilde as a painter would have belonged to the school who feel that the subject itself, its meaning, its moral, intellectual, or sentimental appeal are not the affair of the painter, but only the visual impression of the thing, its lights and tones and reflections and contrasts.

Curiously enough, the French poets of the new schools of the eighteen-eighties did not imitate their own painters, but left this visual impressionism to the English poets. The impressionism of Verlaine, Rimbaud, and Mallarmé is more closely akin to music than to painting. They gained their effect partly through the repetition of suggestive sounds, a trick to which Poe contributed his influence. And this musical suggestiveness is present in the English group as well, as for example, in William Sharp's *Mandolin* and Henley's *London Voluntaries*, which is divided into movements, like a symphony.

Although we have given credit to Wilde for having first printed poems of this Whistler-like inspiration, Henley was writing in the same manner a few years earlier; but his work did not get into print until 1888. Henley became a friend of Whistler, and as an art critic was very conscious of the importance of the modern painters and wrote sympathetic interpretations of them to the British public. And George Moore praised Whistler and Monet and Degas in his very significant book, *Modern Painting*, in 1891, the year in which William Sharp's *Sospiri di Roma* appeared.

Sharp, like Henley, had been an impressionist in poetry almost from the beginning of his career. Through the eighties, he wrote sequences of eight-line imagist poems with such titles as *Dawn amid Scotch Firs, Phosphorescent Sea,* and in the *Australian Transcripts, — Black Swans on the Murray Lagoons, Mid-noon in January,* etc. And through the nineties came Arthur Symons's volumes touched strongly with the impressionistic method, and there were also Laurence Binyon's *Visions* and John Davidson's *Thames Embankment,* less effective than either Henley's or Symons's London sketches, but done with something of this manner.

The course that this movement in poetry has run since the eighteen-nineties has its parallel in the later history of painting. The post-impressionists in painting have gone so far that they develop only a single very limited aspect of the theme before them and let that stand alone. And the descendants of the poetic impressionists, the modern Imagists, have likewise allowed a single image, one suggestive flash from the world of infinite colors and sounds, to stand on their page as a complete poem. Evidently again we find the roots of our contemporary poetry in the work of these new experimenters in the eighties and nineties.

It was, in fact, the sense of experiment that marked the whole interesting group. In their revolt from the Victorians they not only tried new diction and held to a new idea of what makes poetry, but also looked for new rhythms. This was indeed a very hard task, for Tennyson and Swinburne had developed the old rhythms to the highest degree of technical perfection, and Swinburne, especially, had found new rhythms and new melodies undreamed of before. And Andrew Lang, Edmund Gosse, and Austin Dobson had found pleasure in rediscovering the complicated Old French forms — triolets, rondeaus, and ballades.

Again Henley seems to have led the way. He early began to try free verse — evidently as a reaction from the perfect use of very difficult fixed forms. It was not the free verse of Whitman that he tried, although this doubtless influenced him to try for freedom in rhythm. His free verse, like some of Matthew Arnold's experiments, varies constantly in the length of the lines, but one feels in the rhythm almost always a constant rhythmic pattern. Whitman's verse throws this over and we have always the natural rhythm of prose phrases. Although Henley went from one extreme to the other —ballades to free verse — he could find no publisher for his work for more than ten years; but he continued using free verse for much of his work even down to his last volume, *Hawthorn and Lavender,* in 1901. William Sharp, the other most striking impressionist, also wrote one volume, the *Sospiri di Roma,* in free verse, using for the most part short rhythmic phrases varied by longer sweeps, and he returned to this form in certain of the poems written under the pseudonym of Fiona Macleod. His type of free verse is exactly that used by the poets of the twentieth century. Another pioneer in this movement was John Todhunter, the Irish poet, whose volume *The Banshee and Other Poems* (1888) was written chiefly in unrhymed free-verse stanzas, for example:

> And the nations hear in the void and quaking time of night,
> Sad unto dawning, dirges,
> Solemn dirges,
> And snatches of bardic song,
> Their souls quake in the void and quaking time of night,
> And they dream of the weird of kings,
> And tyrannies moulting, sick
> In the dreadful wind of change.

Todhunter may possibly have taken his idea from the Ossianic poems, although the character of the rhythm is quite different. It is nearer to the style of the free ode, of which there were plentiful examples from the time of Cowley on for three hundred years. William Sharp's free-verse poems are very far from these tempestuous ode-like verses. He may have been influenced by the French experimenters who followed Gustave Kahn in the brief-lived review, *La Vogue,* in 1886. Several volumes of French *vers libre* and a great deal of discussion of it appeared between 1887 and 1891, the year of Sharp's volume. But free verse was only an experiment; it took no hold of the eighteen-nineties. Henley was the only English poet who kept on at it during the period. The epidemic of formlessness which broke out in England and America ten years or more ago was a second start in the search for new rhythms.

The poets who were most under the influence of the French, Dowson and Symons, did not go in for free verse, but they tried the experiment of writing French alexandrines in English. This was really as bold an innovation as writing free verse, for modern English and French poetry depend upon entirely different prosodic principles. English fixed verse has a definite rhythmical pattern that is repeated from line to line; each of the measures which compose the line has in theory the same number of syllables. The phrases thrown across this pattern are made to fit it. If necessary, slight stresses may be placed on unimportant words like prepositions or even articles in order to bring out clearly the underlying pattern. Sometimes the phrases have strong accents of their own that conflict with the pattern rhythm, and we feel a struggle of two forces in the rhythm of the poem. Free verse, of course, avoids this struggle by dropping out the fixed pattern. Now French verse is made on a very different principle. The number of syllables in the whole line is, in theory, kept constant, but the accents — which are the accents of prose — divide the line into measures with varying number of syllables. That is, the rhythm of a French poem varies its character from line to line; there is no fixed pattern, and there is no struggle of forces. The number of syllables in the whole line is in theory kept constant, but the rhythm is the rhythm of the phrase groups into which the syllables naturally fall. For example, the alexandrine is a line of twelve syllables divided by a slight pause somewhere in the middle, and the rhythm breaks into four, or occasionally three, and very rarely even five phrase units. That is, the rhythm of the

French alexandrine varies its character from line to line; there is imposed no fixed pattern, and there is no struggle of forces. Here is the *Brise Marine* of Mallarmé, marked with accents which indicate a possible (though of course not the only) metrical reading:

La chair est triste, hélas! et j'ai lu tous les livres.
Fuir! là-bas fuir! Je sens que des oiseaux sont ivres
D'être parmi l'écume inconnue et les cieux!
Rien, ni les vieux jardins reflétés par les yeux
Ne retiendra ce cœur qui dans la mer se trempe
O nuits! ni la clarté déserte de ma lampe
Sur le vide papier que la blancheur défend
Et ni la jeune femme allaitant son enfant.
Je pâtirai! Steamér balançant ta mâture
Lève l'ancre pour une exotique nature!
Un Ennui, désolé par les cruels espoirs,
Croit encore à l'adieu suprême, des mouchoirs!
Et, peut-être, les mâts, invitant les orages
Sont-ils de ceux qu'un vent penche sur les naufrages
Perdus, sans mâts, sans mâts, ni fertiles îlots . . .
Mais, ô mon cœur, entends le chant des matelots!

And below is Arthur Symons's excellent translation of the same poem. It may be read by superimposing an English iambic pattern, but the effect is that of monotonous six-measure lines. This is a meter that has been rejected by most English poets, probably because it breaks too symmetrically in half. If, however, you read the translation in the manner of the French original, you have a new and quite different rhythmical effect. In this reading, which is indicated by accent marks, the lines are divided into constantly varied rhythmic sweeps of short phrases. The strongest accents come upon the three or four most important syllables in the line, and on the last syllable.

The flesh is sad, alas! and all the books are read.
Flight, only flight! I feel that birds are wild to tread
The floor of unknown foam, and to attain the skies!
Nought, neither ancient gardens mirrored in the eyes,
Shall hold this heart that bathes in waters its delight,
O nights! nor yet my waking lamp, whose lonely light
Shadows the vacant paper, whiteness profits best,
Nor the young wife who rocks her baby on her breast.
I will depart! O steamer, swaying rope and spar,
Lift anchor for exotic lands that lie afar!
A weariness, outworn by cruel hopes, still clings
To the last farewell handkerchief's last beckonings!
And are not these, the masts inviting storms, not these
That an awakening wind bends over wrecking seas,
Lost, not a sail, a sail, a flowering isle, ere long?
But, O my heart, hear thou, hear thou the sailor's song!

The famous *Cynara* of Dowson seems also intended to be
read in this way. The refrain line falls very naturally into
a trimeter reading:

I have been faithful to thee, Cynara, in my fashion.

One poet of the nineties worked in exactly the opposite
direction from these proselike rhythms of French alexandrines and of the free-verse experiments. Rudyard Kipling
wrote, as apparently Swinburne did, by fitting his words to
a clearly marked verse tune which beat strongly in his head
before he began his poem. Poets of this type with a very
definite musical sense create verse rhythms that are so like
musical rhythms that they seize the reader's ear with the
intense insistence of a fine tune. The great body of English poetry has been written on a base of iambic rhythm,
though, of course, nearly every poet in the nineteenth century tried experiments with other types, and there are
hundreds of poems that show a new sense of more intricate
music. The versatile Tennyson did some notable things
in new verse tunes. But it was Swinburne with his classical

ear and his musical sense that freed English verse from its
adherence to simple patterns. And the banjo music of
Kipling has carried this freedom on until the modern lyrist
has almost as wide a choice of rhythms as the musician.

Kipling's most distinctive contribution to our rhythm is
his making dipodic verse — what in musical scansion would
be verse read in four-four time — a form for serious as well
as light poetry. His volumes of verse have many examples
of most striking variations of this kind of rhythm, so rich
in possibilities. This four-four time makes the best reading
of Tennyson's *All Along the Valley* and of Browning's
Toccata of Galuppi; but such use of it was rare before
Kipling wrote *Mandalay, The Long Trail, The Song of the
English, The Last Chantey, The Merchantmen, The Song
of the Banjo,* and *Anchor Song,* and many other poems that
cling to the memory of any one who has read them once.

To see the different possibilities in this type of rhythm
one has but to compare the " tunes " of a few lines from
different poems. The syllables indicated by an accent mark
divide the line into equal measures. The other syllables
that the reader finds important can be accented slightly
without disturbing the rapid flow of the verse:

By the óld Moulmein Pagóda, lookin' éastward to the séa,
There's a Búrma girl a-séttin', an' I knów she thinks o' mé . . .

Compare this with *The Long Trail,* in which the rapid flow
of four syllables to each foot in the first and third lines is
contrasted with the slower movement of two syllables to a
foot in the second and fourth, when all the lines are read in
four-four time.

There's a whísper down the fíeld where the yéar has shot her
   yíeld,
   And the rícks stand gráy to the sún,
Singing: Óver then, come óver, for the bée has quit the clóver,
   And your Énglish súmmer's dóne."

And again, notice the difference in the music of the *Anchor*

Song, which comes from fitting two, three, or four syllables
into a pattern of four-four time; and sometimes a pause like
a rest in music contributes to the rhythmic effect:

> Heh! Walk her round. Heave, ah, heave her short again!
> Over, snatch her over, there, and hold her on the pawl.
> Loose all sail, and brace your yards back and full — ,
> Ready jib to pay her off and heave short all!

In the mark that Kipling has made with this rhythm on
the verse of the nineteen hundreds we have one more
example of our thesis that the poetry of the nineties should
not be thought of as the end of the Victorian period but as
the definite beginning of almost every movement that we
call new in our modern poetry. Alfred Noyes and Walter
de la Mare have made this four-four time the basis of much
of their verse music, which is, after all, their chief claim
to consideration as poets. It is, for example, the same
mixing of measures of two syllables with measures of four,
read in four-four time, that Kipling used, which gives the
interesting change in tempo in the delightful nonsense of
Walter de la Mare's *Mocking Fairy:*

> "Won't you look out of your window, Mrs. Gill?"
>   Quoth the fairy nidding, nodding in the garden;
> "Can't you look out of your window, Mrs. Gill?"
>   Quoth the fairy laughing softly in the garden.
> But the air was still, the cherry boughs were still,
> And the ivy-tod 'neath the empty sill,
> And never from her window looked out Mrs. Gill
>   On the fairy shrilly mocking in the garden.

❖

As yet, literary criticism has not found a name for the
modern era in poetry, but when the future has our period
labeled and ticketed, it will be found that the contemporary
movements and schools had their beginnings in the eighteen-
nineties. Victoria outlived her own age by at least a

decade, and there are a few legitimists among the poets even now who are true to her tradition, but her reign in literature really came to an end about 1890. The attitude of appreciating life as it is, which marked the poetry of Henley and Kipling, has continued to be the mood of the most vigorous of the modern men on both sides of the Atlantic. There is beauty in the sheer actuality of life, whether in the city, on the farm, at sea, or in war, or in industry. It may be accepted and felt intensely without rhetorical argument and without the insincere screen of sentiment. This is the point of view of John Masefield, Rupert Brooke, Wilfrid Gibson, Siegfried Sassoon, and Robert Graves in England and of Robert Frost and Carl Sandburg in America. Another important point of view, the impressionistic, which may be considered as a part of the same attitude toward visible life around us, has also continued in a very striking group of modern poets. The impressionism of Henley, Arthur Symons, and William Sharp has become the imagism of Richard Aldington, H. D., and Amy Lowell. The other important direction which the poetry of the nineties took in the mysticism of Lionel Johnson, Francis Thompson, A. E., and Yeats has had no conspicuous following. The mystic's refuge, which evoked the finest poetry of that decade, is still open for us, but few of the singers of today have sought it.

The technique of the modern school also has its beginning with these poets of the nineties. The avoidance of " poetical " words and of an inverted word order, which all except the surviving Victorians sought, has become an essential principle with the moderns. Even the conservatives in thought express themselves as nearly as possible in the direct diction of speech. The free verse of Henley has, with the added influence of Whitman, enlarged our means of poetic expression, and the modern poets with their subtler handling of it have made it a definitely accepted form. In all these ways the present generation of poets are the direct descendants of the men who started new movements in the nineties, so that one may say that our modern age very definitely began then.

The output of poetry in the decade was very large. It was a time when the minor poet could have his place. John Lane, one of the greatest friends poetry ever had, brought out scores of little volumes in finely printed editions, now the joy of the collector. The first decade of the new century was not so rich in production, but since 1910 poetry, both old and new, has enjoyed a popularity unprecedented in literary history. Everybody reads poetry and almost everybody seems to write it. The minor poet appears everywhere, in newspapers, in magazines, in college classrooms, in salons, in women's clubs, in poetry societies, and in innumerable anthologies. But in spite of all this interest and stimulus, the poetry remains minor. The quality probably averages higher than ever before, but almost no truly great figures have emerged. The Victorian era had two major poets in Tennyson and Browning; and in the second class there were Rossetti, Morris, Swinburne, and Arnold, the last two with breadth and intensity enough to be ranked almost as majors. And then, in a third group one would put Clough, James Thomson, Mrs. Browning, Christina Rossetti, Patmore, and Fitzgerald. The work of all these poets covers a period of about fifty years. In the ten years represented in the present collection, there were no new major poets, and Francis Thompson and Yeats are the only two who deserve a place in the second class. But the group of minor men after them is brilliant and significant: Henley, Kipling, Wilde, Symons, Johnson, Dowson, A. E. Housman. After all, new major poets are not to be expected of every decade; and this group of minors is not only more interesting than the Victorian poets of the third class, but it is hard to find any ten years in the history of poetry that produced minor poets of more distinction. It was a decade that accomplished much of high intrinsic worth and handed on important influences to the new century. Has the first quarter of this century as much to show of permanent worth as those brilliant ten years?

ROBERT LOUIS STEVENSON [1]

THE VAGABOND

(To an air of Schubert)

Give to me the life I love,
   Let the lave go by me,
Give the jolly heaven above
   And the byway nigh me.
Bed in the bush with stars to see,
   Bread I dip in the river —
There's the life for a man like me,
   There's the life forever.

Let the blow fall soon or late,
   Let what will be o'er me;
Give the face of earth around
   And the road before me.
Wealth I seek not, hope nor love,
   Nor a friend to know me;
All I seek, the heaven above
   And the road below me.

Or let autumn fall on me
   Where afield I linger,
Silencing the bird on tree,
   Biting the blue finger:
White as meal the frosty field —
   Warm the fireside haven —
Not to autumn will I yield,
   Not to winter even!

Let the blow fall soon or late,
   Let what will be o'er me;
Give the face of earth around,
   And the road before me.

[1] The poems of R. L. Stevenson are reprinted by permission of Charles Scribner's Sons, New York.

Wealth I ask not, hope nor love,
Nor a friend to know me.
All I ask, the heaven above,
And the road below me.

MY WIFE

Trusty, dusky, vivid, true,
With eyes of gold and bramble-dew,
Steel-true and blade-straight,
The great artificer
Made my mate.

Honour, anger, valour, fire;
A love that life could never tire,
Death quench or evil stir,
The mighty master
Gave to her.

Teacher, tender, comrade, wife,
A fellow-farer true through life,
Heart-whole and soul-free
The august father
Gave to me.

RUDYARD KIPLING [1]

SESTINA OF THE TRAMP–ROYAL [2]

Speakin' in general, I 've tried 'em all —
The 'appy roads that take you o'er the world.
Speakin' in general, I 've found them good
For such as cannot use one bed too long,
But must get 'ence, the same as I 've done,
An' go observin' matters till they die.

[1] The poems of Rudyard Kipling are reprinted by permission of the author and of Doubleday, Page & Co., New York. Copyright, Rudyard Kipling.
[2] From *The Seven Seas.*

What do it matter where or 'ow we die,
So long as we've our 'ealth to watch it all —
The different ways that different things are done,
An' men an' women lovin' in this world;
Takin' our chances as they come along,
An' when they ain't, pretendin' they are good?

In cash or credit — no, it aren't no good;
You 'ave to 'ave the 'abit or you'd die,
Unless you lived your life but one day long,
Nor didn't prophesy nor fret at all,
But drew your tucker some'ow from the world,
An' never bothered what you might ha' done.

But, Gawd, what things are they I 'aven't done!
I've turned my 'and to most, an' turned it good,
In various situations round the world —
For 'im that doth not work must surely die;
But that's no reason man should labour all
'Is life on one same shift; life's none so long.

Therefore, from job to job I've moved along.
Pay couldn't 'old me when my time was done,
For something in my 'ead upset me all,
Till I 'ad dropped whatever 'twas for good,
An', out at sea, be'eld the dock-lights die,
An' met my mate — the wind that tramps the world.

It's like a book, I think, this bloomin' world,
Which you can read and care for just so long,
But presently you feel that you will die
Unless you get the page you're readin' done,
An' turn another — likely not so good;
But what you're after is to turn 'em all.

Gawd bless this world! Whatever she 'ath done —
Excep' when awful long — I've found it good.
So write, before I die, " 'E liked it all! "

THE SONG OF THE BANJO [1]

You couldn't pack a Broadwood half a mile —
  You mustn't leave a fiddle in the damp —
You couldn't raft an organ up the Nile,
  And play it in an Equatorial swamp.
I travel with the cooking-pots and pails —
  I'm sandwiched 'tween the coffee and the pork —
And when the dusky column checks and tails,
  You should hear me spur the rearguard to a walk!

    With my *" Pilly-willy-winky-winky popp! "*
      [Oh, it's any tune that comes into my head!]
    So I keep 'em moving forward till they drop;
      So I play 'em up to water and to bed.

In the silence of the camp before the fight,
  When it's good to make your will and say your prayer,
You can hear my *strumpty-tumpty* overnight,
  Explaining ten to one was always fair.
I'm the Prophet of the Utterly Absurd,
  Of the Patently Impossible and Vain —
And when the Thing that Couldn't has occurred,
  Give me time to change my leg and go again.

    With my *" Tumpa-tumpa-tumpa-tum-pa tump! "*
      In the desert where the dung-fed camp-smoke curled
    There was never voice before us till I led our lonely
      chorus,
      I — the war-drum of the White Man round the
      world!

By the bitter road the Younger Son must tread,
  Ere he win to hearth and saddle of his own, —
'Mid the riot of the shearers at the shed,
  In the silence of the herder's hut alone —

[1] From *The Seven Seas.*

In the twilight, on a bucket upside down,
Hear me babble what the weakest won't confess —
I am Memory and Torment — I am Town!
I am all that ever went with evening dress!

  With my *" Tunk-a tunka-tunka-tunka tunk! "*
    [So the lights — the London Lights — grow near
    and plain!]
  So I rowel 'em afresh towards the Devil and the Flesh,
    Till I bring my broken rankers home again.

In desire of many marvels over sea,
  Where the new-raised tropic city sweats and roars,
I have sailed with Young Ulysses from the quay
  Till the anchor rumbled down on stranger shores.
He is blooded to the open and the sky,
  He is taken in a snare that shall not fail,
He shall hear me singing strongly, till he die,
  Like the shouting of a backstay in a gale.

  With my *" Hya! Heeya! Heeya! Hullah! Haul! "*
    [O the green that thunders aft along the deck!]
  Are you sick o' towns and men? You must sign and
    sail again,
    For it's " Johnny Bowlegs, pack your kit and trek! "

Through the gorge that gives the stars at noonday clear —
Up the pass that packs the scud beneath our wheel —
Round the bluff that sinks her thousand fathom sheer —
  Down the valley with our guttering brakes asqueal:
Where the trestle groans and quivers in the snow,
  Where the many-shedded levels loop and twine,
Hear me lead my reckless children from below
  Till we sing the Song of Roland to the pine.

  With my *" Tinka-tinka-tinka-tinka-tink! "*
    [Oh the axe has cleared the mountain, croup and
    crest!]
  And we ride the iron stallions down to drink,
    Through the cañons to the waters of the West!

And the tunes that mean so much to you alone —
  Common tunes that make you choke and blow your nose,
Vulgar tunes that bring the laugh that brings the groan —
  I can rip your very heartstrings out with those;
With the feasting, and the folly, and the fun —
  And the lying, and the lusting, and the drink,
And the merry play that drops you, when you're done,
  To the thoughts that burn like irons if you think.

  With my " *Plunka-lunka-lunka-lunka-lunk!* "
    Here's a trifle on account of pleasure past,
    Ere the wit that made you win gives you eyes to see
      your sin
    And — the heavier repentance at the last!

Let the organ moan her sorrow to the roof —
  I have told the naked stars the Grief of Man!
Let the trumpet snare the foeman to the proof —
  I have known Defeat, and mocked it as we ran!
My bray ye may not alter nor mistake
  When I stand to jeer the fatted Soul of Things,
But the Song of Lost Endeavour that I make,
  Is it hidden in the twanging of the strings?

  With my " *Ta-ra-rara-rara-ra-ra-rrrp!* "
    [Is it naught to you that hear and pass me by?]
    But the word — the word is mine, when the order
      moves the line
    And the lean, locked ranks go roaring down to die!

The grandam of my grandam was the Lyre —
  [O the blue below the little fisher-huts!]
That the Stealer stooping beachward filled with fire,
  Till she bore my iron head and ringing guts!
By the wisdom of the centuries I speak —
  To the tune of yestermorn I set the truth —
I, the joy of life unquestioned — I, the Greek —
  I, the everlasting Wonder-song of Youth!

With my " *Tinka-tinka-tinka-tinka-tink!* "
  [What d' ye lack, my noble masters? What d' ye
    lack?]
So I draw the world together link by link:
  Yea, from Delos up to Limerick and back!

TOMMY [1]

I went into a public-'ouse to get a pint o' beer,
The publican 'e up an' sez, " We serve no red-coats here."
The girls be'ind the bar they laughed an' giggled fit to die,
I outs into the street again an' to myself sez I:
  O it's Tommy this, an' Tommy that, an' " Tommy, go
    away ";
  But it's " Thank you, Mister Atkins," when the band
    begins to play,
  The band begins to play, my boys, the band begins to
    play,
  O it's " Thank you, Mister Atkins," when the band begins
    to play.

I went into a theatre as sober as could be,
They gave a drunk civilian room, but 'adn't none for me;
They sent me to the gallery or round the music-'alls,
But when it comes to fightin', Lord! they'll shove me in
  the stalls!
  For it's Tommy this, an' Tommy that, an' " Tommy,
    wait outside ";
  But it's " Special train for Atkins " when the trooper's on
    the tide,
  The troopship's on the tide, my boys, the troopship's on
    the tide,
  O it's " Special train for Atkins " when the trooper's on
    the tide.

[1] From *Barrack Room Ballads and Other Verses.*

Yes, makin' mock o' uniforms that guard you while you
 sleep
Is cheaper than them uniforms, an' they're starvation
 cheap;
An' hustlin' drunken soldiers when they're goin' large a bit
Is five times better business than paradin' in full kit.
> Then it's Tommy this, an' Tommy that, an' " Tommy,
> 'ow's yer soul? "
> But it's " Thin red line of 'eroes " when the drums begin
> to roll,
> The drums begin to roll, my boys, the drums begin to
> roll,
> O it's " Thin red line of 'eroes " when the drums begin to
> roll.

We aren't no thin red 'eroes, nor we aren't no blackguards
 too,
But single men in barricks, most remarkable like you;
An' if sometimes our conduck isn't all your fancy paints,
Why, single men in barricks don't grow into plaster saints;
> While it's Tommy this, an' Tommy that, an' " Tommy,
> fall be'ind,"
> But it's " Please to walk in front, sir," when there's
> trouble in the wind,
> There's trouble in the wind, my boys, there's trouble in
> the wind,
> O it's " Please to walk in front, sir," when there's trouble
> in the wind.

You talk o' better food for us, an' schools, an' fires, an' all:
We'll wait for extry rations if you treat us rational.
Don't mess about the cook-room slops, but prove it to our
 face
The Widow's Uniform is not the soldier-man's disgrace.
> For it's Tommy this, an' Tommy that, an' " Chuck him
> out, the brute! "
> But it's " Saviour of 'is country " when the guns begin to
> shoot;

An' it's Tommy this, an' Tommy that, an' anything you
    please;
An' Tommy ain't a bloomin' fool — you bet that Tommy
    sees!

THE CONUNDRUM OF THE WORKSHOPS [1]

When the flush of a new-born sun fell first on Eden's green
    and gold,
Our father Adam sat under the Tree and scratched with a
    stick in the mould;
And the first rude sketch that the world had seen was joy to
    his mighty heart,
Till the Devil whispered behind the leaves, " It's pretty,
    but is it Art? "

Wherefore he called to his wife, and fled to fashion his
    work anew —
The first of his race who cared a fig for the first, most
    dread review;
And he left his lore to the use of his sons — and that was a
    glorious gain
When the Devil chuckled " Is it Art? " in the ear of the
    branded Cain.

They builded a tower to shiver the sky and wrench the
    the stars apart,
Till the Devil grunted behind the bricks: " It's striking,
    but is it Art? "
The stone was dropped at the quarry-side and the idle
    derrick swung,
While each man talked of the aims of Art, and each in an
    alien tongue.

[1] From *Barrack Room Ballads and Other Verses.*

They fought and they talked in the North and the South;
    they talked and they fought in the West,
Till the waters rose on the pitiful land, and the poor Red
    Clay had rest —
Had rest till the dank blank-canvas dawn when the dove
    was preened to start,
And the Devil bubbled below the keel: " It's human, but is
    it Art? "

The tale is as old as the Eden Tree — and new as the new-
    cut tooth —
For each man knows ere his lip-thatch grows he is master
    of Art and Truth;
And each man hears as the twilight nears, to the beat of
    his dying heart,
The Devil drum on the darkened pane: " You did it, but
    was it Art? "

We have learned to whittle the Eden Tree to the shape of
    a surplice-peg,
We have learned to bottle our parents twain in the yelk of
    an addled egg,
We know that the tail must wag the dog, for the horse is
    drawn by the cart;
But the Devil whoops, as he whooped of old: " It's clever,
    but is it Art?"

When the flicker of London sun falls faint on the Club-
    room's green and gold,
The sons of Adam sit them down and scratch with their
    pens in the mould —
They scratch with their pens in the mould of their graves,
    and the ink and the anguish start,
For the Devil mutters behind the leaves: " It's pretty, but
    is it Art? "

Now, if we could win to the Eden Tree where the Four
Great Rivers flow,
And the Wreath of Eve is red on the turf as she left it
long ago,
And if we could come when the sentry slept and softly
scurry through,
By the favour of God we might know as much — as our
father Adam knew!

TOMLINSON [1]

Now Tomlinson gave up the ghost in his house in Berkeley
Square,
And a Spirit came to his bedside and gripped him by the
hair —
A Spirit gripped him by the hair and carried him far away,
Till he heard as the roar of a rain-fed ford the roar of the
Milky Way:
Till he heard the roar of the Milky Way die down and
drone and cease,
And they came to the Gate within the Wall where Peter
holds the keys.
" Stand up, stand up now, Tomlinson, and answer loud and
high
" The good that ye did for the sake of men or ever ye came
to die —
" The good that ye did for the sake of men in little earth
so lone! "
And the naked soul of Tomlinson grew white as a rain-
washed bone.

" O I have a friend on earth," he said, " that was my priest
and guide,
" And well would he answer all for me if he were at my
side."

[1] From *Barrack Room Ballads and Other Verses.*

— " For that ye strove in neighbour-love it shall be written
    fair,
" But now ye wait at Heaven's Gate and not in Berkeley
    Square:
" Though we called your friend from his bed this night, he
    could not speak for you,
" For the race is run by one and one and never by two and
    two."
Then Tomlinson looked up and down, and little gain was
    there,
For the naked stars grinned overhead, and he saw that his
    soul was bare:
The Wind that blows between the Worlds, it cut him like
    a knife,
And Tomlinson took up the tale and spoke of his good in
    life.
" O this I have read in a book," he said, " and that was told
    to me,
" And this I have thought that another man thought of a
    Prince in Muscovy."
The good souls flocked like homing doves and bade him
    clear the path,
And Peter twirled the jangling keys in weariness and wrath.
" Ye have read, ye have heard, ye have thought," he said,
    " and the tale is yet to run:
" By the worth of the body that once ye had, give answer —
    what ha' ye done? "
Then Tomlinson looked back and forth, and little good it
    bore,
For the darkness stayed at his shoulder-blade and Heaven's
    Gate before: —
" O this I have felt, and this I have guessed, and this I
    have heard men say,
" And this they wrote that another man wrote of a carl in
    Norroway."
" Ye have read, ye have felt, ye have guessed, good lack!
    Ye have hampered Heaven's Gate;
" There's little room between the stars in idleness to prate!

" O none may reach by hired speech of neighbour, priest,
  and kin
" Through borrowed deed to God's good meed that lies so
  fair within;
" Get hence, get hence to the Lord of Wrong, for doom has
  yet to run,
" And . . . the faith that ye share with Berkeley Square
  uphold you, Tomlinson! "

. . . .

The Spirit gripped him by the hair, and sun by sun they
  fell
Till they came to the belt of Naughty Stars that rim the
  mouth of Hell:
The first are red with pride and wrath, the next are white
  with pain,
But the third are black with clinkered sin that cannot burn
  again:
They may hold their path, they may leave their path, with
  never a soul to mark,
They may burn or freeze, but they must not cease in the
  Scorn of the Outer Dark.
The Wind that blows between the Worlds, it nipped him
  to the bone,
And he yearned to the flare of Hell-gate there as the light
  of his own hearthstone.
The Devil he sat behind the bars, where the desperate
  legions drew,
But he caught the hasting Tomlinson and would not let
  him through.
" Wot ye the price of good pit-coal that I must pay? "
  said he,
" That ye rank yoursel' so fit for Hell and ask no leave of
  me?
" I am all o'er-sib to Adam's breed that ye should give me
  scorn,
" For I strove with God for your First Father the day that
  he was born.

" Sit down, sit down upon the slag, and answer loud and
high
" The harm that ye did to the Sons of Men or ever you
came to die."
And Tomlinson looked up and up, and saw against the night
The belly of a tortured star blood-red in Hell-Mouth light;
And Tomlinson looked down and down, and saw beneath
his feet
The frontlet of a tortured star milk-white in Hell-Mouth
heat.
" O I had a love on earth," said he, " that kissed me to my
fall,
" And if ye would call my love to me I know she would
answer all."
—" All that ye did in love forbid it shall be written fair,
" But now ye wait at Hell-Mouth Gate and not in Berkeley
Square:
" Though we whistled your love from her bed to-night, I
trow she would not run,
" For the sin ye do by two and two ye must pay for one
by one! "
The Wind that blows between the Worlds, it cut him like
a knife,
And Tomlinson took up the tale and spoke of his sin in
life: —
" Once I ha' laughed at the power of Love and twice at the
grip of the Grave,
" And thrice I ha' patted my God on the head that men
might call me brave."
The Devil he blew on a brandered soul and set it aside to
cool:
" Do ye think I would waste my good pit-coal on the hide
of a brain-sick fool?
" I see no worth in the hobnailed mirth or the jolthead jest
ye did
"That I should waken my gentlemen that are sleeping three
on a grid."

Then Tomlinson looked back and forth, and there was little
   grace,
For Hell-Gate filled the houseless soul with the Fear of
   Naked Space.
"Nay, this I ha' heard," quo' Tomlinson, " and this was
   noised abroad,
" And this I ha' got from a Belgian book on the word of
   a dead French lord."
— " Ye ha' heard, ye ha' read, ye ha' got, good lack! and
   the tale begins afresh —
" Have ye sinned one sin for the pride o' the eye or the
   sinful lust of the flesh? "
Then Tomlinson he gripped the bars and yammered, " Let
   me in —
" For I mind that I borrowed my neighbour's wife to sin
   the deadly sin."
The Devil he grinned behind the bars, and banked the fires
   high:
" Did ye read of that sin in a book? " said he; and Tomlin-
   son said " Ay! "
The Devil he blew upon his nails, and the little devils ran,
And he said, " Go husk this whimpering thief that comes in
   the guise of a man:
" Winnow him out 'twixt star and star, and sieve his proper
   worth:
" There's sore decline in Adam's line if this be spawn of
   earth."
Empusa's crew, so naked-new they may not face the fire,
But weep that they bin too small to sin to the height of
   their desire,
Over the coal they chased the Soul, and racked it all
   abroad,
As children rifle a caddis-case or the raven's foolish hoard.
And back they came with the tattered Thing, as children
   after play,
And they said: " The soul that he got from God he has
   bartered clean away.

" We have threshed a stook of print and book, and winnowed
a chattering wind

" And many a soul wherefrom he stole, but his we cannot
find:

" We have handled him, we have dandled him, we have
seared him to the bone,

" And, Sire, if tooth and nail show truth he has no soul of
his own."

The Devil he bowed his head on his breast and rumbled
deep and low: —

" I'm all o'er-sib to Adam's breed that I should bid him go.

" Yet close we lie, and deep we lie, and if I gave him place,

" My gentlemen that are so proud would flout me to my
face;

" They'd call my house a common stews and me a careless
host,

" And — I would not anger my gentlemen for the sake of a
shiftless ghost."

The Devil he looked at the mangled Soul that prayed to
feel the flame,

And he thought of Holy Charity, but he thought of his
own good name: —

" Now ye could haste my coal to waste, and sit ye down
to fry:

" Did ye think of that theft for yourself? " said he; and
Tomlinson said " Ay! "

The Devil he blew an outward breath, for his heart was free
from care: —

" Ye have scarce the soul of a louse," he said, " but the
roots of sin are there.

" And for that sin should ye come in were I the lord alone.

" But sinful pride has rule inside — ay, mightier than my
own.

" Honour and Wit, fore-damned they sit, to each his Priest
and Whore:

" Nay, scarce I dare myself go there, and you they'd torture
sore.

" Ye are neither spirit nor spirk," he said; " ye are neither
    book nor brute —
" Go, get ye back to the flesh again for the sake of Man's
    repute.
" I'm all o'er-sib to Adam's breed that I should mock your
    pain,
" But look that ye win to worthier sin ere ye come back
    again.
" Get hence, the hearse is at your door — the grim black
    stallions wait —
" They bear your clay to place to-day.   Speed, lest ye come
    too late!
" Go back to Earth with a lip unsealed — go back with
    an open eye,
" And carry my word to the Sons of Men or ever ye come
    to die:
" That the sin they do by two and two they must pay for
    one by one —
" And . . . the God that you took from a printed book be
    with you, Tomlinson! "

THE EXPLORER [1]

" There's no sense in going further — it's the edge of culti-
    vation,"
    So they said, and I believed it — broke my land and
    sowed my crop —
Built my barns and strung my fences in the little border
    station
    Tucked away below the foothills where the trails run out
    and stop.

Till a voice, as bad as Conscience, rang interminable
    changes
    On one everlasting Whisper day and night repeated — so:

[1] From *The Five Nations.*

" Something hidden. Go and find it. Go and look behind
    the Ranges —
  " Something lost behind the Ranges. Lost and waiting
    for you. Go! "

So I went, worn out of patience; never told my nearest
    neighbours —
  Stole away with pack and ponies — left 'em drinking in
    the town;
And the faith that moveth mountains didn't seem to help
    my labours
  As I faced the sheer main-ranges, whipping up and lead-
    ing down.

March by march I puzzled through 'em, turning flanks and
    dodging shoulders,
  Hurried on in hope of water, headed back for lack of
    grass;
Till I camped above the tree-line — drifted snow and naked
    boulders —
  Felt free air astir to windward — knew I'd stumbled on
    the Pass.

" Thought to name it for the finder; but that night the
    Norther found me —
  Froze and killed the plains-bred ponies; so I called the
    camp Despair
(It's the Railway Cap to-day, though). Then my Whisper
    waked to hound me: —
  " Something lost behind the Ranges. Over yonder! Go
    you there! "

Then I knew, the while I doubted — knew His Hand was
    certain o'er me.
  Still — it might be self-delusion — scores of better men
    had died —

I could reach the township living, but . . . He knows
  what terrors tore me . . .
  But I didn't . . . but I didn't. I went down the other
  side,

Till the snow ran out in flowers, and the flowers turned to
  aloes,
  And the aloes sprung to thickets and a brimming stream
  ran by;
But the thickets dwined to thorn-scrub, and the water
  drained to shallows,
  And I dropped again on desert — blasted earth, and
  blasting sky. . . .

I remember lighting fires; I remember sitting by 'em;
  I remember seeing faces, hearing voices through the
  smoke;
I remember they were fancy — for I threw a stone to try
  'em.
  " Something lost behind the Ranges " was the only word
  they spoke.

I remember going crazy. I remember that I knew it
  When I heard myself hallooing to the funny folk I saw.
Very full of dreams that desert: but my two legs took me
  through it. . .
  And I used to watch 'em moving with the toes all black
  and raw.

But at last the country altered — White Man's country past
  disputing —
  Rolling grass and open timber, with a hint of hills
  behind —
There I found me food and water, and I lay a week re-
  cruiting.
  Got my strength and lost my nightmares. Then I entered on my find.

Thence I ran my first rough survey — chose my trees and
　blazed and ringed 'em —
　Week by week I pried and sampled — week by week
　　my findings grew.
Saul he went to look for donkeys, and by God he found a
　kingdom!
　But by God, who sent His Whisper, I had struck the
　　worth of two!

Up along the hostile mountains, where the hair-poised
　snow-slide shivers —
　Down and through the big fat marshes that the virgin
　　ore-bed stains,
Till I heard the mile-wide mutterings of unimagined rivers,
　And beyond the nameless timber saw illimitable plains!

Plotted sites of future cities, traced the easy grades between
　'em;
　Watched unharnessed rapids wasting fifty thousand head
　　an hour;
Counted leagues of water-frontage through the axe-ripe
　woods that screen 'em —
　Saw the plant to feed a people — up and waiting for the
　　power!

Well I know who'll take the credit — all the clever chaps
　that followed —
　Came, a dozen men together — never knew my desert
　　fears;
Tracked me by the camps I'd quitted, used the water-holes
　I'd hollowed
　They'll go back and do the talking. *They'll* be called
　　the Pioneers!

They will find my sites of townships — not the cities that
　I set there.
　They will rediscover rivers — not my rivers heard at
　　night.

By my own old marks and bearings they will show me how
 to get there,
 By the lonely cairns I builded they will guide my feet
 aright.

Have I named one single river? Have I claimed one single
 acre?
 Have I kept one single nugget — (barring samples)?
 No, not I!
Because my price was paid me ten times over by my
 Maker.
 But you wouldn't understand it. You go up and occupy.

Ores you'll find there; wood and cattle; water-transit sure
 and steady
 (That should keep the railway rates down), coal and
 iron at your doors.
God took care to hide that country till He judged His
 people ready,
 Then He chose me for His Whisper, and I've found it,
 and it's yours!

Yes, your " Never-never country " — yes, your " edge of
 cultivation "
 And " no sense in going further " — till I crossed the
 range to see.
God forgive me! No, *I* didn't. It's God's present to our
 nation.
 Anybody might have found it but — His Whisper came to
 Me!

ANCHOR SONG [1]

Heh! Walk her round. Heave, ah, heave her short again!
 Over, snatch her over, there, and hold her on the pawl.
Loose all sail, and brace your yards back and full —
 Ready jib to pay her off and heave short all!

[1] From *The Seven Seas.*

Well, ah, fare you well; we can stay no more with you, my
 love —
 Down, set down your liquor and your girl from off your
  knee;
   For the wind has come to say:
   " You must take me while you may,
  If you'd go to Mother Carey,
  (Walk her down to Mother Carey!),
 Oh, we're bound to Mother Carey where she feeds her
  chicks at sea! "

Heh! Walk her round. Break, ah, break it out o' that!
 Break our starboard-bower out, apeak, awash, and clear!
Port — port she casts, with the harbour-mud beneath her
 foot,
 And that's the last o' bottom we shall see this year!

Well, ah, fare you well, for we've got to take her out
 again —
 Take her out in ballast, riding light and cargo-free.
  And it's time to clear and quit
  When the hawser grips the bitt,
 So we'll pay you with the foresheet and a promise from
  the sea!

Heh! Tally on. Aft and walk away with her!
 Handsome to the cathead, now; O tally on the íall!
Stop, seize and fish, and easy on the davit-guy.
 Up, well up the fluke of her, and inboard haul!

Well, ah, fare you well, for the Channel wind's took hold
 of us,
 Choking down our voices as we snatch the gaskets free.
  And it's blowing up for night,
  And she's dropping light on light,
 And she's snorting and she's snatching for a breath of
  open sea!

Wheel, full and by; but she'll smell her road alone to-night.
Sick she is and harbour-sick — oh, sick to clear the land!
Roll down to Brest with the old Red Ensign over us —
Carry on and thrash her out with all she'll stand!

Well, ah, fare you well, and it's Ushant slams the door on us,
Whirling like a windmill through the dirty scud to lee:
Till the last, last flicker goes
From the tumbling water-rows,
And we're off to Mother Carey
(Walk her down to Mother Carey!),
Oh, we're bound for Mother Carey where she feeds her
chicks at sea!

WILLIAM ERNEST HENLEY

HAWTHORN AND LAVENDER

(Selections) [1]

❧

When, in what other life,
Where in what old, spent star,
Systems ago, dead vastitudes afar,
Were we two bird and bough, or man and wife?
Or wave and spar?
Or I the beating sea, and you the bar
On which it breaks?   I know not, I!
But this, O this, my very dear, I know:
Your voice awakes old echoes in my heart;
And things I say to you now are said once more;
And, Sweet, when we two part,
I feel I have seen you falter and linger so,
So hesitate, and turn, and cling — yet go,
As once in some immemorable Before,
Once on some fortunate yet thrice-blasted shore.

[1] The lyrics from *Hawthorn and Lavender* and *London Types* are reprinted by permission of Harper & Brothers, New York.

Was it for good?
O, these poor eyes are wet;
And yet, O, yet,
Now that we know, I would not, if I could,
Forget.

❖

Sing to me, sing, and sing again,
    My glad, great-throated nightingale:
Sing, as the good sun through the rain —
    Sing, as the home-wind in the sail!

Sing to me life, and toil, and time,
    O bugle of dawn, O flute of rest!
Sing, and once more, as in the prime,
    There shall be naught but seems the best.

And sing me at the last of love:
    Sing that old magic of the May,
That makes the great world laugh and move
    As lightly as our dream to-day!

❖

Hither, this solemn eventide,
All flushed and mystical and blue,
When the late bird sings
And sweet-breathed garden-ghosts walk sudden and wide,
Hesper, that bringeth all good things,
Brings me a dream of you.
And in my heart, dear heart, it comes and goes,
Even as the south wind lingers and falls and blows,
Even as the south wind sighs and tarries and streams,
Among the living leaves about and round;
With a still, soothing sound,
As of a multitude of dreams
Of love, and the longing of love, and love's delight,

Thronging, ten thousand deep,
Into the uncreating Night,
With semblances and shadows to fulfil,
Amaze, and thrill
The strange, dispeopled silences of Sleep.

LONDON TYPES

BARMAID

Though, if you ask her name, she says *Elise,*
Being plain *Elizabeth,* e'en let it pass,
And own that, if her aspirates take their ease,
She ever makes a point, in washing glass,
Handling the engine, turning taps for *tots,*
And countering change, and scorning what men say,
Of posing as a dove among the pots,
Nor often gives her dignity away.
Her head's a work of art, and if her eyes
Be tired and ignorant, she has a waist;
Cheaply the Mode she shadows; and she tries
From penny novels to amend her taste;
    And, having mopped the zinc for certain years,
    And faced the gas, she fades and disappears.

LONDON VOLUNTARIES

I. *Grave*

St. Margaret's bells,
Quiring their innocent, old-world canticles,
Sing in the storied air,
All rosy-and-golden, as with memories
Of woods at evensong, and sands and seas
Disconsolate for that the night is nigh.
O, the low, lingering lights!   The large last gleam
(Hark! how those brazen choristers cry and call!)

Touching these solemn ancientries, and there,
The silent River ranging tide-mark high
And the callow, grey-faced Hospital,
With the strange glimmer and glamour of a dream!
The Sabbath peace is in the slumbrous trees,
And from the wistful, the fast-widowing sky
(Hark! how those plangent comforters call and cry!)
Falls as in August plots late roseleaves fall.
The sober Sabbath stir —
Leisurely voices, desultory feet! —
Comes from the dry, dust-coloured street,
Where in their summer frocks the girls go by,
And sweethearts lean and loiter and confer,
Just as they did an hundred years ago,
Just as an hundred years to come they will: —
When you and I, Dear Love, lie lost and low,
And sweet-throats none our welkin shall fulfil,
Nor any sunset fade serene and slow;
But, being dead, we shall not grieve to die.

II. *Andante con moto*

Forth from the dust and din,
The crush, the heat, the many-spotted glare,
The odour and sense of life and lust aflare,
The wrangle and jangle of unrests,
Let us take horse, Dear Heart, take horse and win —
As from swart August to the green lap of May —
To quietness and the fresh and fragrant breasts
Of the still, delicious night, not yet aware
In any of her innumerable nests
Of that first sudden plash of dawn,
Clear, sapphirine, luminous, large,
Which tells that soon the flowing springs of day
In deep and ever deeper eddies drawn
Forward and up, in wider and wider way,
Shall float the sands, and brim the shores,
On this our lith of the World, as round it roars

And spins into the outlook of the Sun
(The Lord's first gift, the Lord's especial charge),
With light, with living light, from marge to marge
Until the course He set and staked be run.

Through street and square, through square and street,
Each with his home-grown quality of dark
And violated silence, loud and fleet,
Waylaid by a merry ghost at every lamp,
The hansom wheels and plunges. Hark, O, hark,
Sweet, how the old mare's bit and chain
Ring back a rough refrain
Upon the marked and cheerful tramp
Of her four shoes! Here is the Park,
And O, the languid midsummer wafts adust,
The tired midsummer blooms!
O, the mysterious distances, the glooms
Romantic, the august
And solemn shapes! At night this City of Trees
Turns to a tryst of vague and strange
And monstrous Majesties,
Let loose from some dim underworld to range
These terrene vistas till their twilight sets:
When, dispossessed of wonderfulness, they stand
Beggared and common, plain to all the land
For stooks of leaves! And lo! the Wizard Hour,
His silent, shining sorcery winged with power!
Still, still the streets, between their carcanets
Of linking gold, are avenues of sleep.
But see how gable ends and parapets
In gradual beauty and significance
Emerge! And did you hear
That little twitter-and-cheep,
Breaking inordinately loud and clear
On this still, spectral, exquisite atmosphere?
'Tis a first nest at matins! And behold
A rakehell cat — how furtive and acold!

A spent witch homing from some infamous dance —
Obscene, quick-trotting, see her tip and fade
Through shadowy railings into a pit of shade!
And now! a little wind and shy,
The smell of ships (that earnest of romance),
A sense of space and water, and thereby
A lamplit bridge touching the troubled sky,
And look, O, look! a tangle of silver gleams
And dusky lights, our River and all his dreams,
His dreams that never save in our deaths can die.

What miracle is happening in the air,
Charging the very texture of the grey
With something luminous and rare?
The night goes out like an ill-parcelled fire,
And, as one lights a candle, it is day.
The extinguisher, that perks it like a spire
On the little formal church, is not yet green
Across the water: but the house-tops nigher,
The corner-lines, the chimneys — look how clean,
How new, how naked!   See the batch of boats,
Here at the stairs, washed in the fresh-sprung beam!
And those are barges that were goblin floats,
Black, hag-steered, fraught with devilry and dream!
And in the piles the water frolics clear,
The ripples into loose rings wander and flee,
And we — we can behold that could but hear
The ancient River singing as he goes,
New-mailed in morning, to the ancient Sea.
The gas burns lank and jaded in its glass:
The old Ruffian soon shall yawn himself awake,
And light his pipe, and shoulder his tools, and take
His hobnailed way to work!

                                        Let us too pass —
Pass ere the sun leaps and your shadow shows —
Through these long, blindfold rows
Of casements staring blind to right and left,

Each with his gaze turned inward on some piece
Of life in death's own likeness — Life bereft
Of living looks as by the Great Release —
Pass to an exquisite night's more exquisite close!

Reach upon reach of burial — so they feel,
These colonies of dreams!   And as we steal
Homeward together, but for the buxom breeze,
Fitfully frolicking to heel
With news of dawn-drenched woods and tumbling seas,
We might — thus awed, thus lonely that we are —
Be wandering some dispeopled star,
Some world of memories and unbroken graves,
So broods the abounding Silence near and far:
Till even your footfall craves
Forgiveness of the majesty it braves.

III.   *Scherzando*

Down through the ancient Strand
The spirit of October, mild and boon
And sauntering, takes his way
This golden end of afternoon,
As though the corn stood yellow in all the land,
And the ripe apples dropped to the harvest-moon.

Lo! the round sun, half-down the western slope —
Seen as along an unglazed telescope —
Lingers and lolls, loth to be done with day:
Gifting the long, lean, lanky street
And its abounding confluences of being
With aspects generous and bland;
Making a thousand harnesses to shine
As with new ore from some enchanted mine,
And every horse's coat so full of sheen
He looks new-tailored, and every 'bus feels clean,
And never a hansom but is worth the feeing;

And every jeweller within the pale
Offers a real Arabian Night for sale;
And even the roar
Of the strong streams of toil, that pause and pour
Eastward and westward, sounds suffused —
Seems as it were bemused
And blurred, and like the speech
Of lazy seas on a lotus-haunted beach —
With this enchanted lustrousness,
This mellow magic, that (as a man's caress
Brings back to some faded face, beloved before,
A heavenly shadow of the grace it wore
Ere the poor eyes were minded to beseech)
Old things transfigures, and you hail and bless
Their looks of long-lapsed loveliness once more:
Till Clement's, angular and cold and staid,
Gleams forth in glamour's very stuffs arrayed;
And Bride's, her aëry, unsubstantial charm
Through flight on flight of springing, soaring stone
Grown flushed and warm,
Laughs into life full-mooded and fresh-blown;
And the high majesty of Paul's
Uplifts a voice of living light, and calls —
Calls to his millions to behold and see
How goodly this his London Town can be!

For earth and sky and air
Are golden everywhere,
And golden with a gold so suave and fine
The looking on it lifts the heart like wine.
Trafalgar Square
(The fountains volleying golden glaze)
Shines like an angel-market. High aloft
Over his couchant Lions, in a haze
Shimmering and bland and soft,
A dust of chrysoprase,
Our Sailor takes the golden gaze

Of the saluting sun, and flames superb,
As once he flamed it on his ocean round.
The dingy dreariness of the picture-place,
Turned very nearly bright,
Takes on a luminous transiency of grace,
And shows no more a scandal to the ground.
The very blind man pottering on the kerb
Among the posies and the ostrich feathers
And the rude voices touched with all the weathers
Of the long, varying year,
Shares in the universal alms of light.
The windows, with their fleeting, flickering fires,
The height and spread of frontage shining sheer,
The quiring signs, the rejoicing roofs and spires —
'Tis El Dorado — El Dorado plain,
The Golden City! And when a girl goes by,
Look! as she turns her glancing head,
A call of gold is floated from her ear!
Golden, all golden! In a golden glory,
Long-lapsing down a golden coasted sky,
The day not dies, but seems
Dispersed in wafts and drifts of gold, and shed
Upon a past of golden song and story
And memories of gold and golden dreams.

IV. *Largo e mesto*

Out of the poisonous East,
Over a continent of blight,
Like a maleficent Influence released
From the most squalid cellarage of hell,
The Wind-Fiend, the abominable —
The Hangman Wind that tortures temper and light —
Comes slouching, sullen and obscene,
Hard on the skirts of the embittered night;
And in a cloud unclean
Of excremental humours, roused to strife

By the operation of some ruinous change,
Wherever his evil mandate run and range,
Into a dire intensity of life,
A craftsman at his bench, he settles down
To the grim job of throttling London Town.

So, by a jealous lightlessness beset
That might have oppressed the dragons of old time
Crunching and groping in the abysmal slime,
A cave of cut-throat thoughts and villainous dreams,
Hag-rid and crying with cold and dirt and wet,
The afflicted City, prone from mark to mark
In shameful occultation, seems
A nightmare labyrinthine, dim and drifting,
With wavering gulfs and antic heights, and shifting,
Rent in the stuff of a material dark,
Wherein the lamplight, scattered and sick and pale,
Shows like the leper's living blotch of bale:
Uncoiling monstrous into street on street
Paven with perils, teeming with mischance,
Where man and beast go blindfold and in dread,
Working with oaths and threats and faltering feet
Somewhither in the hideousness ahead;
Working through wicked airs and deadly dews
That make the laden robber grin askance
At the good places in his black romance,
And the poor, loitering harlot rather choose
Go pinched and pined to bed
Than lurk and shiver and curse her wretched way
From arch to arch, scouting some three-penny prey.

Forgot his dawns and far-flushed afterglows,
His green garlands and windy eyots forgot,
The old Father-River flows,
His watchfires cores of menace in the gloom,

As he came oozing from the Pit, and bore,
Sunk in his filthily transfigured sides,
Shoals of dishonoured dead to tumble and rot
In the squalor of the universal shore:
His voices sounding through the gruesome air
As from the Ferry where the Boat of Doom
With her blaspheming cargo reels and rides:
The while his children, the brave ships,
No more adventurous and fair,
Nor tripping it light of heel as home-bound brides,
But infamously enchanted,
Huddle together in the foul eclipse,
Or feel their course by inches desperately,
As through a tangle of alleys murder-haunted,
From sinister reach to reach out — out — to sea.

And Death the while —
Death with his well-worn, lean, professional smile,
Death in his threadbare working trim —
Comes to your bedside, unannounced and bland,
And with expert, inevitable hand
Feels at your windpipe, fingers you in the lung,
Or flicks the clot well into the labouring heart:
Thus signifying unto old and young,
However hard of mouth or wild of whim,
'Tis time — 'tis time by his ancient watch — to part
From books and women and talk and drink and art.
And you go humbly after him
To a mean suburban lodging: on the way
To what or where
Not Death, who is old and very wise, can say:
And you — how should you care
So long as, unreclaimed of hell,
The Wind-Fiend, the insufferable,
Thus vicious and thus patient, sits him down
To the black job of burking London Town?

V. *Allegro maestoso*

Spring winds that blow
As over leagues of myrtle-blooms and may;
Bevies of spring clouds trooping slow,
Like matrons heavy bosomed and aglow
With the mild and placid pride of increase!   Nay,
What makes this insolent and comely stream
Of appetence, this freshet of desire
(Milk from the wild breasts of the wilful Day!),
Down Piccadilly dance and murmur and gleam
In genial wave on wave and gyre on gyre?
Why does that nymph unparalleled splash and churn
The wealth of her enchanted urn
Till, over-billowing all between
Her cheerful margents, grey and living green,
It floats and wanders, glittering and fleeing,
An estuary of the joy of being?
Why should the lovely leafage of the Park
Touch to an ecstasy the act of seeing?
— Sure, sure my paramour, my Bride of Brides,
Lingering and flushed, mysteriously abides
In some dim, eye-proof angle of odorous dark,
Some smiling nook of green-and-golden shade,
In the divine conviction robed and crowned
The globe fulfils his immemorial round
But as the marrying-place of all things made!

There is no man, this deifying day,
But feels the primal blessing in his blood.
There is no woman but disdains —
The sacred impulse of the May
Brightening like sex made sunshine through her veins —
To vail the ensigns of her womanhood.
None but, rejoicing, flaunts them as she goes,
Bounteous in looks of her delicious best,
On her inviolable quest:

These with their hopes, with their sweet secrets those,
But all desirable and frankly fair,
As each were keeping some most prosperous tryst,
And in the knowledge went imparadised!
For look! a magical influence everywhere,
Look how the liberal and transfiguring air
Washes this inn of memorable meetings,
This centre of ravishments and gracious greetings,
Till, through its jocund loveliness of length
A tidal-race of lust from shore to shore,
A brimming reach of beauty met with strength,
It shines and sounds like some miraculous dream,
Some vision multitudinous and agleam,
Of happiness as it shall be evermore!

Praise God for giving
Through this His messenger among the days
His word the life He gave is thrice-worth living!
For Pan, the bountiful, imperious Pan —
Not dead, not dead, as impotent dreamers feigned,
But the gay genius of a million Mays
Renewing his beneficent endeavour! —
Still reigns and triumphs, as he hath triumphed and reigned
Since in the dim blue dawn of time
The universal ebb-and-flow began,
To sound his ancient music, and prevails,
By the persuasion of his mighty rhyme
Here in this radiant and immortal street
Lavishly and omnipotently as ever
In the open hills, the undissembling dales,
The laughing-places of the juvenile earth.
For lo! the wills of man and woman meet,
Meet and are moved, each unto each endeared,
As once in Eden's prodigal bowers befell,
To share his shameless, elemental mirth
In one great act of faith: while deep and strong,
Incomparably nerved and cheered,

The enormous heart of London joys to beat
To the measures of his rough, majestic song;
The lewd, perennial, overmastering spell
That keeps the rolling universe ensphered,
And life, and all for which life lives to long,
Wanton and wondrous and for ever well.

RHYMES AND RHYTHMS

(Selections)

(*To James McNeill Whistler*)

Under a stagnant sky,
Gloom out of gloom uncoiling into gloom,
The River, jaded and forlorn,
Welters and wanders wearily — wretchedly — on;
Yet in and out among the ribs
Of the old skeleton bridge, as in the piles
Of some dead lake-built city, full of skulls,
Worm-worn, rat-riddled, mouldy with memories,
Lingers to babble to a broken tune
(Once, O, the unvoiced music of my heart!)
So melancholy a soliloquy
It sounds as it might tell
The secret of the unending grief-in-grain,
The terror of Time and Change and Death,
That wastes this floating, transitory world.

What of the incantation
That forced the huddled shapes on yonder shore
To take and wear the night
Like a material majesty?
That touched the shafts of wavering fire
About this miserable welter and wash —
(River, O River of Journeys, River of Dreams!)

Into long, shining signals from the panes
Of an enchanted pleasure-house,
Where life and life might live life lost in life
For ever and evermore?

O Death! O Change! O Time!
Without you, O, the insufferable eyes
Of these poor Might-Have-Beens,
These fatuous, ineffectual Yesterdays!

❖

Fresh from his fastnesses
Wholesome and spacious,
The North Wind, the mad huntsman,
Halloas on his white hounds
Over the grey, roaring
Reaches and ridges,
The forest of ocean,
The chace of the world.
Hark to the peal
Of the pack in full cry,
As he thongs them before him,
Swarming voluminous,
Weltering, wide-wallowing,
Till in a ruining
Chaos of energy,
Hurled on their quarry,
They crash into foam!

Old Indefatigable,
Time's right-hand man, the sea
Laughs as in joy
From his millions of wrinkles:
Laughs that his destiny,
Great with the greatness
Of triumphing order,
Shows as a dwarf
By the strength of his heart
And the might of his hands.

Master of masters,
O maker of heroes,
Thunder the brave,
Irresistible message: —
" Life is worth Living
Through every grain of it,
From the foundations
To the last edge
Of the cornerstone, death."

❖

Space and dread and the dark —
Over a livid stretch of sky
Cloud-monsters crawling, like a funeral train
Of huge, primeval presences
Stooping beneath the weight
Of some enormous, rudimentary grief;
While in the haunting loneliness
The far sea waits and wanders with a sound
As of the trailing skirts of Destiny,
Passing unseen
To some immitigable end
With her grey henchman, Death.

What larve, what spectre is this
Thrilling the wilderness to life
As with the bodily shape of Fear?
What but a desperate sense,
A strong foreboding of those dim
Interminable continents, forlorn
And many-silenced, in a dusk
Inviolable utterly, and dead
As the poor dead it huddles and swarms and styes
In hugger-mugger through eternity?

Life — life — let there be life!
Better a thousand times the roaring hours

When wave and wind,
Like the Arch-Murderer in flight
From the Avenger at his heel,
Storms through the desolate fastnesses
And wild waste places of the world!

Life — give me life until the end,
That at the very top of being,
The battle-spirit shouting in my blood,
Out of the reddest hell of the fight
I may be snatched and flung
Into the everlasting lull,
The immortal, incommunicable dream.

INVICTUS [1]

Out of the night that covers me,
  Black as the Pit from pole to pole,
I thank whatever gods may be
  For my unconquerable soul.

In the fell clutch of circumstance
  I have not winced nor cried aloud.
Under the bludgeonings of chance
  My head is bloody, but unbowed.

Beyond this place of wrath and tears
  Looms but the Horror of the shade,
And yet the menace of the years
  Finds, and shall find, me unafraid.

It matters not how strait the gate,
  How charged with punishments the scroll,
I am the master of my fate:
  I am the captain of my soul.

[1] This poem, though published in 1888, and composed as early as 1875, is included here because no selection of Henley's poems would be adequate without it.

LAURENCE BINYON

FOG

Magically awakened to a strange, brown night
The streets lie cold. A hush of heavy gloom
Dulls the noise of the wheels to a murmur dead:
Near and sudden the passing figures loom;
And out of darkness steep on startled sight
The topless walls in apparition emerge.
Nothing revealing but their own thin flames,
The rayless lamps burn faint and bleared and red:
Link-boys' cries, and the shuffle of horses led,
Pierce the thick air; and like a distant dirge,
Melancholy horns wail from the shrouded Thames.
Long the blind morning hooded the dumb town;
Till lo! in an instant winds arose, and the air
Lifted: at once, from a cold and spectral sky
Appears the sun, and laughs in mockery down
On groping travellers far from where they deem,
In unconjectured roads; the dwindled stream
Of traffic in slow confusion crawling by:
The baffled hive of helpless man laid bare.

THE LITTLE DANCERS

Lonely, save for a few faint stars, the sky
Dreams; and lonely, below, the little street
Into its gloom retires, secluded and shy.
Scarcely the dumb roar enters this soft retreat;
And all is dark, save where come flooding rays
From a tavern window; there, to the brisk measure
Of an organ that down in an alley merrily plays,
Two children, all alone and no one by,
Holding their tattered frocks, through an airy maze
Of motion, lightly threaded with nimble feet
Dance sedately: face to face they gaze,
Their eyes shining, grave with a perfect pleasure.

THE DRAY

Huge through the darkened street
The Dray comes, rolling an uneven thunder
Of wheels and trampling feet;
The shaken windows stare in sleepy wonder.

Now through an open space,
Where loitering groups about the tavern's fume
Show many a sullen face
And brawling figure in the lighted gloom,

It moves, a shadowy force
Through misery triumphant: flushed, on high
Guiding his easy course,
A giant sits, with indolent soft eye.

He turns not, that dim crowd
Of listless forms beneath him to behold;
Shawled women with head bowed
Flitting in hasty stealth, and children old:

Calm as some conqueror
Rode through old Rome, nor heeded at his heel,
'Mid the proud spoils of war,
What woeful captives thronged his chariot wheel.

RED NIGHT

Rolled in a smouldering mist, wrapped in an ardent cloud,
Over ridged roofs, over the buried roar
That comes and goes
Where shadowy London mutters at the core
Of meeting streets interminably ploughed
Through blackness built and steepled and immense
With felt, unfeatured, waste magnificence,
The night shudders and glows.
Ensanguined skies, that lower and lift and change

Each instant! sullen with a spectral rose
Upon the towered horizon; but more near
A lurid vapour, throbbing up the gloom,
Glares like a furnace fume;
Exhausted pallors hover faint and strange;
Dull fiery flushes melt and reappear;
While over all in lofty glimpses far
Spaces of silence and blue dream disclose
The still eye of a star.

Muffled in burning air, so dumb
Above this monstrous ever-trembling hum,
What hide you, heavens?   What sombre presences,
What powers pass over?   What dim-legioned host,
What peopled pageantries,
With gleam of arms and robes that crimsoned trail,
In silent triumph or huge mockery hail?
O, is it the tumultuous-memoried ghost
Of some lost city, fabulous and frail,
Stoops over London; Susa, Thebes, or Tyre,
Rebuilded out of mist and fire?
No, rather to its secret self revealed
The soul of London burning in the skies
Her desolations and her majesties!

There, there is all unsealed:
Terror and hope, ecstasy and despair
Their apparition yield,
While still through kindled street and shadowy square
The faces pass, the uncounted faces crowd, —
Rages, lamentings, joys, in masks of flesh concealed.

Down a grimed lane, around a bare-benched room,
Seven shapes of men are sunken, heads upon hands bowed.
— O spent and mad desires, lost in the fiery cloud,
What dungeon fled you from?
Across the river's glittering gloom,

Under the towered chimes, a youth steps, bright
With dream that all the future clothes,
Into this new, enchanted land.
Incessant stream the faces into light!
From his wife's hand
Behold a drunkard snatch the toil-earned pence,
And strike her on the patient face with oaths.
But over trees, upon a balcony,
To a young girl life murmurs up immense
Its strange delight,
And in her pulses to her spirit sings.
Along an alley thronged and flaring
A woman's loud self-loathing laughter rings.
The old prowler leers. Fierce cries a mob incense.
(Still the red Night her stormy heart is baring.)
A bent blind beggar taps along the stones.
The indifferent traffic roars and drones.
Blank under a high torch
Gapes a house-ruin, propped with beams; beneath
Some shadow-guarded and neglected porch
A girl and boy
(Whence flowered, O Night, yon soft and fearful rose?)
Press timid lips and breathe,
Speechless, their joy.
Hither and thither goes
The homeless outcast; students turn the page
By lamplight; the physician sentences;
Dull-eyed or jovial, tavern-loungers drink;
The applauded actor steps upon the stage;
Mothers with far thoughts watch upon their knees
Where children slumber; revellers stamp and shout;
Long-parted bosoms meet in sobbed embrace;
Hope, behind doors, ebbs from the waiting face;
Locked bodies sway and swell
With pain of unendurable farewell;
No instant, but some debt of terror's paid,
Some shame exacted, measureless love poured out,

Weak hearts are helped, strong men are torn,
Wild sorrow in dear arms is comforted,
The last peace dawns upon the newly dead,
And in hushed rooms is heard wail of the newly born.

What ferments rise and mingle,
Night, on your cloudy mirror! what young fire
Shoots, and what endless lassitudes expire!
Yet out of one flesh wrought,
None separate, none single!
Hater and hated, seeker and sought,
O restless, O innumerable shapes,
Kneaded by one all-urging thought,
That none diverts, that none escapes;
So thirsted for, if not in pride, in shame,
If not with tenderness, with railing curse,
If not with hands that cherish, hands that maim,
Life, how vast!   Life, how brief!
Eternally wooed and wooing,
That some would stifle, and some hotly seize,
And some by cunning trap into their mesh,
Or plunder in the darkness like a thief;
And these from rapturous pangs of flesh
Would crush to maddening wine, and these
In still renunciation lure to their soul's ease.
Though never in a single heart contained,
Though depth of it no wisest seer may plumb,
Though height of it no hero wholly gained,
Heavenly and human, twined in all our throes
Of passion that in blind heat overflows
To charge the night with thick and shuddering fume,
And felt in every cry, in every deed
Defaced or freed,
Ah, spent at such a dear and cruel cost, —
Possessed a moment, and then, like yon height
Of stars, clouded in our own selves and lost, —
Lives the supreme
Reality, diviner than all dream.

Now all the heaven like a huge smithy glows,
Hollow and palpitating dusk and glare!
Ah, forge of God, where blows
The blast of an incredible flame, what might
Shapes to what uses there
Each obdurate iron or molten fiery part
Of the one infinite wrought human heart,
In tears, love, anger, beauty, and despair
Throbbing forever, under the red night?

A. E. HOUSMAN

A SHROPSHIRE LAD

(Selections)

IV

REVEILLE

Wake: the silver dusk returning
　　Up the beach of darkness brims,
And the ship of sunrise burning
　　Strands upon the eastern rims.

Wake: the vaulted shadow shatters,
　　Trampled to the floor it spanned,
And the tent of night in tatters
　　Straws the sky-pavilioned land.

Up, lad, up, 'tis late for lying:
　　Hear the drums of morning play;
Hark, the empty highways crying
　　" Who'll beyond the hills away? "

Towns and countries woo together,
　　Forelands beacon, belfries call;
Never lad that trod on leather
　　Lived to feast his heart with all.

Up, lad: thews that lie and cumber
  Sunlit pallets never thrive;
Morns abed and daylight slumber
  Were not meant for man alive.

Clay lies still, but blood's a rover:
  Breath's a ware that will not keep;
Up, lad: when the journey's over
  There'll be time enough to sleep.

VII

When smoke stood up from Ludlow,
  And mist blew off from Teme,
And blithe afield to ploughing
  Against the morning beam
  I strode beside my team,

The blackbird in the coppice
  Looked out to see me stride,
And hearkened as I whistled
  The tramping team beside,
  And fluted and replied:

" Lie down, lie down, young yeoman;
  What use to rise and rise?
Rise man a thousand mornings
  Yet down at last he lies,
  And then the man is wise."

I heard the tune he sang me,
  And spied his yellow bill;
I picked a stone and aimed it
  And threw it with a will:
  And then the bird was still.

Then my soul within me
  Took up the blackbird's strain,

And still beside the horses
   Along the dewy lane
   It sang the song again:

"Lie down, lie down, young yeoman;
   The sun moves always west;
The road one treads to labour
   Will lead one home to rest,
   And that will be the best."

IX

On moonlit heath and lonesome bank
   The sheep beside me graze;
And yon the gallows used to clank
   Fast by the four cross ways.

A careless shepherd once would keep
   The flocks by moonlight there,[1]
And high amongst the glimmering sheep
   The dead man stood on air.

They hang us now in Shrewsbury jail:
   The whistles blow forlorn,
And trains all night groan on the rail
   To men that die at morn.

There sleeps in Shrewsbury jail tonight,
   Or wakes, as may betide,
A better lad, if things went right,
   Than most that sleep outside.

And naked to the hangman's noose
   The morning clocks will ring
A neck God made for other use
   Than strangling in a string.

[1] Hanging in chains was called keeping sheep by moonlight.

And sharp the link of life will snap,
 And dead on air will stand
Heels that held up as straight a chap
 As treads upon the land.

So here I'll watch the night and wait
 To see the morning shine,
When he will hear the stroke of eight
 And not the stroke of nine;

And wish my friend as sound a sleep
 As lads' I did not know,
That shepherded the moonlit sheep
 A hundred years ago.

XII

When I watch the living meet,
 And the moving pageant file
Warm and breathing through the street
 Where I lodge a little while,

If the heats of hate and lust
 In the house of flesh are strong,
Let me mind the house of dust
 Where my sojourn shall be long.

In the nation that is not
 Nothing stands that stood before;
There revenges are forgot,
 And the hater hates no more;

Lovers lying two and two
 Ask not whom they sleep beside,
And the bridegroom all night through
 Never turns him to the bride.

XIX

TO AN ATHLETE DYING YOUNG

The time you won your town the race
We chaired you through the market-place;
Man and boy stood cheering by,
And home we brought you shoulder-high.

Today, the road all runners come,
Shoulder-high we bring you home,
And set you at your threshold down,
Townsman of a stiller town.

Smart lad, to slip betimes away
From fields where glory does not stay
And early though the laurel grows
It withers quicker than the rose.

Eyes the shady night has shut
Cannot see the record cut,
And silence sounds no worse than cheers
After earth has stopped the ears:

Now you will not swell the rout
Of lads that wore their honours out,
Runners whom renown outran
And the name died before the man.

So set, before its echoes fade,
The fleet foot on the sill of shade,
And hold to the low lintel up
The still-defended challenge-cup.

And round that early-laurelled head
Will flock to gaze the strengthless dead,
And find unwithered on its curls
The garland briefer than a girl's.

XXIII

The lads in their hundreds to Ludlow come in for the fair,
  There's men from the barn and the forge and the mill
    and the fold,
The lads for the girls and the lads for the liquor are there,
  And there with the rest are the lads that will never be
    old.

There's chaps from the town and the field and the till and
    the cart,
  And many to count are the stalwart, and many the brave,
And many the handsome of face and the handsome of heart,
  And few that will carry their looks or their truth to the
    grave.

I wish one could know them, I wish there were tokens to
    tell
  The fortunate fellows that now you can never discern;
And then one could talk with them friendly and wish them
    farewell
  And watch them depart on the way that they will not
    return.

But now you may stare as you like and there's nothing to
    scan;
  And brushing your elbow unguessed-at and not to be told
They carry back bright to the coiner the mintage of man,
  The lads that will die in their glory and never be old.

XXIV

  Say, lad, have you things to do?
    Quick then, while your day's at prime.
  Quick, and if 'tis work for two,
    Here am I, man: now's your time.

Send me now, and I shall go;
  Call me, I shall hear you call;
Use me ere they lay me low
  Where a man's no use at all;

Ere the wholesome flesh decay,
  And the willing nerve be numb,
And the lips lack breath to say,
  " No, my lad, I cannot come."

XXVII

" Is my team ploughing,
    That I was used to drive
And hear the harness jingle
    When I was man alive? "

Ay, the horses trample,
    The harness jingles now;
No change though you lie under
    The land you used to plough.

" Is football playing
    Along the river shore,
With lads to chase the leather,
    Now I stand up no more? "

Ay, the ball is flying,
    The lads play heart and soul;
The goal stands up, the keeper
    Stands up to keep the goal.

" Is my girl happy,
    That I thought hard to leave,
And has she tired of weeping
    As she lies down at eve? "

Ay, she lies down lightly,
  She lies not down to weep:
Your girl is well contented.
  Be still, my lad, and sleep.

" Is my friend hearty,
  Now I am thin and pine,
And has he found to sleep in
  A better bed than mine? "

Yes, lad, I lie easy,
  I lie as lads would choose;
I cheer a dead man's sweetheart,
  Never ask me whose.

XXXIII

If truth in hearts that perish
  Could move the powers on high,
I think the love I bear you
  Should make you not to die.

Sure, sure, if stedfast meaning,
  If single thought could save,
The world might end tomorrow,
  You should not see the grave.

This long and sure-set liking,
  This boundless will to please,
— Oh, you should live forever
  If there were help in these.

But now, since all is idle,
  To this lost heart be kind,
Ere to a town you journey
  Where friends are ill to find.

XXXVI

White in the moon the long road lies,
　The moon stands blank above;
White in the moon the long road lies
　That leads me from my love.

Still hangs the hedge without a gust,
　Still, still the shadows stay:
My feet upon the moonlit dust
　Pursue the ceaseless way.

The world is round, so travellers tell,
　And straight though reach the track,
Trudge on, trudge on, 'twill all be well,
　The way will guide one back.

But ere the circle homeward hies
　Far, far must it remove:
White in the moon the long road lies
　That leads me from my love.

XLIII

THE IMMORTAL PART

When I meet the morning beam,
Or lay me down at night to dream,
I hear my bones within me say,
" Another night, another day.

" When shall this slough of sense be cast,
This dust of thoughts be laid at last,
The man of flesh and soul be slain
And the man of bone remain?

" This tongue that talks, these lungs that shout,
These thews that hustle us about,

This brain that fills the skull with schemes,
And its humming hive of dreams, —

" These today are proud in power
And lord it in their little hour:
The immortal bones obey control
Of dying flesh and dying soul.

" 'Tis long till eve and morn are gone:
Slow the endless night comes on,
And late to fulness grows the birth
That shall last as long as earth.

" Wanderers eastward, wanderers west,
Know you why you cannot rest?
'Tis that every mother's son
Travails with a skeleton.

" Lie down in the bed of dust;
Bear the fruit that bear you must;
Bring the eternal seed to light,
And morn is all the same as night.

" Rest you so from trouble sore,
Fear the heat o' the sun no more,
Nor the snowing winter wild,
Now you labor not with child.

" Empty vessel, garment cast,
We that wore you long shall last.
— Another night, another day."
So my bones within me say.

Therefore they shall do my will
Today while I am master still,
And flesh and soul, now both are strong,
Shall hale the sullen slaves along,

Before this fire of sense decay,
This smoke of thought blow clean away,
And leave with ancient night alone
The stedfast and enduring bone.

XLVII

THE CARPENTER'S SON

" Here the hangman stops his cart:
Now the best of friends must part.
Fare you well, for ill fare I:
Live, lads, and I will die.

" Oh, at home had I but stayed
'Prenticed to my father's trade,
Had I stuck to plane and adze,
I had not been lost, my lads.

" Then I might have built perhaps
Gallows-trees for other chaps,
Never dangled on my own,
Had I but left ill alone.

" Now, you see, they hang me high,
And the people passing by
Stop to shake their fists and curse;
So 'tis come from ill to worse.

" Here hang I, and right and left
Two poor fellows hang for theft:
All the same's the luck we prove,
Though the midmost hangs for love.

" Comrades all, that stand and gaze,
Walk henceforth in other ways;
See my neck and save your own:
Comrades all, leave ill alone.

" Make some day a decent end,
Shrewder fellows than your friend.
Fare you well, for ill fare I:
Live, lads, and I will die."

LIV

With rue my heart is laden
　　For golden friends I had,
For many a rose-lipt maiden
　　And many a lightfoot lad.

By brooks too broad for leaping
　　The lightfoot boys are laid;
The rose-lipt girls are sleeping
　　In fields where roses fade.

LXIII

I hoed and trenched and weeded,
　　And took the flowers to fair:
I brought them home unheeded;
　　The hue was not the wear.

So up and down I sow them
　　For lads like me to find,
When I shall lie below them,
　　A dead man out of mind.

Some seed the birds devour,
　　And some the season mars,
But here and there will flower
　　The solitary stars,

And fields will yearly bear them
　　As light-leaved spring comes on,
And luckless lads will wear them
　　When I am dead and gone.

THOMAS HARDY [1]

DRUMMER HODGE

They throw in Drummer Hodge, to rest
  Uncoffined — just as found:
His landmark is a kopje crest
  That breaks the veldt around;
And foreign constellations west
  Each night above his mound.

Young Hodge the Drummer never knew —
  Fresh from his Wessex home —
The meaning of the broad Karoo,
  The Bush, the dusty loam,
And why uprose to nightly view
  Strange stars amid the gloam.

Yet portion of that unknown plain
  Will Hodge forever be;
His homely Northern breast and brain
  Grow up a Southern tree,
And strange-eyed constellations reign
  His stars eternally.

THE DARKLING THRUSH

I leant upon a coppice gate
  When Frost was spectre-gray,
And Winter's dregs made desolate
  The weakening eye of day.
The tangled bine-stems scored the sky
  Like strings from broken lyres,
And all mankind that haunted nigh
  Had sought their household fires.

[1] The poems of Thomas Hardy are reprinted by permission of the author.

The land's sharp features seemed to be
 The Century's corpse outleant,
His crypt the cloudy canopy,
 The wind his death-lament.
The ancient pulse of germ and birth
 Was shrunken hard and dry,
And every spirit upon earth
 Seemed fervourless as I.

At once a voice outburst among
 The bleak twigs overhead
In a full-hearted evensong
 Of joy illimited;
An aged thrush, frail, gaunt, and small,
 In blast-beruffled plume,
Had chosen thus to fling his soul
 Upon the growing gloom.

So little cause for carollings
 Of such ecstatic sound
Was written on terrestrial things
 Afar or nigh around,
That I could think there trembled through
 His happy good-night air
Some blessed Hope, whereof he knew
 And I was unaware.

December 1900.

THE SUBALTERNS

" Poor wanderer," said the leaden sky,
 " I fain would lighten thee,
But there be laws in force on high
 Which say it must not be."

—" I would not freeze thee, shorn one," cried
 The North, " knew I but how
To warm my breath, to slack my stride;
 But I am ruled as thou."

-- " To-morrow I attack thee, wight,"
　Said Sickness. " Yet I swear
I bear thy little ark no spite,
　But am bid enter there."

— " Come hither, Son," I heard Death say;
　" I did not will a grave
Should end thy pilgrimage to-day,
　But I, too, am a slave! "

We smiled upon each other then,
　And life to me had less
Of that fell look it wore ere when
　They owned their passiveness.

BY THE EARTH'S CORPSE

" O Lord, why grievest Thou? —
　Since Life has ceased to be
Upon this globe, now cold
　As lunar land and sea,
And humankind, and fowl, and fur
　Are gone eternally,
All is the same to Thee as ere
　They knew mortality."

" O Time," replied the Lord,
　" Thou read'st me ill, I ween;
Were all *the same,* I should not grieve
　At that late earthly scene,
Now blestly past — though planned by me
　With interest close and keen! —
Nay, nay: things now are *not* the same
　As they have earlier been.

" Written indelibly
　On my eternal mind
Are all the wrongs endured
　By Earth's poor patient kind,

Which my too oft unconscious hand
  Let enter undesigned.
No god can cancel deeds foredone,
  Or thy old coils unwind!

" As when, in Noë's days,
  I whelmed the plains with sea,
So at this last, when flesh
  And herb but fossils be,
And, all extinct, their piteous dust
  Revolves obliviously,
That I made Earth, and life, and man,
  It still repenteth me! "

GOD–FORGOTTEN

I towered far, and lo! I stood within
The presence of the Lord Most High,
Sent thither by the sons of Earth, to win
    Some answer to their cry.

— " The Earth, say'st thou?   The Human race?
By Me created?   Sad its lot?
Nay: I have no remembrance of such place:
    Such world I fashioned not." —

— " O Lord, forgive me when I say
Thou spakest the word that made it all."
" The Earth of men — let me bethink me . . . Yea!
    I dimly do recall

" Some tiny sphere I built long back
(Mid millions of such shapes of mine)
So named . . . It perished, surely — not a wrack
    Remaining, or a sign?

" It lost my interest from the first,
My aims therefor succeeding ill;

Haply it died of doing as it durst? " —
 " Lord, it existeth still." —

 " Dark, then, its life! For not a cry
 Of aught it bears do I now hear;
Of its own act the threads were snapt whereby
  Its plaints had reached mine ear.

 " It used to ask for gifts of good,
 Till came its severance, self-entailed,
When sudden silence on that side ensued,
  And has till now prevailed.

 " All other orbs have kept in touch;
 Their voicings reach me speedily:
Thy people took upon them overmuch
  In sundering them from me!

 " And it is strange — though sad enough —
 Earth's race should think that one whose call
Frames, daily, shining spheres of flawless stuff
  Must heed their tainted ball! . . .

 " But sayest it is by pangs distraught,
 And strife, and silent suffering? —
Deep grieved am I that injury should be wrought
  Even on so poor a thing!

 " Thou shouldst have learnt that *Not to Mend*
 For Me could mean but *Not to Know:*
Hence, Messengers! and straightway put an end
  To what men undergo." . . .

 Homing at dawn, I thought to see
 One of the Messengers standing by.
— Oh, childish thought! . . . Yet oft it comes to me
  When trouble hovers nigh.

EDMUND GOSSE

IMPRESSION

In these restrained and careful times
Our knowledge petrifies our rhymes;
Ah! for that reckless fire men had
When it was witty to be mad.

When wild conceits were piled in scores,
And lit by flaring metaphors,
When all was crazed and out of tune, —
Yet throbbed with music of the moon.

If we could dare to write as ill
As some whose voices haunt us still,
Even we, perchance, might call our own
Their deep enchanting undertone.

We are too diffident and nice,
Too learned and too over-wise,
Too much afraid of faults to be
The flutes of bold sincerity.

For as this sweet life passes by,
We blink and nod with critic eye;
We've no words rude enough to give
Its charm so frank and fugitive.

The green and scarlet of the Park,
The undulating streets at dark,
The brown smoke blown across the blue,
This coloured city we walk through, —

The pallid faces full of pain,
The field-smell of the passing wain,
The laughter, longing, perfume, strife,
The daily spectacle of life; —

Ah! how shall this be given to rhyme,
By rhymesters of a knowing time?
Ah! for the age when verse was glad,
Being godlike, to be bad and mad.

A DREAM OF NOVEMBER

Far, far away, I know not where, I know not how,
    The skies are gray, the boughs are bare, bare boughs in
      flower;
Long lilac silk is softly drawn from bough to bough,
    With flowers of milk and buds of fawn, a broidered
      shower.

Beneath that tent an Empress sits, with slanted eyes,
    And wafts of scent from censers flit, a lilac flood;
Around her throne bloom peach and plum in lacquered dyes,
    And many a blown chrysanthemum, and many a bud.

She sits and dreams, while bonzes twain strike some rich
      bell,
    Whose music seems a metal rain of radiant dye;
In this strange birth of various blooms, I cannot tell
    Which sprang from earth, which slipped from looms,
      which sank from sky.

Beneath her wings of lilac dim, in robes of blue,
    The Empress sings a wordless hymn that thrills her
      bower;
My trance unweaves, and winds, and shreds, and weaves
    anew
    Dark bronze, bright leaves, pure silken threads, in triple
      flower.

WILLIAM SHARP

HIGH NOON AT MIDSUMMER ON
THE CAMPAGNA

High noon,
And from the purple-veilèd hills
To where Rome lies in azure mist,
Scarce any breath of wind
Upon this vast and solitary waste,
These leagues of sunscorch'd grass
Where i' the dawn the scrambling goats maintain
A hardy feast,
And where, when the warm yellow moonlight floods the flats,
Gaunt laggard sheep browse spectrally for hours
While not less gaunt and spectral shepherds stand
Brooding, or with hollow vacant eyes
Stare down the long perspectives of the dusk.
Now not a breath:
No sound;
No living thing,
Save where the beetle jars his crackling shards,
Or where the hoarse cicala fills
The heavy heated hour with palpitant whirr.
Yet hark!
Comes not a low deep whisper from the ground,
A sigh as though the immemorial past
Breathed here a long, slow, breath?
Hush'd nations sleep below; lost empires here
Are dust; and deeper still,
Dim shadowy peoples are the mould that warms
The roots of every flower that blooms and blows:
Even as we, too, bloom and fade,
Who are so fain
To be as the Night that dies not, but forever
Weaves her immortal web of starry fires;
To be as Time itself,

Time, whose vast holocausts
Lie here, deep buried from the ken of men,
Here, where no breath of wind
Ruffles the brooding heat,
The breathless blazing heat
Of Noon.

THE WHITE PEACOCK

Here where the sunlight
Floodeth the garden,
Where the pomegranate
Reareth its glory
Of gorgeous blossom;
Where the oleanders
Dream through the noontides;
And, like surf o' the sea
Round cliffs of basalt,
The thick magnolias
In billowy masses
Front the sombre green of the ilexes:
Here where the heat lies
Pale blue in the hollows,
Where blue are the shadows
On the fronds of the cactus,
Where pale blue the gleaming
Of fir and cypress,
With the cones upon them
Amber or glowing
With virgin gold:
Here where the honey-flower
Makes the heat fragrant,
As though from the gardens
Of Gulistan,
Where the bulbul singeth
Through a mist of roses
A breath were borne:

Here where the dream-flowers,
The cream-white poppies
Silently waver,
And where the Scirocco,
Faint in the hollows,
Foldeth his soft white wings in the sunlight,
And lieth sleeping
Deep in the heart of
A sea of white violets:
Here, as the breath, as the soul of this beauty
Moveth in silence, and dreamlike, and slowly,
White as a snow-drift in mountain valleys
When softly upon it the gold light lingers:
White as the foam o' the sea that is driven
O'er billows of azure agleam with sun-yellow:
Cream-white and soft as the breasts of a girl,
Moves the White Peacock, as though through the noontide
A dream of the moonlight were real for a moment.
Dim on the beautiful fan that he spreadeth,
Foldeth and spreadeth abroad in the sunlight,
Dim on the cream-white are blue adumbrations,
Shadows so pale in their delicate blueness
That visions they seem as of vanishing violets,
The fragrant white violets veined with azure,
Pale, pale as the breath of blue smoke in far woodlands.
Here, as the breath, as the soul of this beauty,
White as a cloud through the heats of the noontide
Moves the White Peacock.

AL FAR DELLA NOTTE

Hark!
As a bubbling fount
That suddenly wells
And rises in tall spiral waves and flying spray,
The high, sweet, quavering, throbbing voice
Of the nightingale!

Not yet the purple veil of dusk has fallen,
But o'er the yellow band
That binds the west
The vesper star beats like the pulse of heaven.

Up from the fields
The peasants troop
Singing their songs of love:
And oft the twang of thin string'd music breaks
High o'er the welcoming shouts,
The homing laughter.
The whirling bats are out,
And to and fro
The blue swifts wheel
Where, i' the shallows of the dusk,
The grey moths flutter
Over the pale blooms
Of the night-flowering bay.
Softly adown the slopes,
And o'er the plain,
Ave Maria
Solemnly soundeth.
The long day is over.
Dusk, and silence now:
And Night, that is as dew
On the Flower of the World.

FIONA MACLEOD (William Sharp)

THE ROSE OF FLAME

Oh, fair immaculate rose of the world, rose of my dream,
my Rose!
Beyond the ultimate gates of dream I have heard thy mystical call:
It is where the rainbow of hope suspends and the river of
rapture flows —
And the cool sweet dews from the wells of peace forever fall.

And all my heart is aflame because of the rapture and peace,
And I dream, in my waking dreams and deep in the dreams
    of sleep,
Till the high sweet wonderful call that shall be the call of
    release
Shall ring in my ears as I sink from gulf to gulf and from
    deep to deep —

Sink deep, sink deep beyond the ultimate dreams of all
    desire —
Beyond the uttermost limit of all that the craving spirit
    knows:
Then, then, oh then I shall be as the inner flame of thy fire,
O fair immaculate rose of the world, Rose of my dream,
    my Rose!

THE VOICE AMONG THE DUNES

I have heard the sea-wind sighing
    Where the dune-grasses grow,
The sighing of the dying
    Where the salt tides flow.

For where the salt tides flow
    The sullen dead are lifting
Tired arms, and to and fro
    Are idly drifting.

So through the grey dune-grasses
    Not the wind only cries,
But a dim sea-wrought Shadow
    Breathes drownéd sighs.

THE LOST STAR

A star was loosed from heaven;
    All saw it fall, in wonder,
Where universe clashed universe
    With solar thunder.

The angels praised God's glory,
To send his beacon-flare
To show the terror of darkness
Beneath the Golden Stair.

But God was brooding only
Upon new births of light;
The star was a drop of water
On the lips of Eternal Light.

THE WASHER OF THE FORD

There is a lonely stream in a lone dim land;
It hath white dust for shore it has, white bones bestrew the
strand:
The only thing that liveth there is a naked leaping sword;
But I, who a seer am, have seen the whirling hand
Of the Washer of the Ford.

A shadowy shape of cloud and mist, of gloom and dusk, she
stands,
The Washer of the Ford:
She laughs, at times, and strews the dust through the hollow
of her hands.
She counts the sins of all men there, and slays the red-
stained horde —
The ghosts of all the sins of men must know the whirling
sword
Of the Washer of the Ford.

She stoops and laughs when in the dust she sees a writhing
limb:
" Go back into the ford," she says, " and hither and thither
swim;
Then I shall wash you white as snow, and shall take you
by the hand,
And slay you there in silence with this my whirling brand,

And trample you into the dust of this white, windless
    sand " —
           This is the laughing word
           Of the Washer of the Ford
           Along that silent strand.

THE VALLEY OF WHITE POPPIES

Between the grey pastures and the dark wood
A valley of white poppies is lit by the low moon:
    It is the grave of dreams, a holy rood.

It is quiet there: no wind doth ever fall.
Long, long ago a wind sang once a heart-sweet rune.
    Now the white poppies grow, silent and tall.

A white bird floats there like a drifting leaf:
It feeds upon faint sweet hopes and perishing dreams
    And the still breath of unremembering grief.

And as a silent leaf the white bird passes,
Winnowing the dusk by dim forgetful streams.
    I am alone now among the silent grasses.

THE VALLEY OF PALE BLUE FLOWERS

In a hidden valley a pale blue flower grows.
It is so pale that in the moonshine it is dimmer than dim
    gold,
    And in the starshine paler than the palest rose.

It is the flower of dream. Who holds it is never old.
It is the flower of forgetfulness: and oblivion is youth:
    Breathing it, flame is not empty air, dust is not cold.

Lift it, and there is no memory of sorrow or any ruth;
The grey monotone of the low sky is filled with light;
    The dim, terrible, impalpable lie wears the raiment of
      truth.

I lift it, now, for somewhat in the heart of the night
Fills me with dread. It may be that, as a tiger in his lair,
Memory, crouching, waits to spring into the light.

No, I will clasp it close to my heart, overdroop with my
hair:
I will breathe thy frail faint breath, O pale blue flower,
And then . . . and then . . . nothing shall take me unaware!

Nothing: no thought: no fear: only the invisible power
Of the vast deeps of night, wherein down a shadowy stair
My soul slowly, slowly, slowly, will sink to its ultimate
hour.

ARTHUR SYMONS [1]

SEPTEMBER IDYL: IN THE HAMMOCK:
CHAMÉANE

A sky of green and gold, tremulous, delicate,
Starred with pale blue, and bright with little voices; wind
Lifting the golden outer fringe, autumn has thinned;
A yellow leaf drops rustling, and another: wait,
The leaves begin to whisper, and the voices cease:
I hear the silence; but a voice flutters again,
A little, fluting voice, soft, piercing, as the rain;
I close my eyes, and all my body sways with peace.
Delicate, tremulous, seen under eyelids closed,
The sky of green and gold sways over me, and seems
To fill the languid soul with the desire of dreams;
But the sky fades, and only inner eyelids, rosed
With filtered sunlight falling, shadow as they pass
Not even dreams; until a trailing hand perceives,
Sudden, the earth again, in the crisp touch of leaves,
And the arresting slender fingers of the grass.

[1] The poems of Arthur Symons are reprinted by permission of the author.

TWILIGHT

The pale grey sea crawls stealthily
Up the pale lilac of the beach;
A bluer grey, the waters reach
To where the horizon ends the sea.

Flushed with a tinge of dusky rose,
The clouds, a twilit lavender,
Flood the low sky, and duskier
The mist comes flooding in, and flows

Into the twilight of the land,
And darkness, coming softly down,
Rustles across the fading sand
And folds its arms about the town.

IN AUTUMN

Frail autumn lights upon the leaves
Beacon the ending of the year;
The windy rains are here,
Wet nights, and blowing winds about the eaves.

Here in the valley, mists begin
To breathe about the river side
The breath of autumn-tide;
The dark fields wait to take the harvest in.

And you, and you are far away.
Ah, this it is, and not the rain
Now loud against the pane,
That takes the light and colour from the day!

BEFORE THE SQUALL

The wind is rising on the sea,
The windy white foam-dancers leap;
And the sea moans uneasily,
And turns to sleep, and cannot sleep.

Ridge after rocky ridge uplifts
Wild hands, and hammers at the land,
Scatters in liquid dust, and drifts
To death among the dusty sand.

On the horizon's nearing line,
Where the sky rests, a visible wall,
Grey in the offing, I divine
The sails that fly before the squall.

IN AN OMNIBUS

Your smile is like a treachery,
A treachery adorable;
So smiles the siren where the sea
Sings to the unforgetting shell.

Your fleeting Leonardo face,
Parisian Mona Lisa, dreams
Elusively, but not of streams
Born in a shadow-haunted place.

Of Paris, Paris is your thought,
Of Paris robes, and when to wear
The latest bonnet you have bought
To match the marvel of your hair.

Yet that fine malice of your smile,
That faint and fluctuating glint
Between your eyelids, does it hint
Alone of matters mercantile?

Close lips that keep the secret in,
Half spoken by the stealthy eyes,
Is there indeed no word to win,
No secret, from the vague replies

Of lips and lids that feign to hide
That which they feign to render up?
Is there, in Tantalus' dim cup,
The shadow of water, nought beside?

EMMY

Emmy's exquisite youth and her virginal air,
Eyes and teeth in the flash of a musical smile,
Come to me out of the past, and I see her there
As I saw her once for a while.

Emmy's laughter rings in my ears, as bright,
Fresh and sweet as the voice of a mountain brook,
And still I hear her telling us tales that night,
Out of Boccaccio's book.

There, in the midst of the villainous dancing-hall,
Leaning across the table, over the beer,
While the music maddened the whirling skirts of the ball,
As the midnight hour drew near,

There with the women, haggard, painted, and old,
One fresh bud in a garland withered and stale,
She, with her innocent voice and her clear eyes, told
Tale after shameless tale.

And ever the witching smile, to her face beguiled,
Paused and broadened, and broke in a ripple of fun,
And the soul of a child looked out of the eyes of a child
Or ever the tale was done.

O my child, who wronged you first, and began
First the dance of death that you dance so well?
Soul for soul: and I think the soul of a man
Shall answer for yours in hell.

THE BEGGARS

It is the beggars who possess the earth.
Kings on their throne have but the narrow girth
Of some poor known dominion; these possess
All the unknown, and that vast happiness
Of the uncertainty of human things.
Wandering on eternal wanderings,
They know the world; and, tasting but the bread
Of charity, know man; and, strangely led
By some vague, certain, and appointed hand,
Know fate; and, being lonely, understand
Some little of the thing without a name
That sits by the roadside and talks with them,
When they are silent; for the soul is shy
If more than its own shadow loiter by.
They and the birds are old acquaintances,
Knowing the dawn together; theirs it is
To settle on the dusty land like crows,
The ragged vagabonds of the air; who knows
How they too shall be fed, day after day,
And surer than the birds, for are not they
The prodigal sons of God, our piteous
Aliens, outcast and accusing us?
Do they not ask of us their own, and wait,
Humbly, among the dogs about the gate,
While we are feasting? They will wait till night:
Who shall wait longer?

Dim, shadowy, white,
The highway calls; they follow till it ends,
And all the way they walk among their friends,
Sun, wind, and rain, their tearful sister rain,
Their brother wind.   Forest and hill and plain
Know them and are forgotten.   Grey and old,
Their feet begin to linger, brown arms fold
The heavy peace of earth about their heart,
And soon, and without trouble, they depart
On the last journey.

As the beggar lies,
With naked face, remembering the skies,
I think he only wonders: Shall I find
A good road still, a hayrick to my mind,
A tavern now and then upon the road?
He has been earth's guest; he goes; the old abode
Drops to the old horizon, and the day
Is over, and the dark is on the way.

THE OLD WOMEN

They pass upon their old, tremulous feet,
Creeping with little satchels down the street,
And they remember, many years ago,
Passing that way in silks.   They wander, slow
And solitary, through the city ways,
And they alone remember those old days
Men have forgotten.   In their shaking heads
A dancer of old carnivals yet treads
The measure of past waltzes, and they see
The candles lit again, the patchouli
Sweeten the air, and the warm cloud of musk
Enchant the passing of the passionate dusk.
Then you will see a light begin to creep
Under the earthen eyelids, dimmed with sleep,

And a new tremor, happy and uncouth,
Jerking about the corners of the mouth.
Then the old head drops down again, and shakes,
Muttering.

Sometimes, when the swift gaslight wakes
The dreams and fever of the sleepless town,
A shaking huddled thing in a black gown
Will steal at midnight, carrying with her
Violet little bags of lavender,
Into the tap-room full of noisy light;
Or, at the crowded earlier hour of night,
Sidle, with matches, up to some who stand
About a stage-door, and, with furtive hand,
Appealing: " I too was a dancer, when
Your fathers would have been young gentlemen! "
And sometimes, out of some lean ancient throat,
A broken voice, with here and there a note
Of unspoilt crystal, suddenly will arise
Into the night, while a cracked fiddle cries
Pantingly after; and you know she sings
The passing of light, famous, passing things.
And sometimes, in the hours past midnight, reels
Out of an alley upon staggering heels,
Or into the dark keeping of the stones
About a doorway, a vague thing of bones
And draggled hair.

And all these have been loved.
And not one ruinous body has not moved
The heart of man's desire, nor has not seemed
Immortal in the eyes of one who dreamed
The dream that men call love. This is the end
Of much fair flesh; it is for this you tend
Your delicate bodies many careful years,
To be this thing of laughter and of tears,
To be this living judgment of the dead,
An old grey woman with a shaking head.

DIVISIONS ON A GROUND — NO. II

The sorrowful, who have loved, I pity not;
But those, not having loved, who do rejoice
To have escaped the cruelty of love,
I pity, as I pity the unborn.
Love is, indeed, as life is, full of care,
The tyrant of the soul, the death of peace,
Rash father and blind parricide of joy;
And it were better never to have been,
If slothful ease, calm hours, are all of life,
Than to have chosen such a bedfellow.
Yet, if not rest, but rapture, and to attain
The wisdom that is silence in the stars
When the great morning-song is quieted,
Be more of life than these, and worth the pain
Of living, then choose love, although he bring
Mountainous griefs, griefs that have made men mad.
Be sorrowful, all ye that have not loved,
Bow down, be sorrowful exceedingly,
Cover your heads from the embracing air,
And from the eye of the sun, lest ye be shamed;
Earth would be naked of you; ye have known
Only to hide from living; life rejects
The burden of your uncompanioned days.
This is of all things saddest in the world,
Not that men love, not that men die for love,
But that they dare be cowards of their joy,
Even unto death; who, dying without love,
Drop into narrow graves to shiver there
Among the winds of time, till time's last wind
Cleanse off the poor, lonely, and finite dust
From earth made ready for eternity.

DIVISIONS ON A GROUND — NO. III

Let me hear music, for I am not sad,
But half in love with sadness.   To dream so,
And dream, and so forget the dream, and so
Dream I am dreaming!   This old little voice,
Which pants and flutters in the clavichord,
Has the bird's wings in it, and women's tears,
The dust has drunken long ago, and sighs
As of a voiceless crying of old love
That died and never spoke; and then the soul
Of one who sought for wisdom; and these cry
Out of the disappointment of the grave.
And something, in the old and little voice,
Calls from so farther off than far away,
I tremble, hearing it, lest it draw me forth,
This flickering self, desiring to be gone,
Into the boundless and abrupt abyss
Whereat begins infinity; and there
This flickering self wander eternally
Among the soulless, uncreated winds
Which storm against the barriers of the world.
But most I hear the pleading and sad voice
Of beauty, sad because it cannot speak
Out of harsh stones and out of evil noise,
And out of thwarted faces, and the gleam
Of things corrupted, and all ruinous things.
This is the voice that cries, and would be heard,
And can but speak in music.   Venerable
And ageless beauty of the world, whose breath
Is life in all things, I have seen your form
In cloud, and grass, and wave, and glory of man,
Flawless, but I have heard your very voice
Here only, here only human, and here sad
Only of all your voices upon earth.

PROLOGUE: BEFORE THE CURTAIN

We are the puppets of a shadow-play,
We dream the plot is woven of our hearts,
Passionately we play the self-same parts
Our fathers have played passionately yesterday,
And our sons play to-morrow. There's no speech
In all desire, nor any idle word,
Men have not said and women have not heard;
And when we lean and whisper each to each
Until the silence quickens to a kiss,
Even so the actor and the actress played
The lovers yesterday; when the lights fade
Before our feet, and the obscure abyss
Opens, and darkness falls about our eyes,
'Tis only that some momentary rage
Or rapture blinds us to forget the stage,
Like the wise actor, most in this thing wise.
We pass, and have our gesture; love and pain
And hope and apprehension and regret
Weave ordered lines into a pattern set
Not for our pleasure, and for us in vain.
The gesture is eternal; we who pass
Pass on the gesture; we, who pass, pass on
One after one into oblivion,
As shadows dim and vanish from a glass.

EPILOGUE: CREDO

Each, in himself, his hour to be and cease
Endures alone, but who of men shall dare,
Sole with himself, his single burden bear,
All the long day until the night's release?
Yet ere night falls, and the last shadows close,
This labour of himself is each man's lot;
All he has gained of earth shall be forgot,

Himself he leaves behind him when he goes.
If he has any valiancy within,
If he has made his life his very own,
If he has loved or laboured, and has known
A strenuous virtue, or a strenuous sin;
Then, being dead, his life was not all vain,
For he has saved what most desire to lose,
And he has chosen what the few must choose,
Since life, once lived, shall not return again.
For of our time we lose so large a part
In serious trifles, and so oft let slip
The wine of every moment, at the lip
Its moment, and the moment of the heart.
We are awake so little on the earth,
And we shall sleep so long, and rise so late,
If there is any knocking at that gate
Which is the gate of death, the gate of birth.

VIOLET

This was a sweet white wildwood violet
I found among the painted slips that grow
Where, under hot-house glass, the flowers forget
How the sun shines, and how the cool winds blow.

The violet took the orchid's colouring,
Tricked out its dainty fairness like the rest;
Yet still its breath was as the breath of Spring,
And the wood's heart was wild within its breast.

The orchid mostly is the flower I love,
And violets, the mere violets of the wood,
For all their sweetness, have not power to move
The curiosity that rules my blood.

Yet here, in this spice-laden atmosphere,
Where only nature is a thing unreal,
I found in just a violet, planted here,
The artificial flower of my ideal.

OPALS

My soul is like this cloudy, flaming opal ring.
The fields of earth are in it, green and glimmering,
The waves of the blue sky, night's purple flower of noon,
The vanishing cold scintillations of the moon,
And the red heart that is a flame within a flame.
And as the opal dies, and is reborn the same,
And all the fire that is its life-blood seems to dart
Through the veined variable intricacies of its heart,
And ever wandering ever wanders back again,
So must my swift soul constant to itself remain.
Opal, have I not been as variable as you?
But, cloudy opal flaming green and red and blue,
Are you not ever constant in your varying,
Even as my soul, O captive opal of my ring?

FROM ROMANCES SANS PAROLES

(Translated from Paul Verlaine)

Tears in my heart that weeps,
Like the rain upon the town.
What drowsy languor steeps
In tears my heart that weeps?

O sweet sound of the rain
On earth and on the roofs!
For a heart's weary pain
O the song of the rain!

Vain tears, vain tears, my heart!
What, none hath done thee wrong?
Tears without reason start
From my disheartened heart.

This is the weariest woe,
O heart, of love and hate
Too weary, not to know
Why thou hast all this woe.

WIND ON THE SEA

The loneliness of the sea is in my heart,
And the wind is not more lonely than this grey mind.
I have thought far thoughts, I have loved, I have loved, and
    I find
Love gone, thought weary, and I, alas, left behind.

The loneliness of my heart is in the sea,
And my mind is not more lonely than this grey wind.
Who shall stay the feet of the sea, or bind
The wings of the wind? only the feet of mankind
Grow old in the place of their sorrow, and bitter is the heart
That may not wander as the wind or return as the sea.

THE LAST MEMORY

When I am old, and think of the old days,
And warm my hands before a little blaze,
Having forgotten love, hope, fear, desire,
I shall see, smiling out of the pale fire,
One face, mysterious and exquisite;
And I shall gaze, and ponder over it,
Wondering, was it Leonardo wrought
That stealthy ardency, where passionate thought
Burns inward, a revealing flame, and glows
To the last ecstasy, which is repose?
Was it Bronzino, those Borghese eyes?
And, musing thus among my memories,
O unforgotten! you will come to seem,
As pictures do, remembered, some old dream.
And I shall think of you as something strange,
And beautiful, and full of helpless change,

Which I beheld and carried in my heart;
But you, I loved, will have become a part
Of the eternal mystery, and love
Like a dim pain; and I shall bend above
My little fire, and shiver, being cold,
When you are no more young, and I am old.

THE LOOM OF DREAMS

I broider the world upon a loom,
I broider with dreams my tapestry;
Here in a little lonely room
I am master of the earth and sea,
And the planets come to me.

I broider my life into the frame,
I broider my love, thread upon thread;
The world goes by with its glory and shame,
Crowns are bartered and blood is shed;
I sit and broider my dreams instead.

And the only world is the world of my dreams,
And my weaving the only happiness;
For what is the world but what it seems?
And who knows but that God, beyond our guess,
Sits weaving worlds out of loneliness.

ERNEST DOWSON

VITAE SUMMA BREVIS SPEM NOS
VETAT INCOHARE LONGAM

They are not long, the weeping and the laughter,
  Love and desire and hate:
I think they have no portion in us after
  We pass the gate.

They are not long, the days of wine and roses:
    Out of a misty dream
Our path emerges for a while, then closes
    Within a dream.

NUNS OF THE PERPETUAL
ADORATION

Calm, sad, secure; behind high convent walls,
    These watch the sacred lamp, these watch and pray:
And it is one with them when evening falls,
    And one with them the cold return of day.

These heed not time; their nights and days they make
    Into a long, returning rosary,
Whereon their lives are threaded for Christ's sake;
    Meekness and vigilance and chastity.

A vowed patrol, in silent companies,
    Life-long they keep before the living Christ.
In the dim church, their prayers and penances
    Are fragrant incense to the Sacrificed.

Outside, the world is wild and passionate;
    Man's weary laughter and his sick despair
Entreat at their impenetrable gate:
    They heed no voices in their dream of prayer.

They saw the glory of the world displayed;
    They saw the bitter of it, and the sweet;
They knew the roses of the world should fade,
    And be trod under by the hurrying feet.

Therefore they rather put away desire,
    And crossed their hands and came to sanctuary;
And veiled their heads and put on coarse attire:
    Because their comeliness was vanity.

And there they rest; they have serene insight
  Of the illuminating dawn to be:
Mary's sweet Star dispels for them the night,
  The proper darkness of humanity.

Calm, sad, secure; with faces worn and mild:
  Surely their choice of vigil is the best?
Yea! for our roses fade, the world is wild;
  But there, beside the altar, there, is rest.

TO ONE IN BEDLAM

With delicate, mad hands, behind his sordid bars,
Surely he hath his posies, which they tear and twine;
Those scentless wisps of straw, that miserably line
His strait, caged universe, whereat the dull world stares,

Pedant and pitiful. O, how his rapt gaze wars
With their stupidity! Know they what dreams divine
Lift his long, laughing reveries like enchanted wine,
And make his melancholy germane to the stars?

O lamentable brother! if those pity thee,
Am I not fain of all thy lone eyes promise me;
Half a fool's kingdom, far from men who sow and reap,
All their days, vanity? Better than mortal flowers,
Thy moon-kissed roses seem: better than love or sleep,
The star-crowned solitude of thine oblivious hours!

AMOR PROFANUS

Beyond the pale of memory,
In some mysterious dusky grove;
A place of shadows utterly,
Where never coos the turtle-dove,
A world forgotten of the sun:
I dreamed we met when day was done,
And marvelled at our ancient love.

Met there by chance, long kept apart,
We wandered through the darkling glades;
And that old language of the heart
We sought to speak: alas! poor shades!
Over our pallid lips had run
The waters of oblivion,
Which crown all loves of men or maids.

In vain we stammered: from afar
Our old desire shone cold and dead:
That time was distant as a star,
When eyes were bright and lips were red.
And still we went with downcast eye
And no delight in being nigh,
Poor shadows most uncomforted.

Ah, Lalage! while life is ours,
Hoard not thy beauty rose and white,
But pluck the pretty, fleeting flowers
That deck our little path of light:
For all too soon we twain shall tread
The bitter pastures of the dead:
Estranged, sad spectres of the night.

YVONNE OF BRITTANY

In your mother's apple-orchard,
    Just a year ago, last spring:
Do you remember, Yvonne!
    The dear trees lavishing
Rain of their starry blossoms
    To make you a coronet?
Do you remember, Yvonne?
    As I remember yet.

In your mother's apple-orchard,
    When the world was left behind:
You were shy, so shy, Yvonne!
    But your eyes were calm and kind.

We spoke of the apple harvest,
    When the cider press is set,
And such-like trifles, Yvonne!
    That doubtless you forget.

In the still, soft Breton twilight,
    We were silent; words were few,
Till your mother came out chiding,
    For the grass was bright with dew:
But I know your heart was beating,
    Like a fluttered, frightened dove.
Do you ever remember, Yvonne?
    That first faint flash of love?

In the fulness of midsummer,
    When the apple-bloom was shed,
Oh, brave was your surrender,
    Though shy the words you said.
I was so glad, so glad, Yvonne!
    To have led you home at last;
Do you ever remember, Yvonne!
    How swiftly the days passed?

In your mother's apple-orchard
    It is grown too dark to stray,
There is none to chide you, Yvonne!
    You are over far away.
There is dew on your grave grass, Yvonne!
    But your feet it shall not wet:
No, you never remember, Yvonne!
    And I shall soon forget.

BENEDICTIO DOMINI

Without, the sullen noises of the street!
    The voice of London, inarticulate,
Hoarse and blaspheming, surges in to meet
    The silent blessing of the Immaculate.

Dark is the church, and dim the worshippers,
 Hushed with bowed heads as though by some old spell,
While through the incense-laden air there stirs
 The admonition of a silver bell.

Dark is the church, save where the altar stands,
 Dressed like a bride, illustrious with light,
Where one old priest exalts with tremulous hands
 The one true solace of man's fallen plight.

Strange silence here: without, the sounding street
 Heralds the world's swift passage to the fire:
O Benediction, perfect and complete!
 When shall men cease to suffer and desire?

NON SUM QUALIS ERAM BONAE
SUB REGNO CYNARAE

Last night, ah, yesternight, betwixt her lips and mine
There fell thy shadow, Cynara! thy breath was shed
Upon my soul between the kisses and the wine;
And I was desolate and sick of an old passion,
 Yea, I was desolate and bowed my head:
I have been faithful to thee, Cynara! in my fashion.

All night upon mine heart I felt her warm heart beat,
Night-long within mine arms in love and sleep she lay;
Surely the kisses of her bought red mouth were sweet;
But I was desolate and sick of an old passion,
 When I awoke and found the dawn was gray:
I have been faithful to thee, Cynara! in my fashion.

I have forgot much, Cynara! gone with the wind,
Flung roses, roses riotously with the throng,
Dancing, to put thy pale, lost lilies out of mind;
But I was desolate and sick of an old passion,
 Yea, all the time, because the dance was long:
I have been faithful to thee, Cynara! in my fashion.

I cried for madder music and for stronger wine,
But when the feast is finished and the lamps expire,
Then falls thy shadow, Cynara! the night is thine;
And I am desolate and sick of an old passion,
    Yea, hungry for the lips of my desire:
I have been faithful to thee, Cynara! in my fashion.

EXILE

By the sad waters of separation
    Where we have wandered by divers ways,
I have but the shadow and imitation
    Of the old memorial days.

In music I have no consolation,
    No roses are pale enough for me;
The sound of the waters of separation
    Surpasseth roses and melody.

By the sad waters of separation
    Dimly I hear of an hidden place
The sigh of mine ancient adoration:
    Hardly can I remember your face.

If you be dead, no proclamation
    Sprang to me over the waste, gray sea:
Living, the waters of separation
    Sever for ever your soul from me.

No man knoweth our desolation;
    Memory pales of the old delight;
While the sad waters of separation
    Bear us on to the ultimate night.

SPLEEN

I was not sorrowful, I could not weep,
And all my memories were put to sleep.

I watched the river grow more white and strange,
All day till evening I watched it change.

All day till evening I watched the rain
Beat wearily upon the window pane.

I was not sorrowful, but only tired
Of everything that ever I desired.

Her lips, her eyes, all day became to me
The shadow of a shadow utterly.

All day mine hunger for her heart became
Oblivion, until the evening came,

And left me sorrowful, inclined to weep,
With all my memories that could not sleep.

YOU WOULD HAVE UNDERSTOOD ME

> Ah, dans ces mornes séjours
> Les jamais sont les toujours.
> PAUL VERLAINE.

You would have understood me, had you waited;
    I could have loved you, dear! as well as he:
Had we not been impatient, dear! and fated
        Always to disagree.

What is the use of speech? Silence were fitter:
    Lest we should still be wishing things unsaid.
Though all the words we ever spake were bitter,
        Shall I reproach you dead?

Nay, let this earth, your portion, likewise cover
    All the old anger, setting us apart:
Always, in all, in truth was I your lover;
        Always, I held your heart.

I have met other women who were tender,
  As you were cold, dear! with a grace as rare.
Think you, I turned to them, or made surrender,
  I who had found you fair?

Had we been patient, dear! ah, had you waited,
  I had fought death for you, better than he:
But from the very first, dear! we were fated
  Always to disagree.

Late, late, I come to you, now death discloses
  Love that in life was not to be our part:
On your low lying mound between the roses,
  Sadly I cast my heart.

I would not waken you: nay! this is fitter;
  Death and the darkness give you unto me;
Here we who loved so, were so cold and bitter,
  Hardly can disagree.

VAIN RESOLVES

I said: " There is an end of my desire:
  Now have I sown, and I have harvested,
And these are ashes of an ancient fire,
  Which, verily, shall not be quickened.
Now will I take me to a place of peace,
  Forget mine heart's desire;
In solitude and prayer, work out my soul's release.

" I shall forget her eyes, how cold they were;
  Forget her voice, how soft it was and low,
With all my singing that she did not hear,
  And all my service that she did not know.
I shall not hold the merest memory
  Of any days that were,
Within those solitudes where I will fasten me."

And once she passed, and once she raised her eyes,
    And smiled for courtesy, and nothing said:
And suddenly the old flame did uprise,
    And all my dead desire was quickened.
Yea! as it hath been, it shall ever be,
    Most passionless, pure eyes!
Which never shall grow soft, nor change, nor pity me.

EXTREME UNCTION

Upon the eyes, the lips, the feet,
    On all the passages of sense,
The atoning oil is spread with sweet
    Renewal of lost innocence.

The feet, that lately ran so fast
    To meet desire, are soothly sealed;
The eyes, that were so often cast
    On vanity, are touched and healed.

From troublous sights and sounds set free;
    In such a twilight hour of breath,
Shall one retrace his life, or see,
    Through shadows, the true face of death?

Vials of mercy!   Sacring oils!
    I know not where nor when I come,
Nor through what wanderings and toils,
    To crave of you Viaticum.

Yet, when the walls of flesh grow weak,
    In such an hour, it well may be,
Through mist and darkness, light will break,
    And each anointed sense will see.

IMPENITENTIA ULTIMA

Before my light goes out for ever if God should give me a
    choice of graces,
    I would not reck of length of days, nor crave for things
      to be;
But cry: "One day of the great lost days, one face of all
    the faces,
    Grant me to see and touch once more and nothing more
      to see.

" For, Lord, I was free of all Thy flowers, but I chose the
    world's sad roses,
    And that is why my feet are torn and mine eyes are blind
      with sweat,
But at Thy terrible judgment-seat, when this my tired life
    closes,
    I am ready to reap whereof I sowed, and pay my righteous
      debt.

" But once before the sand is run and the silver thread is
    broken,
    Give me a grace and cast aside the veil of dolorous years,
Grant me one hour of all mine hours, and let me see for a
    token
    Her pure and pitiful eyes shine out, and bathe her feet
      with tears."

Her pitiful hands should calm, and her hair stream down
    and blind me,
    Out of the sight of night, and out of the reach of fear,
And her eyes should be my light whilst the sun went out
    behind me,
    And the viols in her voice be the last sound in mine ear.

Before the ruining waters fall and my life be carried under,
    And Thine anger cleave me through as a child cuts down
      a flower,

I will praise Thee, Lord, in Hell, while my limbs are racked
    asunder,
  For the last sad sight of her face and the little grace of
    an hour.

CARTHUSIANS

Through what long heaviness, assayed in what strange fire,
  Have these white monks been brought into the way of
    peace,
Despising the world's wisdom and the world's desire,
  Which from the body of this death bring no release?

Within their austere walls no voices penetrate;
  A sacred silence only, as of death, obtains;
Nothing finds entry here of loud or passionate;
  This quiet is the exceeding profit of their pains.

From many lands they came, in divers fiery ways;
  Each knew at last the vanity of earthly joys;
And one was crowned with thorns, and one was crowned
    with bays,
  And each was tired at last of the world's foolish noise.

It was not theirs with Dominic to preach God's holy wrath,
  They were too stern to bear sweet Francis' gentle sway;
Theirs was a higher calling and a steeper path,
  To dwell alone with Christ, to meditate and pray.

A cloistered company, they are companionless,
  None knoweth here the secret of his brother's heart:
They are but come together for more loneliness,
  Whose bond is solitude and silence all their part.

O beatific life! Who is there shall gainsay,
  Your great refusal's victory, your little loss,
Deserting vanity for the more perfect way,
  The sweeter service of the most dolorous Cross.

Ye shall prevail at last!   Surely ye shall prevail!
   Your silence and austerity shall win at last:
Desire and mirth, the world's ephemeral lights shall fail,
   The sweet star of your queen is never overcast.

We fling up flowers and laugh, we laugh across the wine;
   With wine we dull our souls and careful strains of art;
Our cups are polished skulls round which the roses twine:
   None dares to look at Death who leers and lurks apart.

Move on, white company, whom that has not sufficed!
   Our viols cease, our wine is death, our roses fail:
Pray for our heedlessness, O dwellers with the Christ!
   Though the world fall apart, surely ye shall prevail.

DREGS

The fire is out, and spent the warmth thereof
(This is the end of every song man sings!)
The golden wine is drunk, the dregs remain,
Bitter as wormwood and as salt as pain;
And health and hope have gone the way of love
Into the drear oblivion of lost things.
Ghosts go along with us until the end;
This was a mistress, this, perhaps, a friend.
With pale, indifferent eyes, we sit and wait
For the dropt curtain and the closing gate:
This is the end of all the songs man sings.

RONDEAU

Ah, Manon, say, why is it we
Are one and all so fain of thee?
Thy rich red beauty debonnaire
In very truth is not more fair,
Than the shy grace and purity

That clothe the maiden maidenly;
Her gray eyes shine more tendorly
And not less bright than thine her hair,
   Ah, Manon, say!
Expound, I pray, the mystery
Why wine-stained lip and languid eye,
And most unsaintly Maenad air,
Should move us more than all the rare
White roses of virginity?
   Ah, Manon, say!

LIBERA ME

Goddess the laughter-loving, Aphrodite, befriend!
Long have I served thine altars, serve me now at the end,
Let me have peace of thee, truce of thee, golden one, send.

Heart of my heart have I offered thee, pain of my pain,
Yielding my life for the love of thee into thy chain;
Lady and goddess be merciful, loose me again.

All things I had that were fairest, my dearest and best,
Fed the fierce flames on thine altar: ah, surely, my breast
Shrined thee alone among goddesses, spurning the rest.

Blossom of youth thou hast plucked of me, flower of my
    days;
Stinted I nought in thine honouring, walked in thy ways,
Song of my soul pouring out to thee, all in thy praise.

Fierce was the flame while it lasted, and strong was thy wine,
Meet for immortals that die not, for throats such as thine,
Too fierce for bodies of mortals, too potent for mine.

Blossom and bloom hast thou taken, now render to me
Ashes of life that remain to me, few though they be,
Truce of the love of thee, Cyprian, let me go free.

Goddess the laughter-loving, Aphrodite, restore
Life to the limbs of me, liberty, hold me no more
Having the first-fruits and flower of me, cast me the core.

A LAST WORD

Let us go hence: the night is now at hand;
   The day is overworn, the birds all flown;
   And we have reaped the crops the gods have sown;
Despair and death; deep darkness o'er the land,
Broods like an owl; we cannot understand
   Laughter or tears, for we have only known
   Surpassing vanity: vain things alone
Have driven our perverse and aimless band.

Let us go hence, somewhither strange and cold,
   To Hollow Lands where just men and unjust
Find end of labour, where's rest for the old,
   Freedom to all from love and fear and lust.
Twine our torn hands!   O pray the earth enfold
   Our life-sick hearts and turn them into dust.

LIONEL JOHNSON

TO MORFYDD

A voice on the winds,
A voice by the waters,
   Wanders and cries:
Oh! what are the winds?
And what are the waters?
   Mine are your eyes!

Western the winds are,
And western the waters,
   Where the light lies:

Oh! what are the winds?
And what are the waters?
   Mine are your eyes!

Cold, cold, grow the winds,
And wild grow the waters,
   Where the sun dies:
Oh! what are the winds?
And what are the waters?
   Mine are your eyes!

And down the night winds,
And down the night waters,
   The music flies:
Oh! what are the winds?
And what are the waters?
Cold be the winds,
And wild be the waters,
   So mine be your eyes!

TO MORFYDD DEAD

II

Morfydd at midnight
Met the Nameless Ones:
Now she wanders on the winds,
   White and lone.
I would give the light
Of eternal suns,
To be with her on the winds,
   No more lone!

Oh, wild sea of air!
Oh, night's vast sweet noon!
We would wander through the night,
   Star and star.

Nay! but she, most fair!
Sun to me and moon:
I the vassal of her flight,
Far and far.

Morfydd at midnight
Met the Nameless Ones:
Now she wanders on the winds,
White and lone.
Take from me the light,
God! of all Thy suns:
Give me her, who on the winds
Wanders lone!

A STRANGER

Her face was like sad things: was like the lights
Of a great city, seen from far off fields,
Or seen from sea: sad things, as are the fires
Lit in a land of furnaces by night:
Sad things, as are the reaches of a stream
Flowing beneath a golden moon alone.
And her clear voice, full of remembrances,
Came like faint music down the distant air.
As though she had a spirit of dead joy
About her, looked the sorrow of her ways:
If light there be, the dark hills are to climb
First: and if calm, far over the long sea.
Fallen from all the world apart she seemed,
Into a silence and a memory.
What had the thin hands done, that now they strained
Together in such passion?   And those eyes,
What saw they long ago, that now they dreamed
Along the busy streets, blind but to dreams?
Her white lips mocked the world, and all therein:
She had known more than this; she wanted not
This, who had known the past so great a thing.

Moving about our ways, herself she moved
In things done, years remembered, places gone.
Lonely, amid the living crowds, as dead,
She walked with wonderful and sad regard:
With us, her passing image: but herself
Far over the dark hills and the long sea.

FRIENDS

IV

O patron Saints of all my friends!
O guardian Angels of them all!
With them begins, with them still ends,
    My prayer's most passionate call.

You know my voice: you know their names,
That wing so its least selfish tone
Across your white celestial flames,
    And up to the White Throne.

Heaven were not Heaven, and they not there;
Heaven were no Heaven, my friends away:
O Saints and Angels! hear the prayer,
    I pray you every day.

THE CHURCH OF A DREAM

Sadly the dead leaves rustle in the whistling wind,
Around the weather-worn, gray church, low down the vale:
The Saints in golden vesture shake before the gale;
The glorious windows shake, where still they dwell en-
    shrined;
Old Saints by long dead, shrivelled hands, long since
    designed:
There still, although the world autumnal be, and pale,
Still in their golden vesture the old saints prevail;
Alone with Christ, desolate else, left by mankind.

Only one ancient Priest offers the Sacrifice,
Murmuring holy Latin immemorial:
Swaying with tremulous hands the old censer full of spice,
In gray, sweet incense clouds; blue, sweet clouds mystical:
To him, in place of men, for he is old, suffice
Melancholy remembrances and vesperal.

THE AGE OF A DREAM

Imageries of dreams reveal a gracious age:
Black armour, falling lace, and altar lights at morn.
The courtesy of Saints, their gentleness and scorn,
Lights on an earth more fair, than shone from Plato's page:
The courtesy of knights, fair calm and sacred rage:
The courtesy of love, sorrow for love's sake borne.
Vanished, those high conceits!   Desolate and forlorn,
We hunger against hope for that lost heritage.

Gone now, the carven work!   Ruined, the golden shrine!
No more the glorious organs pour their voice divine;
No more rich frankincense drifts through the Holy Place:
Now from the broken tower, what solemn bell still tolls,
Mourning what piteous death?   Answer, O saddened souls!
Who mourn the death of beauty and the death of grace.

A PROSELYTE

Heart of magnificent desire:
O equal of the lordly sun!
Since thou hast cast on me thy fire,
My cloistral peace, so hardly won,
   Breaks from its trance:
    One glance
From thee hath all its joy undone.

Of lonely quiet was my dream;
Day gliding into fellow day,
With the mere motion of a stream:
But now in vehement disarray
  Go time and thought,
    Distraught
With passion kindled at thy ray.

Heart of tumultuary might,
O greater than the mountain flame,
That leaps upon the fearful night!
On me thy devastation came,
  Sudden and swift;
    A gift
Of joyous torment without name.

Thy spirit stings my spirit: thou
Takest by storm and ecstasy
The cloister of my soul. And now,
With ardour that is agony,
  I do thy will;
    Yet still
Hear voices of calm memory.

THE PRECEPT OF SILENCE

I know you: solitary griefs,
Desolate passions, aching hours!
I know you: tremulous beliefs,
Agonized hopes, and ashen flowers!

The winds are sometimes sad to me;
The starry spaces, full of fear:
Mine is the sorrow on the sea,
And mine the sigh of places drear.

Some players upon plaintive strings
Publish their wistfulness abroad:
I have not spoken of these things,
    Save to one man, and unto God.

MYSTIC AND CAVALIER

Go from me: I am one of those, who fall.
What! hath no cold wind swept your heart at all,
In my sad company?   Before the end,
    Go from me, dear my friend!

Yours are the victories of light: your feet
Rest from good toil, where rest is brave and sweet.
But after warfare in a mourning gloom,
    I rest in clouds of doom.

Have you not read so, looking in these eyes?
Is it the common light of the pure skies,
Lights up their shadowy depths?   The end is set:
    Though the end be not yet.

When gracious music stirs, and all is bright,
And beauty triumphs through a courtly night;
When I too joy, a man like other men:
    Yet, am I like them, then?

And in the battle, when the horsemen sweep
Against a thousand deaths, and fall on sleep:
Who ever sought that sudden calm, if I
    Sought not?   Yet, could not die.

Seek with thine eyes to pierce this crystal sphere:
Canst read a fate there, prosperous and clear?
Only the mists, only the weeping clouds:
    Dimness, and airy shrouds.

Beneath, what angels are at work?   What powers
Prepare the secret of the fatal hours?
See! the mists tremble, and the clouds are stirred:
  When comes the calling word?

The clouds are breaking from the crystal ball,
Breaking and clearing: and I look to fall.
When the cold winds and airs of portent sweep,
  My spirit may have sleep.

O rich and sounding voices of the air!
Interpreters and prophets of despair:
Priests of a fearful sacrament!   I come,
  To make with you mine home.

THE DARK ANGEL

Dark Angel, with thine aching lust
To rid the world of penitence:
Malicious Angel, who still dost
My soul such subtile violence!

Because of thee, no thought, no thing,
Abides for me undesecrate:
Dark Angel, ever on the wing,
Who never reachest me too late!

When music sounds, then changest thou
Its silvery to a sultry fire:
Nor will thine envious heart allow
Delight untortured by desire.

Through thee, the gracious Muses turn
To Furies, O mine Enemy!
And all the things of beauty burn
With flames of evil ecstasy.

Because of thee, the land of dreams
Becomes a gathering place of fears:
Until tormented slumber seems
One vehemence of useless tears.

When sunlight glows upon the flowers,
Or ripples down the dancing sea:
Thou, with thy troop of passionate powers,
Beleaguerest, bewilderest, me.

Within the breath of autumn woods,
Within the wintry silences:
Thy venomous spirit stirs and broods,
O Master of impieties!

The ardour of red flame is thine,
And thine the steely soul of ice:
Thou poisonest the fair design
Of nature, with unfair device.

Apples of ashes, golden bright;
Waters of bitterness, how sweet!
O banquet of a foul delight,
Prepared by thee, dark Paraclete!

Thou art the whisper in the gloom,
The hinting tone, the haunting laugh:
Thou art the adorner of my tomb,
The minstrel of mine epitaph.

I fight thee, in the Holy Name!
Yet, what thou dost, is what God saith:
Tempter! should I escape thy flame,
Thou wilt have helped my soul from Death:

The second Death, that never dies,
That cannot die, when time is dead:
Live Death, wherein the lost soul cries,
Eternally uncomforted.

Dark Angel, with thine aching lust!
Of two defeats, of two despairs:
Less dread, a change to drifting dust,
Than thine eternity of cares.

Do what thou wilt, thou shalt not so,
Dark Angel! triumph over me:
Lonely, unto the Lone I go;
Divine, to the Divinity.

THE DARKNESS

Master of spirits! hear me: King of souls!
I kneel before thine altar, the long night,
Besieging Thee with penetrable prayers;
And all I ask, light from the Face of God.
Thy darkness Thou hast given me enough,
The dark clouds of Thine angry majesty:
Now give me light!   I cannot always walk
Surely beneath the full and starless night.
Lighten me, fallen down, I know not where,
Save, to the shadows and the fear of death.
Thy Saints in light see light, and sing for joy:
Safe from the dark, safe from the dark and cold.
But from my dark comes only doubt of light:
Disloyalty, that trembles to despair.
Now bring me out of night, and with the sun
Clothe me, and crown me with Thy seven stars,
Thy spirits in the hollow of Thine hand.
Thou from the still throne of Thy tabernacle
Wilt come to me in glory, O Lord God!
Thou wilt, I doubt Thee not: I worship Thee
Before Thine holy altar, the long night.
Else have I nothing in the world, but death:
Thine hounding winds rush by me day and night,
Thy seas roar in mine ears: I have no rest,
No peace, but am afflicted constantly,
Driven from wilderness to wilderness.

And yet Thou hast a perfect house of light,
Above the four great winds, an house of peace:
Its beauty of the crystal and the dew,
Guard Angels and Archangels, in their hands
The blade of a sword shaken. Thither bring
Thy servant: when the black night falls on me,
With bitter voices tempting in the gloom,
Send out Thine armies, flaming ministers,
And shine upon the night: for what I would,
I cannot, save these help me. O Lord God!
Now, when my prayers upon Thine altar lie,
When Thy dark anger is too hard for me:
Through vision of Thyself, through flying fire,
Have mercy, and give light, and stablish me!

WILLIAM BUTLER YEATS [1]

THE LAKE ISLE OF INNISFREE

I will arise and go now, and go to Innisfree,
   And a small cabin build there, of clay and wattles made;
Nine bean rows will I have there, a hive for the honey bee,
   And live alone in the bee-loud glade.

And I shall have some peace there, for peace comes drop-
    ping slow,
   Dropping from the veils of the morning to where the
    cricket sings;
There midnight's all a glimmer, and noon a purple glow,
   And evening full of the linnet's wings.

I will arise and go now, for always night and day
   I hear lake water lapping with low sounds by the shore;
While I stand on the roadway, or on the pavements gray,
   I hear it in the deep heart's core.

---

[1] The poems of William Butler Yeats are reprinted by permission of the Macmillan Company, New York.

WHEN YOU ARE OLD

When you are old and gray and full of sleep,
And nodding by the fire, take down this book,
And slowly read, and dream of the soft look
Your eyes had once, and of their shadows deep;

How many loved your moments of glad grace,
And loved your beauty with love false or true;
But one man loved the pilgrim soul in you,
And loved the sorrows of your changing face.

And bending down beside the glowing bars
Murmur, a little sadly, how love fled
And paced upon the mountains overhead
And hid his face amid a crowd of stars.

THE LOVER TELLS OF THE ROSE
IN HIS HEART

All things uncomely and broken, all things worn out and old,
The cry of a child by the roadway, the creak of a lumbering
    cart,
The heavy steps of the ploughman, splashing the wintry
    mould,
Are wronging your image that blossoms a rose in the deeps
    of my heart.

The wrong of unshapely things is a wrong too great to be
    told;
I hunger to build them anew and sit on a green knoll apart,
With the earth and the sky and the water, remade, like a
    casket of gold
For my dreams of your image that blossoms a rose in the
    deeps of my heart.

HE REMEMBERS FORGOTTEN BEAUTY

When my arms wrap you round I press
My heart upon the loveliness
That has long faded from the world;
The jewelled crowns that kings have hurled
In shadowy pools, when armies fled;
The love-tales wrought with silken thread
By dreaming ladies upon cloth
That has made fat the murderous moth;
The roses that of old time were
Woven by ladies in their hair,
The dew-cold lilies ladies bore
Through many a sacred corridor
Where such gray clouds of incense rose
That only the gods' eyes did not close:
For that pale breast and lingering hand
Come from a more dream-heavy land,
A more dream-heavy hour than this;
And when you sigh from kiss to kiss
I hear white Beauty sighing, too,
For hours when all must fade like dew
But flame on flame, deep under deep,
Throne over throne, where in half sleep
Their swords upon their iron knees
Brood her high lonely mysteries.

THE SORROW OF LOVE

The quarrel of the sparrows in the eaves,
The full round moon and the star-laden sky,
And the loud song of the ever-singing leaves,
Had hid away earth's old and weary cry.

And then you came with those red mournful lips,
And with you came the whole of the world's tears,

And all the trouble of her labouring ships,
And all the trouble of her myriad years.

And now the sparrows warring in the eaves,
The curd-pale moon, the white stars in the sky,
And the loud chaunting of the unquiet leaves,
Are shaken with earth's old and weary cry.

INTO THE TWILIGHT

Out-worn heart, in a time out-worn,
Come clear of the nets of wrong and right;
Laugh heart again in the gray twilight,
Sigh, heart, again in the dew of the morn.

Your mother Eire is always young,
Dew ever shining and twilight gray;
Though hopes fall from you and love decay,
Burning in fires of a slanderous tongue.

Come, heart, where hill is heaped upon hill:
For there the mystical brotherhood
Of sun and moon and hollow and wood
And river and stream work out their will;

And God stands winding His lonely horn,
And time and the world are ever in flight;
And love is less kind than the gray twilight,
And hope is less dear than the dew of the morn.

THE ROSE OF THE WORLD

Who dreamed that beauty passes like a dream?
For these red lips, with all their mournful pride,
Mournful that no new wonder may betide,
Troy passed away in one high funeral gleam,
And Usna's children died.

We and the labouring world are passing by:
Amid men's souls, that waver and give place,
Like the pale waters in their wintry race,
Under the passing stars, foam of the sky,
Lives on this lonely face.

Bow down, archangels, in your dim abode:
Before you were, or any hearts to beat,
Weary and kind one lingered by His seat;
He made the world to be a grassy road
Before her wandering feet.

THE SECRET ROSE

Far off, most secret, and inviolate Rose,
Enfold me in my hour of hours; where those
Who sought thee in the Holy Sepulchre,
Or in the wine vat, dwell beyond the stir
And tumult of defeated dreams; and deep
Among pale eyelids, heavy with the sleep
Men have named beauty. Thy great leaves enfold
The ancient beards, the helms of ruby and gold
Of the crowned Magi; and the king whose eyes
Saw the Pierced Hands and Rood of elder rise
In druid vapour and make the torches dim;
Till vain frenzy awoke and he died; and him
Who met Fand walking among flaming dew
By a gray shore where the wind never blew,
And lost the world and Emer for a kiss;
And him who drove the gods out of their liss,
And till a hundred morns had flowered red,
Feasted and wept the barrows of his dead;
And the proud dreaming king who flung the crown
And sorrow away, and calling bard and clown
Dwelt among wine-stained wanderers in deep woods;
And him who sold tillage, and house, and goods,

And sought through lands and islands numberless years,
Until he found with laughter and with tears,
A woman, of so shining loveliness,
That men threshed corn at midnight by a tress,
A little stolen tress. I, too, await
The hour of thy great wind of love and hate.
When shall the stars be blown about the sky,
Like the sparks blown out of a smithy, and die?
Surely thine hour has come, thy great wind blows,
Far off, most secret, and inviolate Rose?

TO THE ROSE UPON THE ROOD OF TIME

Red Rose, proud Rose, sad Rose of all my days!
Come near me, while I sing the ancient ways:
Cuchulain battling with the bitter tide;
The Druid, gray, wood-nurtured, quiet-eyed,
Who cast round Fergus dreams, and ruin untold;
And thine own sadness, whereof stars, grown old
In dancing silver sandalled on the sea,
Sing in their high and lonely melody.
Come near, that no more blinded by man's fate,
I find under the boughs of love and hate,
In all poor foolish things that live a day,
Eternal beauty wandering on her way.
Come near, come near, come near — Ah, leave me still
A little space for the rose-breath to fill!
Lest I no more hear common things that crave;
The weak worm hiding down in its small cave,
The field mouse running by me in the grass,
The heavy mortal hopes that toil and pass;
But seek alone to hear the strange things said
By God to the bright hearts of those long dead,
And learn to chaunt a tongue men do not know.
Come near; I would, before my time to go,
Sing of old Eire and the ancient ways:
Red Rose, proud Rose, sad Rose of all my days.

G. A. GREENE

SONG OF THE SONGSMITHS

(First Anniversary of the Rhymers' Club)

Here do we meet again,
  After a full year's time:
Here do we meet again,
Meet with our old refrain,
  Praise of the regal rhyme.
Songsmiths like them who of old
Fashioned their speech of gold
  In a far, forgotten clime,
We at that ancient fire
With our young bright breath suspire,
  And hammer the golden rhyme,
  Hammer the ringing rhyme
    Till the echoes tire.

Who is it jeers at our song?
  Scoffs at an art sublime?
Who is it jeers at our song?
We who know right from wrong
  Worship the godlike rhyme.
Still on the world-wide breeze,
Over the surge of the seas,
  Comes like an echoed chime
The voice of all passions that play
In the dim heart of man alway,
  With the rush of a rolling rhyme,
  The lilt of a lulling rhyme,
    To the end of day.

Ours is the prentice-hand;
  Yet 'tis in us no crime,
Here in the misty land,
To seek for the fire that was fanned
  By kings of the kingly rhyme.

They have gone down to the shade,
Leaving the songs they made
  A wreath for the brows of Time.
Still is the great world young;
Not yet is the lyre unstrung,
  As it shakes to the quivering rhyme,
  Sighs for the resonant rhyme
    Of the songs unsung.

Ours are the echoes at least
  That fell from that golden prime;
Ours are the echoes at least,
Ours are the crumbs from the feast
  At the feet of the queenly rhyme:
Ours be the task to prolong
The joy and the sorrow of song
  In the midst of years that begrime;
In the clinging mist of the years,
With reverent toil and with tears,
  To hammer the golden rhyme,
  Hammer the ringing rhyme
    Till the mad world hears.

DRIFTING

As one that drifting in an open boat
  Down a broad river, singing, wayfareth,
While on the banks few listeners hear the note,

And pause and hearken, till the lapsing stream
  Seaward bears on the bark whence murmureth
Music that fails and dies, a flying dream:

Such is my song. Borne downward on the tide,
  I cannot tell what echoes of my breath
Are caught by listeners on the riverside:
  I and my songs glide onward unto death.

BEYOND?

What lies beyond the splendour of the sun,
  Beyond his flashing belt of sister-spheres?
  What deeps are they whereinto disappears
The visitant comet's sword, of fire fine-spun?

What rests beyond the myriad lights that run
  Their nightly race around our human fears?
  Hope-signals raised on multitudinous spears
Of armies captained by the Eternal One?

Beyond the sun, and far beyond the stars,
  Beyond the weariness of this our day,
Beyond this fretting at the prison-bars,
  The urgent soul, divine in soulless clay,
Bids us set forth, through endless avatars,
  To seek where God hath hidden Himself away.

VICTOR PLARR

TO A BRETON BEGGAR

(Dol Cathedral)

In the brown shadow of the transept door,
  Grey kings and granite prophets overhead,
Which are so ancient they can age no more,
  A beggar begs his bread.

He too is old, — so old, and worn, and still,
  He seems a part of those gaunt sculptures there,
By wizard masons dowered with power and will
  To moan sometimes in prayer: —

To moan in prayer, moving thin carven lips,
    And with faint senses striving to drink in
Some golden sound which peradventure slips
    From the altar's heart within.

What is thy prayer?   Is it a plaintive praise,
    An intercession, or an anguished plaint;
Remorse, O sinner, for wild vanished days,
    Or ecstasy, O saint?

And through long hours, when thou art wont to sit
    In moveless silence, what inspires thy thought?
Is thine an utter drowsing; or shall wit
    Still travail, memory-fraught?

Hear'st thou old battles?   Wast thou one of those
    Whose angry fire-locks made the hillsides ring,
When, clad in skins and rags, the Chouans rose
    To die for Church and King?

Or dost thou view, in weird and sad array,
    The long-dead Cymry — they of whom men tell
That always to the war they marched away,
    And that they always fell?

So moving are thine eyes which cannot see,
    So great a resignation haunts thy face,
I often think that I behold in thee
    The symbol of thy race:

Not as it was when bards Armorican
    Sang the high pageant of their Age of Gold;
But as it is, a sombre long-tressed man,
    Exceedingly poor and old.

With somewhat in his eyes for some to read,
    Albeit dimmed with years and scarcely felt, —
The mystery of an antique deathless Creed,
    The glamour of the Celt.

EPITAPHIUM CITHARISTRIAE

Stand not uttering sedately
  Trite oblivious praise above her!
Rather say you saw her lately
  Lightly kissing her last lover.

Whisper not, " There is a reason
  Why we bring her no white blossom."
Since the snowy bloom's in season
  Strow it on her sleeping bosom!

Oh, for it would be a pity
  To o'erpraise her or to flout her.
She was wild, and sweet, and witty —
  Let's not say dull things about her.

THE NIGHT–JAR [1]

On the river, in the shallows, on the shore,
  Are the darkness and the silence of the tomb;
O'er the woods the sunset tinged an hour before
      Utter gloom.

'Twixt the ramparts of the mighty aspen trees,
  In midstream, the pallid waters gleam afar,
Not a ripple on their surface, not a breeze,
      Not a star.

Where the shadow of the ruined water-mill
  Hides the mill-pool and its anchored lily fleet,
And the warm air seems to slumber over-still,
      Over-sweet,

[1] " They are the witches among birds."

Hark the Night-jar!   In the meadows by the stream
  Sounds the bird's unearthly note: I like it well,
For it lulls you as the mystery of a dream,
              Or a spell.

All the nightingales along the bowery reach
  Plain together when the midnight moon is bright:
This bird only knows by heart the secret speech
              Of dark night.

Turn the boat now! row away, friends; let us hence,
  Lest the glamour of the night's o'er-trancing breath
Plunge us one and all into that dream intense
              Which is Death!

TO A GREEK GEM

Was it the signet of an Antonine —
This middle-finger ring, whose bezel glows
With the most lovely of intaglios
E'er wrought by craftsman in an age divine?
Or was it borne by grim Tiberius' line
At lustful festals and fierce wild beast shows?
Signed it wise edicts, or when Lucan chose
His artful liberal death was it the sign?

I cannot tell, nor can this lucent toy.
I only know that these small graven forms,
This cymbal-playing maenad and this boy,
In their delightful beauty shall live on,
Crannied 'mong crashing rocks, when Time's last storms
Have whelmed us in the sands we build upon.

T. W. ROLLESTON

NIGHT
(After all)

When the time comes for me to die,
  To-morrow, or some other day,
If God should bid me make reply,
  " What would'st thou? " I shall say,

O God, Thy world was great and fair;
  Yet give me to forget it clean!
Vex me no more with things that were,
  And things that might have been.

I loved, I toiled, throve ill or well,
  — Lived certain years and murmured not.
Now grant me in that land to dwell
  Where all things are forgot.

For others, Lord, Thy purging fires,
  The loves reknit, the crown, the palm.
For me, the death of all desires
  In deep, eternal calm.

NOON–DAY
(Elegiacs)

Wind, O wind of the Spring, thine old enchantment renew-
    ing,
  How at the shock of thy might wakens a cry within me!
Out of what wonderful lands never trodden by man, never
    told of,
  Lands where never a ship anchored or trafficker fared,
Comest thou, breathing like flame till the brown earth flames
    into blossom,
  Quickening the sap of old woods swayed in thy stormy
    embrace,

Rousing in depths of the heart the wild waves of an infinite
longing,
Longing for freedom and life, longing for Springs that
are dead?
Surely the far blue sea, foam-flecked with the speed of thy
coming,
Brightened in laughter abroad, sang at the feet of the
isles,
Stirred in a tumult of joy, as my soul stirs trembling with
passion,
Trembling with passion and hope, wild with the spirit of
Spring.
Ah, what dreams re-arise, half pain half bliss to remember,
Hearing the storm of thy song, blown from the height of
the skies:
*Something remains upon earth to be done, to be dared, to
be sought for.*
Up with the anchor again! out with the sails to the blast!
*Out to the shock of the seas that encircle the Fortunate
Islands,*
*Vision and promise and prize, home of the Wind of the
Spring!*

JOHN TODHUNTER

EUTHANASIA

(Fin de siècle)

Yes, this rich death were best:
Lay poison on thy lips, kiss me to sleep,
Or on the siren billow of thy breast
Bring some voluptuous Lethe for life's pain,
Some languorous nepenthe that will creep
Drowsily from vein to vein;
That slowly, drowsily, will steep
Sense after sense, till, down long gulfs of rest
Whirled like a leaf, I sink to the lone deep.

It shall be afternoon,
And roses, roses breathing in the air!
Deliciously the splendour of deep June,
    Tempered through amber draperies, round us fall;
        And, like a dream of Titian, let thy hair
            Bosom and arms glow all,
        Clouds of love's sunset, o'er me there:
    Kiss that last kiss; then low some golden tune
        Sing, for the dirge of our superb despair.

    So let the clock tick on,
Measuring the soft pulsations of Time's wing,
While to the pulseless ocean, like a swan
    Abandoned to an unrelenting stream,
        Floating, I hear thee faint and fainter sing;
            Till death athwart my dream
        Shall glide, robed like a Magian king,
    And ease with poppies of oblivion
        This heart, the scorpion Life no more may sting.

THE SONG OF TRISTRAM

The star of love is trembling in the west,
    Night hears the desolate sea with moan on moan
    Sigh for the storm, who on his mountains lone
Smites his wild harp and dreams of her wild breast.
    I am thy storm, Isolt, and thou my sea!
        Isolt!
    My passionate sea!

The storm to her wild breast, the passionate sea
    To his fierce arms: we to the rapturous leap
    Of mated spirits mingling in love's deep,
Flame to flame, I to thee and thou to me!
    Thou to mine arms, Isolt, I to thy breast!
        Isolt!
    I to thy breast!

ARTHUR CECIL HILLIER

IN EXCELSIS

Above the world at our window seat
All the murmur of London rises high,
From the hansoms racing along the street,
And the flaring stalls and the passers-by.

As the lamps of a rolling carriage gleam
You may catch for a moment a woman's face,
And a soft-robed figure — a vanishing dream
Of a white burnoose and a flutter of lace.

One argent star o'er the clock-tower wakes
More pure than the spark of a Northern night,
Where the sleeping woodlands and lonely lakes
Wed the splendour of frost to the glory of light.

Above the world at our window-sill
O'er the countless roofs of the city of care,
The darkness falls, and my pulses thrill
At the touch of thy cheek and the scent of thine hair.

We have lived here long through the dreary days
Of the sun and the rain and the trodden snow:
We have watched of an evening the heaven ablaze
With the smoky glare of the afterglow.

We have lived together and known great joys
And have sorrowed for much beyond recall,
And been soiled with the dust and deafened with noise,
And the crowd heeds not, but the stars know all.

RICHARD LE GALLIENNE

A BALLAD OF LONDON

Ah, London! London! our delight,
Great flower that opens but at night,
Great City of the midnight sun,
Whose day begins when day is done.

Lamp after lamp against the sky
Opens a sudden beaming eye,
Leaping alight on either hand,
The iron lilies of the Strand.

Like dragonflies, the hansoms hover,
With jewelled eyes, to catch the lover,
The streets are full of lights and loves,
Soft gowns, and flutter of soiled doves.

The human moths about the light
Dash and cling close in dazed delight,
And burn and laugh, the world and wife,
For this is London, this is life!

Upon thy petals butterflies,
But at thy root, some say, there lies,
A world of weeping trodden things,
Poor worms that have not eyes or wings.

From out corruption of their woe
Springs this bright flower that charms us so,
Men die and rot deep out of sight
To keep this jungle-flower bright.

Paris and London, World-Flowers twain
Wherewith the World-Tree blooms again,
Since Time hath gathered Babylon,
And withered Rome still withers on.

Sidon and Tyre were such as ye,
How bright they shone upon the tree!
But Time hath gathered, both are gone,
And no man sails to Babylon.

Ah, London! London! our delight,
For thee, too, the eternal night,
And Circe Paris hath no charm
To stay Time's unrelenting arm.

BEAUTY ACCURST

I am so fair that wheresoe'er I wend
 Men yearn with strange desire to kiss my face,
Stretch out their hands to touch me as I pass,
 And women follow me from place to place.

A poet writing honey of his dear
 Leaves the wet page, — ah, leaves it long to dry,
The bride forgets it is her marriage morn,
 The bridegroom too forgets as I go by.

Within the street where my strange feet shall stray
 All markets hush and traffickers forget,
In my gold head forget their meaner gold,
 The poor man grows unmindful of his debt.

Two lovers kissing in a secret place,
 Should I draw nigh, will never kiss again;
I come between the king and his desire,
 And where I am all loving else is vain.

Lo! as I walk along the woodland way
 Strange creatures leer at me with uncouth love,
And from the grass reach upward to my breast,
 And to my mouth lean from the boughs above.

The sleepy kine move round me in desire
  And press their oozy lips upon my hair,
Toads kiss my feet and creatures of the mire,
  The snails will leave their shells to watch me there.

But all this worship — what is it to me?
  I smite the ox and crush the toad in death,
I only know I am so very fair
  And that the world was made to give me breath.

I only wait the hour when God shall rise
  Up from the star where he so long hath sat,
And bow before the wonder of my eyes,
  And set *me* there — I am so fair as that.

JOHN DAVIDSON

A BALLAD OF HEAVEN

He wrought at one great work for years;
  The world passed by with lofty look:
Sometimes his eyes were dashed with tears;
  Sometimes his lips with laughter shook.

His wife and child went clothed in rags,
  And in a windy garret starved:
He trod his measures on the flags,
  And high on heaven his music carved.

Wistful he grew but never feared;
  For always on the midnight skies
His rich orchestral score appeared
  In stars and zones and galaxies.

He thought to copy down his score:
  The moonlight was his lamp: he said,
" Listen, my love; " but on the floor
  His wife and child were lying dead.

Her hollow eyes were open wide;
   He deemed she heard with special zest:
Her death's-head infant coldly eyed
   The desert of her shrunken breast.

" Listen, my love: my work is done;
   I tremble as I touch the page
To sign the sentence of the sun
   And crown the great eternal age.

" The slow adagio begins;
   The winding-sheets are ravelled out
That swathe the minds of men, the sins
   That wrap their rotting souls about.

" The dead are heralded along;
   With silver trumps and golden drums,
And flutes and oboes, keen and strong,
   My brave andante singing comes.

" Then like a python's sumptuous dress
   The frame of things is cast away,
And out of Time's obscure distress,
   The thundering scherzo crashes Day.

" For three great orchestras I hope
   My mighty music shall be scored:
On three high hills they shall have scope
   With heaven's vault for a sounding-board.

" Sleep well, love; let your eyelids fall;
   Cover the child; goodnight, and if . . .
What?   Speak . . . the traitorous end of all!
   Both . . . cold and hungry . . . cold and stiff!

" But no, God means us well, I trust:
   Dear ones, be happy, hope is nigh:
We are too young to fall to dust,
   And too unsatisfied to die."

He lifted up against his breast
　　The woman's body stark and wan;
And to her withered bosom pressed
　　The little skin-clad skeleton.

" You see you are alive," he cried.
　　He rocked them gently to and fro.
" No, no, my love, you have not died;
　　Nor you, my little fellow; no."

Long in his arms he strained his dead
　　And crooned an antique lullaby;
Then laid them on the lowly bed,
　　And broke down with a doleful cry.

" The love, the hope, the blood, the brain,
　　Of her and me, the budding life,
And my great music — all in vain!
　　My unscored work, my child, my wife!

" We drop into oblivion,
　　And nourish some suburban sod:
My work, this woman, this my son,
　　Are now no more: there is no God.

" The world's a dustbin; we are due,
　　And death's cart waits: be life accurst! "
He stumbled down beside the two,
　　And clasping them, his great heart burst.

Straightway he stood at heaven's gate,
　　Abashed and trembling for his sin:
I trow he had not long to wait,
　　For God came out and let him in.

And then there ran a radiant pair,
　　Ruddy with haste and eager-eyed
To meet him first upon the stair —
　　His wife and child beatified.

They clad him in a robe of light,
   And gave him heavenly food to eat;
Great seraphs praised him to the height,
   Archangels sat about his feet.

God, smiling, took him by the hand,
   And led him to the brink of heaven:
He saw where systems whirling stand,
   Where galaxies like snow are driven.

Dead silence reigned; a shudder ran
   Through space; Time furled his wearied wings;
A slow adagio then began
   Sweetly resolving troubled things.

The dead were heralded along:
   As if with drums and trumps of flame,
And flutes and oboes keen and strong,
   A brave andante singing came.

Then like a python's sumptuous dress
   The frame of things was cast away.
And out of Time's obscure distress
   The conquering scherzo thundered Day.

He doubted; but God said " Even so;
   Nothing is lost that's wrought with tears:
The music that you made below
   Is now the music of the spheres."

THE MERCHANTMAN

The Markethaunters

Now, while our money is piping hot
   From the mint of our toil that coins the sheaves,
Merchantman, merchantman, what have you got
   In your tabernacle hung with leaves?

What have you got?
  The sun rides high;
Our money is hot;
  We must buy, buy, buy!

The Merchantman

I come from the elfin king's demesne
  With chrysolite, hyacinth, tourmaline;
I have emeralds here of living green;
  I have rubies, each like a cup of wine;
And diamonds, diamonds that never have been
  Outshone by eyes the most divine!

The Markethaunters

Jewellery? — Baubles; bad for the soul;
  Desire of the heart and lust of the eye!
Diamonds, indeed!   We wanted coal.
  What else do you sell?   Come, sound your cry!
      Our money is hot;
        The night draws nigh;
      What have you got
        That we want to buy?

The Merchantman

I have here enshrined the soul of the rose
  Exhaled in the land of the daystar's birth;
I have casks whose golden staves enclose
  Eternal youth, eternal mirth;
And cordials that bring repose,
  And the tranquil night, and the end of the earth.

The Markethaunters

Rapture of wine?   But it never pays:
  We must keep our common-sense alert.

Raisins are healthier, medicine says —
  Raisins and almonds for dessert.
      But we want to buy;
      For our money is hot,
      And age draws nigh:
      What else have you got?

The Merchantman

I have lamps that gild the lustre of noon;
  Shadowy arrows that pierce the brain;
Dulcimers strung with beams of the moon;
  Psalteries fashion'd of pleasure and pain;
A song and a sword and a haunting tune
  That may never be offer'd the world again.

The Markethaunters

Dulcimers! psalteries!   Whom do you mock?
  Arrows and songs?   We have axes to grind!
Shut up your booth and your mouldering stock,
  For we never shall deal. — Come away; let us find
    What the others have got!
      We must buy, buy, buy;
      For our money is hot,
      And death draws nigh.

AUBREY BEARDSLEY

THE BALLAD OF A BARBER

Here is the tale of Carrousel,
The barber of Meridian Street.
He cut, and coiffed, and shaved so well,
That all the world was at his feet.

The King, the Queen, and all the Court,
To no one else would trust their hair,
And reigning belles of every sort
Owed their successes to his care.

With carriage and with cabriolet
Daily Meridian Street was blocked,
Like bees about a bright bouquet
The beaux about his doorway flocked.

Such was his art he could with ease
Curl wit into the dullest face;
Or to a goddess of old Greece
Add a new wonder and a grace.

All powders, paints, and subtle dyes,
And costliest scents that men distil,
And rare pomades, forgot their price
And marvelled at his splendid skill.

The curling irons in his hand
Almost grew quick enough to speak,
The razor was a magic wand
That understood the softest cheek.

Yet with no pride his heart was moved;
He was so modest in his ways!
His daily task was all he loved,
And now and then a little praise.

An equal care he would bestow
On problems simple or complex;
And nobody had seen him show
A preference for either sex.

How came it then one summer day,
Coiffing the daughter of the King,
He lengthened out the least delay
And loitered in his hairdressing?

The Princess was a pretty child,
Thirteen years old, or thereabout.
She was as joyous and as wild
As spring flowers when the sun is out.

Her gold hair fell down to her feet
And hung about her pretty eyes;
She was as lyrical and sweet
As one of Schubert's melodies.

Three times the barber curled a lock,
And thrice he straightened it again;
And twice the irons scorched her frock,
And twice he stumbled in her train.

His fingers lost their cunning quite,
His ivory combs obeyed no more;
Something or other dimmed his sight,
And moved mysteriously the floor.

He leant upon the toilet table,
His fingers fumbled in his breast;
He felt as foolish as a fable,
And feeble as a pointless jest.

He snatched a bottle of Cologne,
And broke the neck between his hands;
He felt as if he was alone,
And mighty as a king's commands.

The Princess gave a little scream,
Carrousel's cut was sharp and deep;
He left her softly as a dream
That leaves a sleeper to his sleep.

He left the room on pointed feet;
Smiling that things had gone so well.
They hanged him in Meridian Street.
You pray in vain for Carrousel.

THE THREE MUSICIANS

Along the path that skirts the wood,
   The three musicians wend their way,
Pleased with their thoughts, each other's mood,
   Franz Himmel's latest roundelay,
The morning's work, a new-found theme, their breakfast
and the summer day.

One's a soprano, lightly frocked
   In cool, white muslin that just shows
Her brown silk stockings gaily clocked,
   Plump arms and elbows tipped with rose,
And frills of petticoats and things, and outlines as the warm
wind blows.

Beside her a slim, gracious boy
   Hastens to mend her tresses' fall,
And dies her favour to enjoy,
   And dies for *réclame* and recall
At Paris and St. Petersburg, Vienna and St. James's Hall.

The third's a Polish Pianist
   With big engagements everywhere,
A light heart and an iron wrist,
   And shocks and shoals of yellow hair,
And fingers that can trill on sixths and fill beginners with
despair.

The three musicians stroll along
   And pluck the ears of ripened corn,
Break into odds and ends of song,
   And mock the woods with Siegfried's horn,
And fill the air with Gluck, and fill the tweeded tourist's
soul with scorn.

The Polish genius lags behind,
 And, with some poppies in his hand,
Picks out the strings and wood and wind
 Of an imaginary band,
Enchanted that for once his men obey his beat and under-
 stand.

 The charming cantatrice reclines
  And rests a moment where she sees
 Her château's roof that hotly shines
  Amid the dusky summer trees,
And fans herself, half shuts her eyes, and smooths the frock
 about her knees.

 The gracious boy is at her feet,
  And weighs his courage with his chance;
 His fears soon melt in noonday heat.
  The tourist gives a furious glance,
Red as his guide-book grows, moves on, and offers up a
 prayer for France.

JOHN GRAY

WINGS IN THE DARK

Forth into the warm darkness faring wide —
More silent momently the silent quay —
Towards where the ranks of boats rock to the tide,
Muffling their plaintive gurgling jealously.

With gentle nodding of her gracious snout,
One greets her master till he step aboard;
She flaps her wings, impatient to get out;
She runs to plunder, straining every cord.

Full-winged and stealthy like a bird of prey,
All tense the muscles of her seemly flanks;

She, the coy creature that the idle day
Sees idly riding in the idle ranks.

Backward and forth, over the chosen ground,
Like a young horse, she drags the heavy trawl,
Tireless; or speeds her rapturous course unbound,
And passing fishers through the darkness call

Deep greeting, in the jargon of the sea.
Haul upon haul, flounders and soles and dabs,
And phosphorescent animalculae,
Sand, seadrift, weeds, thousands of worthless crabs.

Low on the mud the darkling fishes grope,
Cautious to stir, staring with jewel eyes;
Dogs of the sea, the savage congers mope,
Winding their sulky march Meander-wise.

Suddenly all is light and life and flight,
Upon the sandy bottom, agates strewn.
The fishers mumble, waiting till the night
Urge on the clouds, and cover up the moon.

CHARLEVILLE

(Imitated from the French of Arthur Rimbaud)

The square, with gravel paths and shabby lawns.
Correct, the trees and flowers repress their yawns.
The tradesman brings his favourite conceit,
To air it, while he stifles with the heat.

In the kiosk, the military band.
The shakos nod the time of the quadrilles.
The flaunting dandy strolls about the stand.
The notary, half unconscious of his seals.

On the green seats, small groups of grocermen,
Absorbed, their sticks scooping a little hole
Upon the path, talk market prices; then
Take up a cue: I think, upon the whole . . .

The loutish roughs are larking on the grass.
The sentimental trooper, with a rose
Between his teeth, seeing a baby, grows
More tender, with an eye upon the nurse.

Unbuttoned, like a student, I follow
A couple of girls along the chestnut row.
They know I am following, for they turn and laugh,
Half impudent, half shy, inviting chaff.

I do not say a word.   I only stare
At their round, fluffy necks.   I follow where
The shoulders drop; I struggle to define
The subtle torso's hesitating line.

Only my rustling tread, deliberate, slow;
The rippled silence from the still leaves drips.
They think I am an idiot, they speak low;
— I feel faint kisses creeping on my lips.

LORD ALFRED DOUGLAS

THE CITY OF THE SOUL

IV

Each new hour's passage is the acolyte
Of inarticulate song and syllable,
And every passing moment is a bell,
To mourn the death of undiscerned delight.
Where is the sun that made the noon-day bright,
And where the midnight moon?   O let us tell,
In long carved line and painted parable,
How the white road curves down into the night.

Only to build one crystal barrier
Against this sea which beats upon our days;
To ransom one lost moment with a rhyme
Or if fate cries and grudging gods demur,
To clutch Life's hair, and thrust one naked phrase
Like a lean knife between the ribs of Time.

NAPLES, 1897

SAROJINI CHATTOPÂDHYÂY

EASTERN DANCERS

Eyes ravished with rapture, celestially panting, what pas-
    sionate spirits aflaming with fire
Drink deep of the hush of the hyacinth heavens that glim-
    mer around them in fountains of light?
O wild and entrancing the strain of keen music that
    cleaveth the stars like a wail of desire,
And beautiful dancers with Houri-like faces bewitch the
    voluptuous watches of Night.

The scents of red roses and sandalwood flutter and die in
    the maze of their gem-tangled hair,
And smiles are entwining like magical serpents the poppies
    of lips that are opiate-sweet,
Their glittering garments of purple are burning like tremu-
    lous dawns in the quivering air,
And exquisite, subtle and slow are the tinkle and tread of
    their rhythmical slumber-soft feet.

Now silent, now singing and swaying and swinging, like
    blossoms that bend to the breezes or showers,
Now wantonly winding, they flash, now they falter, and
    lingering languish in radiant choir,
Their jewel-bright arms and warm, wavering, lily-long
    fingers enchant thro' the summer-swift hours,
Eyes ravished with rapture, celestially panting, their pas-
    sionate spirits aflaming with fire.

ALICE MEYNELL [1]

THE SHEPHERDESS

She walks — the lady of my delight —
  A shepherdess of sheep.
Her flocks are thoughts.   She keeps them white;
  She guards them from the steep;
She feeds them on the fragrant height,
  And folds them in for sleep.

She roams maternal hills and bright,
  Dark valleys safe and deep.
Into that tender breast at night
  The chastest stars may peep.
She walks — the lady of my delight —
  A shepherdess of sheep.

She holds her little thoughts in sight,
  Though gay they run and leap.
She is so circumspect and right;
  She has her soul to keep.
She walks — the lady of my delight —
  A shepherdess of sheep.

" I AM THE WAY "

    Thou art the Way.
  Hadst Thou been nothing but the goal,
      I cannot say
  If Thou hadst ever met my soul.

      I cannot see —
  I, child of process — if there lies
      An end for me,
  Full of repose, full of replies.

---

[1] These three poems of Alice Meynell were included in a privately printed volume entitled *Other Poems* (1896).

I'll not reproach
The road that winds, my feet that err.
Access, approach
Art Thou, Time, Way, and Wayfarer.

THE TWO POETS

Whose is the speech
That moves the voices of this lonely beech?
Out of the long west did this wild wind come —
O strong and silent!   And the tree was dumb,
    Ready and dumb, until
The dumb gale struck it in the darkened hill.

Two memories,
Two powers, two promises, two silences
Closed in this cry, closed in these thousand leaves
Articulate. This sudden hour retrieves
    The purpose of the past,
Separate, apart — embraced, embraced at last.

" Whose is the word?
Is it I that spake? Is it thou? Is it I that heard? "
" Thine earth was solitary, yet I found thee! "
" Thy sky was pathless, but I caught, I bound thee,
    Thou visitant divine."
" O thou my Voice, the word was thine." " Was thine."

LAURENCE HOUSMAN

THE GOD AT PLAY

(On a child playing by the water)

In the hollow of his hand
My child holds a little land:
Lord of all that land is he!

There are hills and meadows green,
There a river meets the sea;
And between,
On a rock an island town
Takes its stand,
Looking down
Over all the pleasant lea.
And its ramparts are the band
Of a crown,
Steeple-crested, gemmed and grand,
Lording all that little land,
  So fair to see
In my child's hand!

Out to sea the fighting fleets, —
Round the walls the fighting men
Bannered go.
Faint from inland fold and pen
White flock bleats
And cattle low:
Autumn hoards, and summer heaps,
Ploughman ploughs, and reaper reaps,
Over sluggard winter leaps
Light-foot spring;
Peace is priest, and Plenty king,
Since a kind god wills it so, —
So to be from long ago,
In this lazy little land,
  So fair to see
In my child's hand!

Little land is all asleep,
Resting at the Sabbath-bell:
High upon its rocky perch,
Grounded deep,
Goes the gadding town to church. —
Goes to pray in pious speech,
Goes to let the preacher preach.

And as there folk sit and nod,
All the while a tired god
Lets the river rise and rise,
Sets the shoreward tide to flow
Up the land in soft surprise:
Ah, heigho!
How the happy sheepfolds go,
How the farms like islands show!
How of all the little land
Nothing soon is left to stand
Save the town, a place of woe, —
Spired crown and rampart-band:
This, — of all the little land
    So fair to see
In my child's hand!

THE CITY OF SLEEP

Manikin, maker of dreams,
    Came to the city of sleep:
The watch was on guard, and the gates were barred,
    And the moat was deep.

" Who is on my side, who? "
    Moonbeams rose in a row:
He tuned them loud 'twixt town and cloud
    But his voice was low.

He sang a song of the moon
    For loan of her silver beams;
Misty and fair, and afloat in air,
    Lay the ladder of dreams.

He harped by river and hill;
    And the river forgot to flow,
And the wind in the grass forgot to pass,
    And the grass to grow.

He harped to the heart of earth
  Where honey in hives lies sweet:
And that sound leapt through the gates, and crept
  Through the silent street.

Manikin, maker of dreams,
  He pursed his lips to pipe:
And the strange and the new grew near and true,
  For the time was ripe.

He piped to the hearts of men:
  And dreamers rose up straight,
To drift unbarred by the drowsy guard,
  And beyond the gate.

He piped the dream of the maid:
  And her heart was up and away;
And fast it beat and hurried her feet
  To the gates of day.

He piped the dream of the mother,
  The cry of her babe for food:
And she rose from rest to give it the breast
  And that was good!

He piped the dream of the child:
  And into its hands and feet
Came tunes to play of the live-long day;
  And that was sweet!

He piped to the heart of youth:
  And the heart of youth had sight
Of love to be won, and a race to run;
  And that was right!

He piped the song of age:
  And that was a far-off song, —
When life made haste and the mouth could taste: —
  But that was wrong!

    Manikin, maker of dreams,
        Had piped himself to sleep:
The watch was on guard, and the gates were barred,
        And the moat was deep!

LOVE IMPORTUNATE

    Dark was the night, and dark as night my heart,
    When at my chamber door there knocked a hand.
    Then, with glad start,
    I rose, and oped:
    Nay, not the one I hoped, —
    There Love Himself did stand.

    Ah, me! those eyes I could not meet for shame, —
    So, downward looking, saw the Feet that bled;
    And knew He came,
    Footsore and worn,
    A Lover to man's scorn: —
    Yet could not give Him bread!

    Grieved, from His Feet I feared to lift mine eyes:
    Patiently there He stood while I stayed dumb.
    Till with sharp sighs
    I cried, " Oh, sweet,
    Oh, fearful, bleeding Feet
    Of Love, why are Ye come? "

    " One welcome lacking ever must I roam,
    And footsore needs must be," my Lord confessed:
    " From many a home
    A wanderer still,
    Because your stubborn will
    Denies my Heart its rest."

    Sadly I owned, nought had I here to give:
    Nay, not a bed so made that He might lie.

Could one not live
From Love shut fast,
But to one's door at last
He needs must come to die?

" Why, then," quoth Love, " didst thou so watch and wait?
Whom Love hath made, loveless can find no rest.
In empty state
Can peace have part?
Is not thy very heart
An inn that lacks a guest? "

" Yet there be other inns," I sighed: " fair boards
Where open hearts the feast for Thee prepare
Which peace accords! "
" Let it be so;
That feast I will forego! "
Said Love. " Thou art My care."

Ah, what He further spake I may not tell!
But in the very place, where once lay sin,
Love deigns to dwell;
Nor may I doubt
The door which once shut out
Can closelier shut Love in.

FRANCIS THOMPSON

TO A SNOW-FLAKE

What heart could have thought you? —
Past our devisal
(O filigree petal!)
Fashioned so purely,
Fragilely, surely,
From what Paradisal
Imagineless metal,
Too costly for cost?

Who hammered you, wrought you,
From argentine vapour? —
" God was my shaper.
Passing surmisal,
He hammered, He wrought me,
From curled silver vapour,
To lust of His mind: —
Thou could'st not have thought me!
So purely, so palely,
Tinily, surely,
Mightily, frailly,
Insculped and embossed,
With His hammer of wind,
And His graver of frost."

THE KINGDOM OF GOD

(" In no Strange Land ")

O World invisible, we view thee,
O World intangible, we touch thee,
O World unknowable, we know thee,
Inapprehensible, we clutch thee!

Does the fish soar to find the ocean,
The eagle plunge to find the air —
That we ask of the stars in motion
If they have rumour of thee there?

Not where the wheeling systems darken,
And our benumbed conceiving soars! —
The drift of pinions, would we hearken,
Beats at our own clay-shuttered doors.

The angels keep their ancient places; —
Turn but a stone and start a wing!
'Tis ye, 'tis your estrangèd faces,
That miss the many-splendoured thing.

But (when so sad thou canst not sadder)
Cry,   and upon thy so sore loss
Shall shine the traffic of Jacob's ladder
Pitched betwixt Heaven and Charing Cross.

Yea, in the night, my Soul, my daughter,
Cry, — clinging Heaven by the hems;
And lo, Christ walking on the water
Not of Genesareth, but Thames!

TO DAISIES

Ah, drops of gold in whitening flame
Burning, we know your lovely name —
Daisies, that little children pull!
Like all weak things, over the strong
Ye do not know your power for wrong,
And much abuse your feebleness.
Weak maids, with flutter of a dress,
Increase most heavy tyrannies;
And vengeance unto heaven cries
For multiplied injustice of dove-eyes.
Daisies, that little children pull,
As ye are weak, be merciful!
O hide your eyes! they are to me
Beautiful insupportably.
Or be but conscious ye are fair,
And I your loveliness could bear;
But, being fair so without art,
Ye vex the silted memories of my heart!

As a pale ghost yearning strays
With sundered gaze,
'Mid corporal presences that are
To it impalpable — such a bar
Sets you more distant than the morning-star.
Such wonder is on you and amaze,

I look and marvel if I be
Indeed the phantom, or are ye?
The light is on your innocence
Which fell from me.
The fields ye still inhabit whence
My world-acquainted treading strays,
The country where I did commence;
And though ye shine to me so near,
So close to gross and visible sense,
Between us lies impassable year on year.
To other time and far-off place
Belongs your beauty: silent thus,
Though to others naught you tell,
To me your ranks are rumorous
Of an ancient miracle.

Vain does my touch your petals graze,
I touch you not; and, though ye blossom here,
Your roots are fast in alienated days.
Ye there are anchored, while Time's stream
Has swept me past them: your white ways
And infantile delights do seem
To look in on me like a face,
Dead and sweet, come back through dream,
With tears, because for old embrace
It has no arms. These hands did toy,
Children, with you when I was child,
And in each other's eyes we smiled:
Not yours, not yours the grievous-fair
Apparelling
With which you wet mine eyes; you wear,
Ah me, the garment of the grace
I wove you when I was a boy;
O mine, and not the year's, your stolen Spring!
And since ye wear it,
Hide your sweet selves!   I cannot bear it.
For, when ye break the cloven earth

With your young laughter and endearment,
No blossomy carillon 'tis of mirth
To me; I see my slaughtered joy
Bursting its cerement.

THE HOUND OF HEAVEN

I fled Him, down the nights and down the days;
    I fled Him, down the arches of the years;
I fled Him, down the labyrinthine ways
    Of my own mind; and in the mist of tears
I hid from Him, and under running laughter.
            Up vistaed hopes I sped;
            And shot, precipitated,
Adown Titanic glooms of chasmèd fears,
    From those strong Feet that followed, followed after.
            But with unhurrying chase,
            And unperturbèd pace,
        Deliberate speed, majestic instancy,
            They beat — and a Voice beat
            More instant than the Feet —
        " All things betray thee, who betrayest Me."

            I pleaded, outlaw-wise,
By many a hearted casement, curtained red,
    Trellised with intertwining charities;
(For, though I knew His love Who followèd,
            Yet was I sore adread
Lest, having Him, I must have naught beside);
But, if one little casement parted wide,
    The gust of His approach would clash it to.
    Fear wist not to evade, as Love wist to pursue.
Across the margent of the world I fled,
    And troubled the gold gateways of the stars,
    Smiting for shelter on their clangèd bars;
            Fretted to dulcet jars

And silvern chatter the pale ports o' the moon.
I said to dawn, Be sudden; to eve, Be soon;
  With thy young skiey blossoms heap me over
    From this tremendous Lover!
Float thy vague veil about me, lest He see!
  I tempted all His servitors, but to find
My own betrayal in their constancy,
In faith to Him their fickleness to me,
  Their traitorous trueness, and their loyal deceit.
To all swift things for swiftness did I sue;
  Clung to the whistling mane of every wind.
    But whether they swept, smoothly fleet,
    The long savannahs of the blue;
      Or whether, Thunder-driven,
      They clanged his chariot 'thwart a heaven
Plashy with flying lightnings round the spurn o' their
  feet: —
  Fear wist not to evade as Love wist to pursue.
    Still with unhurrying chase,
    And unperturbèd pace,
    Deliberate speed, majestic instancy,
      Came on the following Feet,
      And a Voice above their beat —
  " Naught shelters thee, who wilt not shelter Me."

I sought no more that after which I strayed
    In face of man or maid;
But still within the little children's eyes
    Seems something, something that replies;
They at least are for me, surely for me!
I turned me to them very wistfully;
But, just as their young eyes grew sudden fair
    With dawning answers there,
Their angel plucked them from me by the hair.
" Come then, ye other children, Nature's — share
With me " (said I) " your delicate fellowship;

Let me greet you lip to lip,
Let me twine with you caresses,
   Wantoning
With our Lady-Mother's vagrant tresses,
   Banqueting
With her in her wind-walled palace,
Underneath her azured daïs,
Quaffing, as your taintless way is,
   From a chalice
Lucent-weeping out of the dayspring."
   So it was done:
I in their delicate fellowship was one —
Drew the bolt of Nature's secrecies.
   I knew all the swift importings
   On the wilful face of skies;
   I knew how the clouds arise
   Spumèd of the wild sea-snortings;
     All that's born or dies
   Rose and drooped with — made them shapers
Of mine own moods, or wailful or divine —
   With them joyed and was bereaven.
   I was heavy with the even,
   When she lit her glimmering tapers
   Round the day's dead sanctities.
   I laughed in the morning's eyes.
I triumphed and I saddened with all weather,
   Heaven and I wept together,
And its sweet tears were salt with mortal mine;
Against the red throb of its sunset-heart
   I laid my own to beat,
   And share commingling heat;
But not by that, by that, was eased my human smart.
In vain my tears were wet on Heaven's grey cheek.
For ah! we know not what each other says,
   These things and I; in sound *I* speak —
Their sound is but their stir, they speak by silences.
Nature, poor stepdame, cannot slake my drouth;

Let her, if she would owe me,
Drop yon blue bosom-veil of sky, and show me
The breasts o' her tenderness:
Never did any milk of hers once bless
    My thirsting mouth.
    Nigh and nigh draws the chase,
    With unperturbèd pace,
Deliberate speed, majestic instancy;
    And past those noisèd Feet
    A voice comes yet more fleet —
"Lo! naught contents thee, who content'st not Me."

Naked I wait Thy love's uplifted stroke!
My harness piece by piece Thou hast hewn from me,
    And smitten me to my knee;
    I am defenceless utterly.
    I slept, methinks, and woke,
And, slowly gazing, find me stripped in sleep.
In the rash lustihead of my young powers,
    I shook the pillaring hours
And pulled my life upon me; grimed with smears,
I stand amid the dust o' the moulded years —
My mangled youth lies dead beneath the heap.
My days have crackled and gone up in smoke,
Have puffed and burst as sun-starts on a stream.
    Yea, faileth now even dream
The dreamer, and the lute the lutanist;
Even the linked fantasies, in whose blossomy twist
I swung the earth a trinket at my wrist,
Are yielding; cords of all too weak account
For earth with heavy griefs so overplussed.
    Ah! is Thy love indeed
A weed, albeit an amaranthine weed,
Suffering no flowers except its own to mount?
    Ah! must —
    Designer infinite! —
Ah! must Thou char the wood ere Thou canst limn with it?

My freshness spent its wavering shower i' the dust;
And now my heart is as a broken fount,
Wherein tear-drippings stagnate, spilt down ever
    From the dank thoughts that shiver
Upon the sighful branches of my mind.
    Such is; what is to be?
The pulp so bitter, how shall taste the rind?
I dimly guess what Time in mists confounds;
Yet ever and anon a trumpet sounds
From the hid battlements of Eternity;
Those shaken mists a space unsettle, then
Round the half-glimpsèd turrets slowly wash again.
    But not ere him who summoneth
    I first have seen, enwound
With glooming robes purpureal, cypress-crowned;
His name I know, and what his trumpet saith.
Whether man's heart or life it be which yields
    Thee harvest, must Thy harvest fields
    Be dunged with rotten death?

    Now of that long pursuit
    Comes on at hand the bruit;
That Voice is round me like a bursting sea:
    " And is thy earth so marred,
    Shattered in shard on shard?
Lo, all things fly thee, for thou fliest Me!
    Strange, piteous, futile thing,
Wherefore should any set thee love apart?
Seeing none but I makes much of naught " (He said),
" And human love needs human meriting:
    How hast thou merited —
Of all man's clotted clay the dingiest clot?
    Alack, thou knowest not
How little worthy of any love thou art!
Whom wilt thou find to love ignoble thee
    Save Me, save only Me?
All which I took from thee I did but take,

Not for thy harms,
But just that thou might'st seek it in My arms.
All which thy child's mistake
Fancies as lost, I have stored for thee at home:
Rise, clasp My hand, and come! "

Halts by me that footfall:
Is my gloom, after all,
Shade of His hand, outstretched caressingly?
" Ah, fondest, blindest, weakest,
I am He Whom thou seekest!
Thou dravest love from thee, who dravest Me."

BEFORE HER PORTRAIT IN YOUTH

As lovers, banished from their lady's face,
And hopeless of her grace,
Fashion a ghostly sweetness in its place,
Fondly adore
Some stealth-won cast attire she wore,
A kerchief, or a glove:
And at the lover's beck
Into the glove there fleets the hand,
Or at impetuous command
Up from the kerchief floats the virgin neck:
So I, in very lowlihead of love, —
Too shyly reverencing
To let one thought's light footfall smooth
Tread near the living, consecrated thing, —
Treasure me thy cast youth.
This outworn vesture, tenantless of thee,
Hath yet my knee,
For that, with show and semblance fair
Of the past Her
Who once the beautiful, discarded raiment bare,
It cheateth me.

As gale to gale drifts breath
Of blossoms' death,
So, dropping down the years from hour to hour
This dead youth's scent is wafted me today:
I sit, and from the fragrance dream the flower.
So, then, she looked (I say);
And so her front sank down
Heavy beneath the poet's iron crown:
On her mouth museful sweet —
(Even as the twin lips meet)
Did thought and sadness greet:
Sighs
In those mournful eyes
So put on visibilities;
As viewless ether turns, in deep on deep, to dyes.
Thus, long ago,
She kept her meditative paces slow
Through maiden meads, with wavèd shadow and gleam
Of locks half-lifted on the winds of dream,
Till love up-caught her to his chariot's glow.
Yet, voluntary, happier Proserpine!
This drooping flower of youth thou lettest fall
I, faring in the cockshut-light, astray,
Find on my 'lated way,
And stoop, and gather for memorial,
And lay it on my bosom, and make it mine.
To this, the all of love the stars allow me,
I dedicate and vow me.
I reach back through the days
A trothed hand to the dead the last trump shall not raise.
The water-wraith that cries
From those eternal sorrows of thy pictured eyes
Entwines and draws me down their soundless intricacies!

EX ORE INFANTIUM

Little Jesus, wast Thou shy
Once, and just so small as I?
And what did it feel like to be
Out of Heaven, and just like me?
Didst Thou sometimes think of *there,*
And ask where all the angels were?
I should think that I would cry
For my house all made of sky;
I would look about the air,
And wonder where my angels were;
And at waking 'twould distress me —
Not an angel there to dress me!
Hadst Thou ever any toys,
Like us little girls and boys?
And didst Thou play in Heaven with all
The angels, that were not too tall,
With stars for marbles?   Did the things
Play *Can you see me?* through their wings?
And did Thy Mother let Thee spoil
Thy robes, with playing on *our* soil?
How nice to have them always new
In Heaven, because 'twas quite clean blue!

Didst Thou kneel at night to pray,
And didst Thou join Thy hands, this way?
And did they tire sometimes, being young,
And make the prayer seem very long?
And dost Thou like it best, that we
Should join our hands to pray to Thee?
I used to think, before I knew,
The prayer not said unless we do.
And did Thy Mother at the night
Kiss Thee, and fold the clothes in right?
And didst Thou feel quite good in bed,
Kissed, and sweet, and Thy prayers said?

Thou canst not have forgotten all
That it feels like to be small:
And Thou know'st I cannot pray
To Thee in my father's way —
When Thou wast so little, say,
Couldst Thou talk Thy Father's way?

So, a little Child, come down
And hear a child's tongue like Thy own;
Take me by the hand and walk,
And listen to my baby-talk.
To Thy Father show my prayer
(He will look, Thou art so fair),
And say: " O Father, I, Thy Son,
Bring the prayer of a little one."

And He will smile, that children's tongue
Has not changed since Thou wast young!

DAISY

Where the thistle lifts a purple crown
    Six foot out of the turf,
And the harebell shakes on the windy hill —
    O the breath of the distant surf! —

The hills look over on the South,
    And southward dreams the sea;
And, with the sea-breeze hand in hand,
    Came innocence and she.

Where 'mid the gorse the raspberry
    Red for the gatherer springs,
Two children did we stray and talk
    Wise, idle, childish things.

She listened with big-lipped surprise,
    Breast-deep 'mid flower and spine:
Her skin was like a grape, whose veins
    Run snow instead of wine.

She knew not those sweet words she spake,
  Nor knew her own sweet way;
But there's never a bird so sweet a song
  Thronged in whose throat that day!

Oh, there were flowers in Storrington
  On the turf and on the spray;
But the sweetest flower on Sussex hills
  Was the Daisy-flower that day!

Her beauty smoothed earth's furrowed face!
  She gave me tokens three: —
A look, a word of her winsome mouth,
  And a wild raspberry.

A berry red, a guileless look,
  A still word, — strings of sand!
And yet they made my wild, wild heart
  Fly down to her little hand.

For, standing artless as the air,
  And candid as the skies,
She took the berries with her hand,
  And the love with her sweet eyes.

The fairest things have fleetest end:
  Their scent survives their close,
But the rose's scent is bitterness
  To him that loved the rose!

She looked a little wistfully,
  Then went her sunshine way: —
The sea's eye had a mist on it,
  And the leaves fell from the day.

She went her unremembering way,
  She went, and left in me
The pang of all the partings gone,
  And partings yet to be.

She left me marvelling why my soul
  Was sad that she was glad;
At all the sadness in the sweet,
  The sweetness in the sad.

Still, still I seemed to see her, still
  Look up with soft replies,
And take the berries with her hand,
  And the love with her lovely eyes.

Nothing begins, and nothing ends,
  That is not paid with moan;
For we are born in other's pain,
  And perish in our own.

THE DREAD OF HEIGHT

*If ye were blind, ye should have no sin: but now ye say:
  We see: your sin remaineth. John* IX. 41.

Not the Circean wine
Most perilous is for pain:
Grapes of the heavens' star-loaden vine,
Whereto the lofty-placed
Thoughts of fair souls attain,
Tempt with a more retributive delight,
And do disrelish all life's sober taste.
'Tis to have drunk too well
The drink that is divine,
Maketh the kind earth waste,
And breath intolerable.

Ah me!
How shall my mouth content it with mortality?
Lo, secret music, sweetest music,
From distances of distance drifting its lone flight,
Down the arcane where Night would perish in night,
Like a god's loosened locks slips undulously:

Music that is too grievous of the height
For safe and low delight,
Too infinite
For bounded hearts which yet would girth the sea!

So let it be,
Though sweet be great, and though my heart be small:
So let it be,
O music, music, though you wake in me
No joy, no joy at all;
Although you only wake
Uttermost sadness, measure of delight,
Which else I could not credit to the height
Did I not know,
That ill is statured to its opposite;
Did I not know,
And even of sadness so,
Of utter sadness, make
Of extreme sad a rod to mete
The incredible excess of unsensed sweet,
And mystic wall of strange felicity.
So let it be,
Though sweet be great, and though my heart be small,
And bitter meat
The food of gods for men to eat;
Yea, John ate daintier, and did tread
Less ways of heat,
Than whom to their wind-carpeted
High banquet-hall,
And golden love-feasts, the fair stars entreat.

But ah! withal,
Some hold, some stay,
O difficult Joy, I pray,
Some arms of thine,
Not only, only arms of mine!
Lest like a weary girl I fall

From clasping love so high,
And lacking thus thine arms, then may
Most hapless I
Turn utterly to love of basest rate;
For low they fall whose fall is from the sky.
Yea, who me shall secure
But I, of height grown desperate,
Surcease my wing, and my lost fate
Be dashed from pure
To broken writhings in the shameful slime:
Lower than man, for I dreamed higher,
Thrust down, by how much I aspire,
And damned with drink of immortality?
For such things be,
Yea, and the lowest reach of reeky Hell
Is but made possible
By foreta'en breath of Heaven's austerest clime.

These tidings from the vast to bring
Needeth not doctor nor divine,
Too well, too well
My flesh doth know the heart-perturbing thing;
That dread theology alone
Is mine,
Most native and my own;
And ever with victorious toil
When I have made
Of the deific peaks dim escalade,
My soul with anguish and recoil
Doth like a city in an earthquake rock,
As at my feet the abyss is cloven then,
With deeper menace than for other men,
Of my potential cousinship with mire;
That all my conquered skies do grow a hollow mock,
My fearful powers retire,
No longer strong,
Reversing the shook banners of their song.

Ah, for a heart less native to high Heaven,
A hooded eye, for jesses and restraint,
Or for a will accipitrine to pursue! —
The veil of tutelar flesh to simple livers given
Or those brave-fledging favours of the Saint,
Whose heavenly falcon-craft doth never taint,
Nor they in sickest time their ample virtue mew.

CONTEMPLATION

This morning saw I, fled the shower,
The earth reclining in a lull of power:
The heavens, pursuing not their path,
Lay stretched out naked after bath,
Or so it seemed; field, water, tree, were still,
Nor was there any purpose on the calm-browed hill.

The hill, which sometimes visibly is
Wrought with unresting energies,
Looked idly; from the musing wood,
And every rock, a life renewed
Exhaled like an unconscious thought
When poets, dreaming unperplexed,
Dream that they dream of nought.
Nature one hour appears a thing unsexed,
Or to such serene balance brought
That her twin natures cease their sweet alarms,
And sleep in one another's arms.
The sun with resting pulses seems to brood,
And slacken its command upon my unurged blood.

The river has not any care
Its passionless water to the sea to bear;
The leaves have brown content;
The wall to me has freshness like a scent,
And takes half animate the air,
Making one life with its green moss and stain;

And life with all things seems too perfect blent
For anything of life to be aware.
The very shades on hill, and tree, and plain,
Where they have fallen doze, and where they doze remain.

No hill can idler be than I;
No stone its inter-particled vibration
Investeth with a stiller lie;
No heaven with a more urgent rest betrays
The eyes that on it gaze.
We are too near akin that thou shouldst cheat
Me, Nature, with thy fair deceit.
In poets floating like a water-flower
Upon the bosom of the glassy hour,
In skies that no man sees to move,
Lurk untumultuous vortices of power,
For joy too native, and for agitation
Too instant, too entire for sense thereof,
Motion like gnats when autumn suns are low,
Perpetual as the prisoned feet of love
On the heart's floors with painèd pace that go.
From stones and poets you may know,
Nothing so active is, as that which least seems so.

For he, that conduit running wine of song,
Then to himself does most belong
When he his mortal house unbars
To the importunate and thronging feet
That round our corporal walls unheeded beat;
Till, all containing, he exalt
His stature to the stars, or stars
Narrow their heaven to his fleshly vault:
When, like a city under ocean,
To human things he grows a desolation,
And is made a habitation
For the fluctuous universe
To lave with unimpeded motion.

He scarcely frets the atmosphere
With breathing, and his body shares
The immobility of rocks;
His heart's a drop-well of tranquillity;
His mind more still is than the limbs of fear,
And yet its unperturbed velocity
The spirit of the simoon mocks.
He round the solemn centre of his soul
Wheels like a dervish, while his being is
Streamed with the set of the world's harmonies,
In the long draft of whatsoever sphere
He lists the sweet and clear
Clangour of his high orbit on to roll,
So gracious is his heavenly grace;
And the bold stars does hear,
Every one in his airy soar,
For evermore
Shout to each other from the peaks of space,
As 'thwart ravines of azure shouts the mountaineer.

A. E.   (G. W. RUSSELL) [1]

BY THE MARGIN OF THE GREAT DEEP

When the breath of twilight blows to flame the misty skies,
All its vaporous sapphire, violet glow and silver gleam
With their magic flood me through the gateway of the eyes;
   I am one with the twilight's dream.

When the trees and skies and fields are one in dusky mood,
Every heart of man is rapt within the mother's breast:
Full of peace and sleep and dreams in the vasty quietude,
   I am one with their hearts at rest.

[1] The poems of A. E. are reprinted by permission of the author.

From our immemorial joys of hearth and home and love
Strayed away along the margin of the unknown tide,
All its reach of soundless calm can thrill me far above
  Word or touch from the lips beside.

Aye, and deep and deep and deeper let me drink and draw
From the olden fountain more than light or peace or dream,
Such primeval being as o'erfills the heart with awe,
  Growing one with its silent stream.

THE GREAT BREATH

Its edges foamed with amethyst and rose,
    Withers once more the old blue flower of day:
There where the ether like a diamond glows
    Its petals fade away.

A shadowy tumult stirs the dusky air;
    Sparkle the delicate dews, the distant snows;
The great deep thrills, for through it everywhere
    The breath of Beauty blows.

I saw how all the trembling ages past,
    Moulded to her by deep and deeper breath,
Neared to the hour when Beauty breathes her last
    And knows herself in death.

IMMORTALITY

We must pass like smoke or live within the spirit's fire;
For we can no more than smoke unto the flame return,
If our thought has changed to dream, our will unto desire.
As smoke we vanish though the fire may burn.

Lights of infinite pity star the grey dusk of our days:
Surely here is soul; with it we have eternal breath:
In the fire of love we live, or pass by many ways,
By unnumbered ways of dream to death.

CHILDHOOD

How I could see through and through you!
So unconscious, tender, kind,
More than ever was known to you
Of the pure ways of your mind.

We who long to rest from strife
Labour sternly as a duty;
But a magic in your life
Charms, unknowing of its beauty.

We are pools whose depths are told;
You are like a mystic fountain,
Issuing ever pure and cold
From the hollows of the mountain.

We are men by anguish taught
To distinguish false from true;
Higher wisdom we have not;
But a joy within guides you.

DUST

I heard them in their sadness say
" The earth rebukes the thought of God;
We are but embers wrapped in clay
A little nobler than the sod."

But I have touched the lips of clay:
Mother, thy rudest sod to me
Is thrilled with fire of hidden day,
And haunted by all mystery.

STAR TEACHERS

Even as a bird sprays many-coloured fires,
The plumes of Paradise, the dying light
Rays through the fevered air in misty spires
That vanish in the height,

Vanish beyond the stars and further dreams,
The heaven of heavens. Here in my thought the dome
Flashes about me with familiar gleams
    Of birthplace and of home.

These myriad eyes that look on me are mine;
Wandering beneath them I have found again
The ancient ample moment, the divine,
    The God-root within men.

For this, for this the lights innumerable
As symbols shine that we the true light win:
For every star and every deep they fill
    Are stars and deeps within.

Heroes and gods beneath them come and go;
Still the heroic, the divine, remain
Breathing from these the strength that quiets woe
    With beauty crowning pain.

ANSWER

The warmth of life is quenched with bitter frost:
Upon the lonely road a child limps by
Skirting the frozen pools: our way is lost:
    Our hearts sink utterly.

But from the snow-patched moorland chill and drear,
Lifting our eyes beyond the spired height,
With white-fire lips apart the dawn breathes clear
    Its soundless hymn of light.

Out of the vast the voice of One replies
Whose words are clouds and stars and night and day,
When for the light the anguished spirit cries
    Deep in its house of clay.

KRISHNA

I am Beauty itself among beautiful things.
BHAGAVAD-GITA

The East was crowned with snow-cold bloom
And hung with veils of pearly fleece:
They died away into the gloom,
Vistas of peace — and deeper peace.

And earth and air and wave and fire
In awe and breathless silence stood;
For One who passed into their choir
Linked them in mystic brotherhood.

Twilight of amethyst, amid
Thy few strange stars that lit the heights,
Where was the secret spirit hid?
Where was Thy place, O Light of Lights?

The flame of Beauty far in space —
Where rose the fire: in Thee? in Me?
Which bowed the elemental race
To adoration silently?

THE SECRET

One thing in all things have I seen:
One thought has haunted earth and air:
Clangour and silence both have been
Its palace chambers.   Everywhere

I saw the mystic vision flow
And live in men and woods and streams,
Until I could no longer know
The dream of life from my own dreams.

Sometimes it rose like fire in me
Within the depths of my own mind,
And spreading to infinity,
It took the voices of the wind:

It scrawled the human mystery —
Dim heraldry — on light and air;
Wavering along the starry sea
I saw the flying vision there.

Each fire that in God's temple lit
Burns fierce before the inner shrine,
Dimmed as my fire grew near to it
And darkened at the light of mine.

At last, at last, the meaning caught —
The Spirit wears its diadem;
It shakes its wondrous plumes of thought
And trails the stars along with them.

KATHARINE TYNAN HINKSON

SHEEP AND LAMBS

All in the April morning,
  April airs were abroad,
The sheep with their little lambs
  Passed me by on the road.

The sheep with their little lambs
  Passed me by on the road;
All in the April evening
  I thought on the Lamb of God.

The lambs were weary, and crying
  With a weak, human cry.
I thought on the Lamb of God
  Going meekly to die.

Up in the blue, blue mountains
    Dewy pastures are sweet:
Rest for the little bodies,
    Rest for the little feet.

But for the Lamb of God,
    Up on the hill-top green,
Only a Cross of shame
    Two stark crosses between.

All in the April evening,
    April airs were abroad;
I saw the sheep with their lambs,
    And thought on the Lamb of God.

AN ISLAND FISHERMAN

I groan as I put out
    My nets on the say,
To hear the little *girshas* shout
    Dancin' among the spray.

Ochone! the childher pass
    An' lave us to our grief;
The stranger took my little lass
    At the fall o' the leaf.

Why would you go so fast
    With him you never knew?
In all the throuble that is past
    I never frowned on you.

The light o' my old eyes!
    The comfort o' my heart!
Waitin' for me your Mother lies
    In blessed Innishart.

Her lone grave 1 keep
   From all the cold world wide,
But you in life an' death will sleep
   The stranger beside.

Ochone! my thoughts are wild:
   But little blame I say;
An ould man hungerin' for his child,
   Fishin' the livelong day.

You will not run again,
   Laughin' to see me land.
Oh, what was pain an' throuble then,
   Holdin' your little hand?

Or when your head let fall
   Its soft curls on my breast?
Why do the childher grow at all
   To love the stranger best?

MOIRA O'NEILL

CORRYMEELA

Over here in England I'm helpin' wi' the hay,
An' I wisht I was in Ireland the livelong day;
Weary on the English hay, an' sorra take the wheat!
Och! Corrymeela an' the blue sky over it.

There's a deep dumb river flowin' by beyont the heavy
   trees,
This livin' air is moithered wi' the hummin' o' the bees;
I wisht I'd hear the Claddagh burn go runnin' through the
   heat
Past Corrymeela wi' the blue sky over it.

The people that's in England is richer nor the Jews,
There's not the smallest young gossoon but thravels in his
    shoes!
I'd give the pipe between me teeth to see a barefut child,
Och! Corrymeela an' the low south wind.

Here's hands so full o' money an' hearts so full o' care,
By the luck o' love!   I'd still go light for all I did go bare.
" God save ye, colleen dhas," I said: the girl she thought
    me wild!
Far Corrymeela, an' the low south wind.

D'ye mind me now, the song at night is mortial hard to
    raise,
The girls are heavy goin' here, the boys are ill to plase;
When once't I'm out this workin' hive, 'tis I'll be back
    again —
Aye, Corrymeela, in the same soft rain.

The puff o' smoke from one ould roof before an English
    town!
For a *shaugh* wid Andy Feelan here I'd give a silver crown,
For a curl o' hair like Mollie's ye'll ask the like in vain,
Sweet Corrymeela, an' the same soft rain.

NORA HOPPER

THE DARK MAN

Rose o' the world, she came to my bed
And changed the dreams of my heart and head;
For joy of mine she left grief of hers
And garlanded me with a crown of furze.

Rose o' the world, they go out and in,
And watch me dream and my mother spin;
And they pity the tears on my sleeping face
While my soul's away in a fairy place.

Rose o' the world, they have words galore,
And wide's the swing of my mother's door;
And soft they speak of my darkened eyes,
But what do they know, who are all so wise?

Rose o' the world, the grief you give
Is worth all days that a man may live;
Worth all shy prayers that the colleens say
On the night that darkens the wedding-day.

Rose o' the world, what man would wed
When he might dream of your face instead?
Might go to his grave with the blessed pain
Of hungering after your face again?

Rose o' the world, they may talk their fill,
For dreams are good, and my life stands still
While their lives' red ashes the gossips stir,
But my fiddle knows, and *I* talk to her.

BEAUTY

Beauty was born of the world's desire
For the wandering water, the wandering fire.
Under the arch of her hurrying feet
She has trodden a world full of bittersweet.

The blood of the violet is in her veins,
Her pulse has the passion of April rains.
Out of the heart of a satin flower
God made her eyelids in one sweet hour.

Out of the wind He made her feet
That they might be lovely, and luring, and fleet.
Out of a cloud He wove her hair
Heavy and black with the rain held there.

What is her name?   There's none that knows —
Mother-o'-mischief, or Mother-o'-rose.
What is her pathway?   None may tell,
But it climbs to heaven and it dips to hell.

The garment on her is mist and fire,
Anger and sorrow and heart's desire.
Her forehead-jewel's an amethyst,
The garland to her is love-in-a-mist.

Her girdle is of the beryl-stone,
And one dark rose for her flower has grown,
Filled to the brim with the strength o' the sun,
A passionate rose, and only one.

The bird in her breast sings all the day long
A wonderful, wistful, whispering song:
The song that is of all passing things,
None knows it — wingless or born with wings.

DORA SIGERSON SHORTER

THE GYPSIES' ROAD

I shall go on the gypsies' road,
  The road that has no ending;
For the sedge is brown on the lone lake side,
  The wild geese eastward tending.

I shall go as the unfetter'd wave,
  From shore to shore, forgetting
The grief that lies 'neath a roof-tree's shade,
  The years that bring regretting.

No law shall dare my wandering stay,
  No man my acres measure;
The world was made for the gypsies' feet,
  The winding road for pleasure.

And I shall drift as the pale leaf stray'd,
  Whither the wild wind listed,
I shall sleep in the dark of the hedge,
  'Neath rose and thorn entwisted.

This was a call in the heart of the night,
  A whispering dream's dear treasure:
" The world was made for the nomads' feet,
  The winding road for pleasure."

I stole at dawn from my roof-tree's shade,
  And the cares that it did cover;
I flew to the heart of the fierce north wind,
  As a maid will greet her lover.

But a thousand hands did draw me back
  And bid me to their tending;
I may not go on the gypsies' road —
  The road that has no ending.

OSCAR WILDE

THE BALLAD OF READING GAOL

In Memoriam
C. T. W.
Sometime Trooper of the Royal Horse Guards.
Obiit H. M. Prison, Reading, Berkshire, July 7, 1896

I

He did not wear his scarlet coat,
  For blood and wine are red,
And blood and wine were on his hands
  When they found him with the dead,
The poor dead woman whom he loved,
  And murdered in her bed.

He walked amongst the Trial Men
  In a suit of shabby gray;
A cricket cap was on his head,
  And his step seemed light and gay;
But I never saw a man who looked
  So wistfully at the day.

I never saw a man who looked
  With such a wistful eye
Upon that little tent of blue
  Which prisoners call the sky,
And at every drifting cloud that went
  With sails of silver by.

I walked, with other souls in pain,
  Within another ring,
And was wondering if the man had done
  A great or little thing,
When a voice behind me whispered low,
  " That fellow's got to swing."

Dear Christ! the very prison walls
  Suddenly seemed to reel,
And the sky above my head became
  Like a casque of scorching steel;
And, though I was a soul in pain,
  My pain I could not feel.

I only knew what hunted thought
  Quickened his step, and why
He looked upon the garish day
  With such a wistful eye;
The man had killed the thing he loved,
  And so he had to die.

Yet each man kills the thing he loves,
  By each let this be heard,

Some do it with a bitter look,
   Some with a flattering word,
The coward does it with a kiss,
   The brave man with a sword!

Some kill their love when they are young,
   And some when they are old;
Some strangle with the hands of Lust,
   Some with the hands of Gold:
The kindest use a knife, because
   The dead so soon grow cold.

Some love too little, some too long,
   Some sell, and others buy;
Some do the deed with many tears,
   And some without a sigh:
For each man kills the thing he loves,
   Yet each man does not die.

He does not die a death of shame
   On a day of dark disgrace,
Nor have a noose about his neck,
   Nor a cloth upon his face,
Nor drop feet foremost through the floor
   Into an empty space.

He does not sit with silent men
   Who watch him night and day;
Who watch him when he tries to weep,
   And when he tries to pray;
Who watch him lest himself should rob
   The prison of its prey.

He does not wake at dawn to see
   Dread figures throng his room,
The shivering Chaplain robed in white,
   The Sheriff stern with gloom,
And the Governor all in shiny black,
   With the yellow face of doom.

He does not rise in piteous haste
   To put on convict clothes,
While some coarse-mouthed Doctor gloats,
     and notes
   Each new and nerve-twitched pose,
Fingering a watch whose little ticks
   Are like horrible hammer-blows.

He does not know that sickening thirst
   That sands one's throat before
The hangman with his gardener's gloves
   Slips through the padded door,
And binds one with three leathern thongs,
   That the throat may thirst no more.

He does not bend his head to hear
   The Burial Office read,
Nor, while the terror of his soul
   Tells him he is not dead,
Cross his own coffin, as he moves
   Into the hideous shed.

He does not stare upon the air
   Through a little roof of glass:
He does not pray with lips of clay
   For his agony to pass;
Nor feel upon his shuddering cheek
   That kiss of Caiaphas.

II

Six weeks our guardsman walked the yard,
   In the suit of shabby gray:
His cricket cap was on his head,
   And his step seemed light and gay,
But I never saw a man who looked
   So wistfully at the day.

I never saw a man who looked
    With such a wistful eye
Upon that little tent of blue
    Which prisoners call the sky,
And at every wandering cloud that trailed
    Its raveled fleeces by.

He did not wring his hands, as do
    Those witless men who dare
To try to rear the changeling Hope
    In the cave of black Despair:
He only looked upon the sun,
    And drank the morning air.

He did not wring his hands nor weep,
    Nor did he peek or pine,
But he drank the air as though it held
    Some healthful anodyne;
With open mouth he drank the sun
    As though it had been wine!

And I and all the souls in pain,
    Who tramped the other ring,
Forgot if we ourselves had done
    A great or little thing,
And watched with gaze of dull amaze
    The man who had to swing.

And strange it was to see him pass
    With a step so light and gay,
And strange it was to see him look
    So wistfully at the day,
And strange it was to think that he
    Had such a debt to pay.

For oak and elm have pleasant leaves
    That in the spring-time shoot:

But grim to see is the gallows-tree,
   With its adder-bitten root,
And, green or dry, a man must die
   Before it bears its fruit!

The loftiest place is that seat of grace
   For which all worldlings try:
But who would stand in hempen band
   Upon a scaffold high,
And through a murderer's collar take
   His last look at the sky?

It is sweet to dance to violins
   When Love and Life are fair:
To dance to flutes, to dance to lutes
   Is delicate and rare;
But it is not sweet with nimble feet
   To dance upon the air!

So with curious eyes and sick surmise
   We watched him day by day,
And wondered if each one of us
   Would end the self-same way,
For none can tell to what red Hell
   His sightless soul may stray.

At last the dead man walked no more
   Amongst the Trial Men,
And I knew that he was standing up
   In the black dock's dreadful pen,
And that never would I see his face
   In God's sweet world again.

Like two doomed ships that pass in storm
   We had crossed each other's way:
But we made no sign, we said no word,
   We had no word to say;
For we did not meet in the holy night,
   But in the shameful day.

A prison wall was round us both,
　Two outcast men we were:
The world had thrust us from its heart,
　And God from out His care;
And the iron gin that waits for Sin
　Had caught us in its snare.

III

In Debtors' Yard the stones are hard,
　And the dripping wall is high,
So it was there he took the air
　Beneath the leaden sky,
And by each side a Warder walked,
　For fear the man might die.

Or else he sat with those who watched
　His anguish night and day;
Who watched him when he rose to weep,
　And when he crouched to pray;
Who watched him lest himself should rob
　Their scaffold of its prey.

The Governor was strong upon
　The Regulations Act:
The Doctor said that Death was but
　A scientific fact:
And twice a day the Chaplain called,
　And left a little tract.

And twice a day he smoked his pipe,
　And drank his quart of beer:
His soul was resolute, and held
　No hiding-place for fear;
He often said that he was glad
　The hangman's hands were near.

But why he said so strange a thing
    No Warder dared to ask:
For he to whom a watcher's doom
    Is given as his task,
Must set a lock upon his lips,
    And make his face a mask.

Or else he might be moved, and try
    To comfort or console:
And what should Human Pity do
    Pent up in Murderers' Hole?
What word of grace in such a place
    Could help a brother's soul?

With slouch and swing around the ring
    We trod the Fools' Parade!
We did not care: we knew we were
    The Devil's Own Brigade:
And shaven head and feet of lead
    Make a merry masquerade.

We tore the tarry rope to shreds
    With blunt and bleeding nails;
We rubbed the doors, and scrubbed the floors,
    And cleaned the shining rails:
And, rank by rank, we soaped the plank,
    And clattered with the pails.

We sewed the sacks, we broke the stones,
    We turned the dusty drill:
We banged the tins, and bawled the hymns,
    And sweated on the mill:
But in the heart of every man
    Terror was lying still.

So still it lay that every day
    Crawled like a weed-clogged wave:

And we forgot the bitter lot
   That waits for fool and knave,
Till once, as we tramped in from work,
   We passed an open grave.

With yawning mouth the yellow hole
   Gaped for a living thing;
The very mud cried out for blood
   To the thirsty asphalt ring:
And we knew that ere one dawn grew fair
   Some prisoner had to swing.

Right in we went, with soul intent
   On Death and Dread and Doom:
The hangman, with his little bag,
   Went shuffling through the gloom:
And each man trembled as he crept
   Into his numbered tomb.

That night the empty corridors
   Were full of forms of Fear,
And up and down the iron town
   Stole feet we could not hear,
And through the bars that hide the stars
   White faces seemed to peer.

He lay as one who lies and dreams
   In a pleasant meadow-land,
The watchers watched him as he slept,
   And could not understand
How one could sleep so sweet a sleep
   With a hangman close at hand.

But there is no sleep when men must weep
   Who never yet have wept:
So we — the fool, the fraud, the knave —
   That endless vigil kept,
And through each brain on hands of pain
   Another's terror crept.

Alas! it is a fearful thing
  To feel another's guilt!
For, right within, the sword of Sin
  Pierced to its poisoned hilt,
And as molten lead were the tears we shed
  For the blood we had not spilt.

The Warders with their shoes of felt
  Crept by each padlocked door,
And peeped and saw, with eyes of awe,
  Gray figures on the floor,
And wondered why men knelt to pray
  Who never prayed before.

All through the night we knelt and prayed,
  Mad mourners of a corse!
The troubled plumes of midnight were
  The plumes upon a hearse:
And bitter wine upon a sponge
  Was the savor of Remorse.

The gray cock crew, the red cock crew,
  But never came the day;
And crooked shapes of Terror crouched,
  In the corners where we lay:
And each evil sprite that walks by night
  Before us seemed to play.

They glided past, they glided fast,
  Like travelers through a mist:
They mocked the moon in a rigadoon
  Of delicate turn and twist,
And with formal pace and loathsome grace
  The phantoms kept their tryst.

With mop and mow, we saw them go,
  Slim shadows hand and hand:

About, about, in ghostly rout
  They trod a saraband:
And the damned grotesques made arabesques,
  Like the wind upon the sand!

With the pirouettes of marionettes,
  They tripped on pointed tread:
But with flutes of Fear they filled the ear,
  As their grisly masque they led,
And loud they sang, and long they sang,
  For they sang to wake the dead.

" *Oho!* " they cried, " *The world is wide,*
  But fettered limbs go lame!
And once, or twice, to throw the dice
  Is a gentlemanly game,
But he does not win who plays with Sin
  In the secret House of Shame."

No things of air these antics were,
  That frolicked with such glee:
To men whose lives were held in gyves,
  And whose feet might not go free,
Ah! wounds of Christ! they were living things,
  Most terrible to see.

Around, around, they waltzed and wound;
  Some wheeled in smirking pairs;
With the mincing step of a demirep
  Some sidled up the stairs:
And with subtle sneer, and fawning leer,
  Each helped us at our prayers.

The morning wind began to moan,
  But still the night went on:
Through its giant loom the web of gloom
  Crept till each thread was spun:
And, as we prayed, we grew afraid
  Of the Justice of the Sun.

The moaning wind went wandering round
  The weeping prison-wall:
Till like a wheel of turning steel
  We felt the minutes crawl:
O moaning wind! what had we done
  To have such a seneschal?

At last I saw the shadowed bars,
  Like a lattice wrought in lead,
Move right across the whitewashed wall
  That faced my three-plank bed,
And I knew that somewhere in the world
  God's dreadful dawn was red.

At six o'clock we cleaned our cells,
  At seven all was still,
But the sough and swing of a mighty wing
  The prison seemed to fill,
For the Lord of Death with icy breath,
  Had entered in to kill.

He did not pass in purple pomp,
  Nor ride a moon-white steed.
Three yards of cord and a sliding board
  Are all the gallows' need:
So with rope of shame the Herald came
  To do the secret deed.

We were as men who through a fen
  Of filthy darkness grope:
We did not dare to breathe a prayer,
  Or to give our anguish scope:
Something was dead in each of us,
  And what was dead was Hope.

For Man's grim Justice goes its way,
  And will not swerve aside:

It slays the weak, it slays the strong,
  It has a deadly stride:
With iron heel it slays the strong,
  The monstrous parricide!

We waited for the stroke of eight:
  Each tongue was thick with thirst:
For the stroke of eight is the stroke of Fate
  That makes a man accursed,
And Fate will use a running noose
  For the best man and the worst.

We had no other thing to do,
  Save to wait for the sign to come:
So, like things of stone in a valley lone,
  Quiet we sat and dumb:
But each man's heart beat thick and quick,
  Like a madman on a drum!

With sudden shock the prison-clock
  Smote on the shivering air,
And from all the jail rose up a wail
  Of impotent despair,
Like the sound that frightened marshes hear
  From some leper in his lair.

And as one sees most fearful things
  In the crystal of a dream,
We saw the greasy hempen rope
  Hooked to the blackened beam,
And heard the prayer the hangman's snare
  Strangled into a scream.

And all the woe that moved him so
  That he gave that bitter cry,
And the wild regrets, and the bloody sweats,
  None knew so well as I:
For he who lives more lives than one
  More deaths than one must die.

IV

There is no chapel on the day
　On which they hang a man:
The Chaplain's heart is far too sick,
　Or his face is far too wan,
Or there is that written in his eyes
　Which none should look upon.

So they kept us close till nigh on noon,
　And then they rang the bell,
And the Warders with their jingling keys
　Opened each listening cell,
And down the iron stair we tramped,
　Each from his separate Hell.

Out into God's sweet air we went,
　But not in wonted way,
For this man's face was white with fear,
　And that man's face was gray,
And I never saw sad men who looked
　So wistfully at the day.

I never saw sad men who looked
　With such a wistful eye
Upon that little tent of blue
　We prisoners called the sky,
And at every careless cloud that passed
　In happy freedom by.

But there were those amongst us all
　Who walked with downcast head,
And knew that, had each got his due,
　They should have died instead:
He had but killed a thing that lived,
　Whilst they had killed the dead.

For he who sins a second time
　Wakes a dead soul to pain,

And draws it from its spotted shroud,
    And makes it bleed again,
And makes it bleed great gouts of blood,
    And makes it bleed in vain!

Like ape or clown, in monstrous garb
    With crooked arrows starred,
Silently we went round and round
    The slippery asphalt yard;
Silently we went round and round,
    And no man spoke a word.

Silently we went round and round,
    And through each hollow mind
The Memory of dreadful things
    Rushed like a dreadful wind,
And Horror stalked before each man,
    And Terror crept behind.

The Warders strutted up and down,
    And kept their herd of brutes,
Their uniforms were spick and span,
    And they wore their Sunday suits,
But we knew the work they had been at,
    By the quicklime on their boots.

For where a grave had opened wide,
    There was no grave at all:
Only a stretch of mud and sand
    By the hideous prison-wall,
And a little heap of burning lime,
    That the man should have his pall.

For he has a pall, this wretched man,
    Such as few men can claim:
Deep down below a prison-yard,
    Naked for greater shame,
He lies, with fetters on each foot,
    Wrapt in a sheet of flame!

And all the while the burning lime
   Eats flesh and bone away,
It eats the brittle bone by night,
   And the soft flesh by day,
It eats the flesh and bone by turns,
   But it eats the heart alway.

For three long years they will not sow
   Or root or seedling there:
For three long years the unblessed spot
   Will sterile be and bare,
And look upon the wondering sky
   With unreproachful stare.

They think a murderer's heart would taint
   Each simple seed they sow.
It is not true! God's kindly earth
   Is kindlier than men know,
And the red rose would but blow more red,
   The white rose whiter blow.

Out of his mouth a red, red rose!
   Out of his heart a white!
For who can say by what strange way,
   Christ brings his will to light,
Since the barren staff the pilgrim bore
   Bloomed in the great Pope's sight?

But neither milk-white rose nor red
   May bloom in prison air;
The shard, the pebble, and the flint,
   Are what they give us there:
For flowers have been known to heal
   A common man's despair.

So never will wine-red rose or white,
   Petal by petal, fall

On that stretch of mud and sand that lies
　By the hideous prison-wall,
To tell the men who tramp the yard
　That God's Son died for all.

Yet though the hideous prison-wall
　Still hems him round and round,
And a spirit may not walk by night
　That is with fetters bound,
And a spirit may but weep that lies
　In such unholy ground,

He is at peace — this wretched man —
　At peace, or will be soon:
There is no thing to make him mad,
　Nor does Terror walk at noon,
For the lampless Earth in which he lies
　Has neither Sun nor Moon.

They hanged him as a beast is hanged:
　They did not even toll
A requiem that might have brought
　Rest to his startled soul,
But hurriedly they took him out,
　And hid him in a hole.

They stripped him of his canvas clothes,
　And gave him to the flies:
They mocked the swollen purple throat,
　And the stark and staring eyes:
And with laughter loud they heaped the shroud
　In which their convict lies.

The Chaplain would not kneel to pray
　By his dishonored grave:
Nor mark it with that blessed Cross
　That Christ for sinners gave,
Because the man was one of those
　Whom Christ came down to save.

Yet all is well; he has but passed
   To Life's appointed bourne:
And alien tears will fill for him
   Pity's long-broken urn,
For his mourners will be outcast men,
   And outcasts always mourn.

V

I know not whether Laws be right,
   Or whether Laws be wrong;
All that we know who lie in jail
   Is that the wall is strong;
And that each day is like a year,
   A year whose days are long.

But this I know, that every Law
   That men have made for Man,
Since first Man took his brother's life,
   And the sad world began,
But straws the wheat and saves the chaff
   Like a most evil fan.

This too I know — and wise it were
   If each could know the same —
That every prison that men build
   Is built with bricks of shame,
And bound with bars lest Christ should see
   How men their brothers maim.

With bars they blur the gracious moon,
   And blind the goodly sun:
And they do well to hide their Hell,
   For in it things are done
That Son of God nor son of Man
   Ever should look upon!

The vilest deeds like poison weeds
   Bloom well in prison-air:

It is only what is good in Man
  That wastes and withers there:
Pale Anguish keeps the heavy gate,
  And the Warder is Despair.

For they starve the little frightened child
  Till it weeps both night and day:
And they scourge the weak, and flog the fool,
  And gibe the old and gray,
And some grow mad, and all grow bad,
  And none a word may say.

Each narrow cell in which we dwell
  Is a foul and dark latrine,
And the fetid breath of living Death
  Chokes up each grated screen,
And all, but Lust, is turned to dust
  In Humanity's machine.

The brackish water that we drink
  Creeps with a loathsome slime,
And the bitter bread they weigh in scales
  Is full of chalk and lime,
And Sleep will not lie down, but walks
  Wild-eyed, and cries to Time.

But though lean Hunger and green Thirst
  Like asp and adder fight,
We have little care of prison fare,
  For what chills and kills outright
Is that every stone one lifts by day
  Becomes one's heart at night.

With midnight always in one's heart,
  And twilight in one's cell,
We turn the crank, or tear the rope,
  Each in his separate Hell,
And the silence is more awful far
  Than the sound of a brazen bell.

And never a human voice comes near
   To speak a gentle word:
And the eye that watches through the door
   Is pitiless and hard:
And by all forgot, we rot and rot,
   With soul and body marred.

And thus we rust Life's iron chain
   Degraded and alone:
And some men curse, and some men weep,
   And some men make no moan:
But God's eternal Laws are kind
   And break the heart of stone.

And every human heart that breaks,
   In prison-cell or yard,
Is as that broken box that gave
   Its treasure to the Lord,
And filled the unclean leper's house
   With the scent of costliest nard.

Ah! happy they whose hearts can break
   And peace of pardon win!
How else may man make straight his plan
   And cleanse his soul from Sin?
How else but through a broken heart
   May Lord Christ enter in?

And he of the swollen purple throat,
   And the stark and staring eyes,
Waits for the holy hands that took
   The Thief to Paradise;
And a broken and a contrite heart
   The Lord will not despise.

The man in red who reads the Law
   Gave him three weeks of life

Three little weeks in which to heal
  His soul of his soul's strife,
And cleanse from every blot of blood
  The hand that held the knife.

And with tears of blood he cleansed the hand,
  The hand that held the steel:
For only blood can wipe out blood,
  And only tears can heal:
And the crimson stain that was of Cain
  Became Christ's snow-white seal.

VI

In Reading gaol by Reading town
  There is a pit of shame,
And in it lies a wretched man
  Eaten by teeth of flame,
In a burning winding-sheet he lies,
  And his grave has got no name.

And there, till Christ call forth the dead,
  In silence let him lie:
No need to waste the foolish tear,
  Or heave a windy sigh:
The man had killed the thing he loved,
  And so he had to die.

And all men kill the thing they love,
  By all let this be heard,
Some do it with a bitter look,
  Some with a flattering word,
The coward does it with a kiss,
  The brave man with a sword!

EUGENE LEE–HAMILTON [1]

WHAT THE SONNET IS

Fourteen small broidered berries on the hem
  Of Circe's mantle, each of magic gold;
    Fourteen of lone Calypso's tears that roll'd
Into the sea, for pearls to come of them;

Fourteen clear signs of omen in the gem
  With which Medea human fate foretold;
    Fourteen small drops, which Faustus, growing old,
Craved of the Fiend, to water Life's dry stem.

It is the pure white diamond Dante brought
  To Beatrice, the sapphire Laura wore
When Petrarch cut it sparkling out of thought;

The ruby Shakespeare hewed from his heart's core;
  The dark, deep emerald that Rossetti wrought
For his own soul, to wear for evermore.

SONNET GOLD

We get it from Etruscan tombs, hid deep
  Beneath the passing ploughshare, or from caves
    Known but to Prospero, where pale-green waves
Have rolled the wreck-gold, which the mermaids keep

And from the caverns, where the gnomes up-heap
  The secret treasures, which the Earth's dwarf slaves
    Coin in her bosom, till the red gold paves
Her whole great heart, where only poets peep;

Or from old missals, where the gold defies
  Time's hand, in saints' bright aureoles, and keeps,
In angels' long straight trumpets, all its flash;

[1] These poems are from *Sonnets of the Wingless Hours*.

But chiefly from the crucible, where lies
    The alchemist's pure dream-gold. — While he sleeps
The poet steals it, leaving him the ash.

THE WAIFS OF TIME

When some great ship has long ago been wreck'd,
    And the repentant waves have long since laid
    Upon the beach the booty that they made,
And few remember still, and none expect,

The Sea will sometimes suddenly eject
    A lonely shattered waif, still undecayed,
    That tells of lives with which an old storm played,
In a carved name that greybeards recollect.

So ever and anon the soundless sea
    Which we call Time, casts up upon the strand
Some tardy waif from lost antiquity;

A stained maimed god, a faun with shattered hand,
    From Art's great wreck is suddenly set free,
And stands before us as immortals stand.

SUNKEN GOLD

In deep green depths rot ingot-laden ships;
    And gold doubloons, that from the drowned hand fell,
    Lie nestled in the ocean-flower's bell
With love's old gifts, once kissed by long-drowned lips;

And round some wrought gold cup the sea-grass whips,
    And hides lost pearls, near pearls still in their shell,
    Where sea-weed forests fill each ocean dell
And seek dim sunlight with their restless tips.

So lie the wasted gifts, the long-lost hopes
    Beneath the now hushed surface of myself,
In lonelier depths than where the diver gropes;

They lie deep, deep; but I at times behold
　In doubtful glimpses, on some reefy shelf,
The gleam of irrecoverable gold.

SEA–SHELL MURMURS

The hollow sea-shell which for years hath stood
　On dusty shelves, when held against the ear
　Proclaims its stormy parent; and we hear
The faint far murmur of the breaking flood.

We hear the sea.　The sea?　It is the blood
　In our own veins, impetuous and near,
　And pulses keeping pace with hope and fear
And with our feelings' every shifting mood.

Lo, in my heart I hear, as in a shell
　The murmur of a world beyond the grave,
Distinct, distinct, though faint and far it be.

Thou fool; this echo is a cheat as well, —
　The hum of earthly instincts; and we crave
A world unreal as the shell-heard sea.

ROMAN BATHS

There were some Roman baths where we spent hours:
　Immense and lonely courts of rock-like brick,
　All overgrown with verdure strong and thick,
And girding sweet wild lawns all full of flowers.

One day, beneath the turf, green with the showers
　Of all the centuries since Geneseric,
　They found rich pavements hidden by Time's trick,
Adorned with tritons, dolphins, doves like ours.

So, underneath the surface of To-day,
　Lies Yesterday, and what we call the Past,
The only thing which never can decay.

Things bygone are the only things that last:
  The Present is mere grass, quick-mown away;
The Past is stone, and stands for ever fast.

WAIFS OF A WORLD

Long ere Columbus in the breeze unfurled
  His venturous sail to hunt the setting sun,
  Long ere he fired his first exultant gun
Where strange canoes all round his flagship whirled,

The unsailed ocean which the west wind curled
  Had borne strange waifs to Europe, one by one;
  Wood carved by Indian hands, and trees like none
Which men then knew, from an untrodden world.

Oh for a waif from o'er the wider sea
  Whose margin is the grave, and where we think
A gem-bepebbled continent may be!

But all in vain we watch upon the brink;
  No waif floats up from black infinity,
Where all who venture out for ever sink.

EPILOGUE

I wrought them like a targe of hammered gold
  On which all Troy is battling round and round;
  Or Circe's cup, embossed with snakes that wound
Through buds and myrtles, fold on scaly fold;

Or like gold coins, which Lydian tombs may hold,
  Stamped with winged racers, in the old red ground;
  Or twined gold armlets from the funeral mound
Of some great viking, terrible of old.

I know not in what metal I have wrought;
  Nor whether what I fashion will be thrust
Beneath the clods that hide forgotten thought;

But if it is of gold it will not rust;
   And when the time is ripe it will be brought
Into the sun, and glitter through its dust.

ROBERT BRIDGES

A PASSER-BY

Whither, O splendid ship, thy white sails crowding,
   Leaning across the bosom of the urgent West,
That fearest nor sea rising, nor sky clouding,
   Whither away, fair rover, and what thy quest?
   Ah! soon, when Winter has all our vales opprest,
When skies are cold and misty, and hail is hurling,
   Wilt thou glide on the blue Pacific, or rest
In a summer haven asleep, thy white sails furling.

I there before thee, in the country that well thou knowest,
   Already arrived am inhaling the odorous air:
I watch thee enter unerringly where thou goest,
   And anchor queen of the strange shipping there,
   Thy sails for awnings spread, thy masts bare;
Nor is aught from the foaming reef to the snow-capped, grandest
   Peak, that is over the feathery palms more fair
Than thou, so upright, so stately, and still thou standest.

And yet, O splendid ship, unhailed and nameless,
   I know not if, aiming a fancy, I rightly divine
That thou hast a purpose joyful, a courage blameless,
   Thy port assured in a happier land than mine.
   But for all I have given thee, beauty enough is thine,
As thou, aslant with trim tackle and shrouding,
   From the proud nostril curve of a prow's line
In the offing scatterest foam, thy white sails crowding.

I HAVE LOVED FLOWERS THAT FADE

I have loved flowers that fade,
Within whose magic tents
Rich hues have marriage made
With sweet unmemoried scents:
A honeymoon delight, —
A joy of love at sight,
That ages in an hour: —
My song be like a flower!

I have loved airs, that die
Before their charm is writ
Along a liquid sky
Trembling to welcome it.
Notes, that with pulse of fire
Proclaim the spirit's desire,
Then die, and are nowhere: —
My song be like an air!

Die, song, die like a breath,
And wither as a bloom:
Fear not a flowery death,
Dread not an airy tomb!
Fly with delight, fly hence!
'Twas thine love's tender sense
To feast; now on thy bier
Beauty shall shed a tear.

A POPPY GROWS UPON THE SHORE

A poppy grows upon the shore,
  Bursts her twin cup in summer late:
Her leaves are glaucous-green and hoar,
  Her petals yellow, delicate.

Oft to her cousins turns her thought,
   In wonder if they care that she
Is fed with spray for dew, and caught
   By every gale that sweeps the sea.

She has no lovers like the red,
   That dances with the noble corn:
Her blossoms on the waves are shed,
   Where she stands shivering and forlorn.

I LOVE ALL BEAUTEOUS THINGS

I love all beauteous things,
   I seek and adore them;
God hath no better praise,
And man in his hasty days
   Is honoured for them.

I too will something make
   And joy in the making;
Altho' to-morrow it seem
Like the empty words of a dream
   Remembered on waking.

ELEGY

The wood is bare: a river-mist is steeping
   The trees that winter's chill of life bereaves:
Only their stiffened boughs break silence, weeping
      Over their fallen leaves;

That lie upon the dank earth brown and rotten,
   Miry and matted in the soaking wet:
Forgotten with the spring, that is forgotten
      By them that can forget.

Yet it was here we walked when ferns were springing,
  And through the mossy bank shot bud and blade: —
Here found in Summer, when the birds were singing,
      A green and pleasant shade.

'Twas here we loved in sunnier days and greener;
  And now, in this disconsolate decay,
I come to see her where I most have seen her,
      And touch the happier day.

For on this path, at every turn and corner,
  The fancy of her figure on me falls:
Yet walks she with the slow step of a mourner,
      Nor hears my voice that calls.

So through my heart there winds a track of feeling,
  A path of memory, that is all her own:
Whereto her phantom beauty ever stealing
      Haunts the sad spot alone.

About her steps the trunks are bare, the branches
  Drip heavy tears upon her downcast head;
And bleed from unseen wounds that no sun stanches,
      For the year's sun is dead.

And dead leaves wrap the fruits that summer planted:
  And birds that love the South have taken wing.
The wanderer, loitering o'er the scene enchanted,
      Weeps, and despairs of spring.

LONDON SNOW

When men were all asleep the snow came flying,
In large white flakes falling on the city brown,
Stealthily and perpetually settling and loosely lying,
  Hushing the latest traffic of the drowsy town;
Deadening, muffling, stifling its murmurs failing;
Lazily and incessantly floating down and down:
  Silently sifting and veiling road, roof and railing;

Hiding difference, making unevenness even,
Into angles and crevices softly drifting and sailing.
     All night it fell, and when full inches seven
It lay in the depth of its uncompacted lightness,
The clouds blew off from a high and frosty heaven;
     And all woke earlier for the unaccustomed brightness
Of the winter dawning, the strange unheavenly glare:
The eye marvelled — marvelled at the dazzling whiteness;
     The ear harkened to the stillness of the solemn air;
No sound of wheel rumbling nor of foot falling,
And the busy morning cries came thin and spare.
     Then boys I heard, as they went to school, calling,
They gathered up the crystal manna to freeze
Their tongues with tasting, their hands with snowballing;
     Or rioted in a drift, plunging up to the knees;
Or peering up from under the white-mossed wonder,
" O look at the trees! " they cried, " O look at the trees! "
With lessened load a few carts creak and blunder,
Following along the white deserted way,
A country company long dispersed asunder:
     When now already the sun, in pale display
Standing by Paul's high dome, spread forth below
His sparkling beams, and awoke the stir of the day.
     For now doors open, and war is waged with the snow;
And trains of sombre men, past tale of number,
Tread long brown paths, as toward their toil they go:
     But even for them awhile no cares encumber
Their minds diverted; the daily word is unspoken,
The daily thoughts of labour and sorrow slumber
At the sight of the beauty that greets them, for the charm
     they have broken.

TRIOLET

All women born are so perverse
No man need boast their love possessing.
If nought seem better, nothing's worse:
All women born are so perverse.

From Adam's wife, that proved a curse
Though God had made her for a blessing,
All women born are so perverse
No man need boast their love possessing.

ROSAMUND MARRIOTT WATSON

A SUMMER NIGHT

*Le vent qui vient à travers la montagne
Me rendra fou.*

The linden leaves are wet,
The gas-lights flare —
Deep yellow jewels set
In dusky air,
In dim air subtly sweet
With vanished rain.

Hush! — from the distant street
Again — again —
Life's music swells and falls,
Despairing — light —
Beyond my garden walls
This summer night.

Where do you call me, where?
O voice that cries!
O murky evening air,
What Paradise,
Unsought, unfound, unknown,
Inviteth me,
With faint night-odours blown?
With murmurous plea?

Future art thou, or Past?
Hope, or Regret?
My heart throbs thick and fast,
Mine eyes are wet,

For well and well I know
Thou hast no share,
Nor hence, nor long ago,
Nor anywhere.

RESURGAM

Though I am old, the world will still be young —
The spring wind breathes on slumbering memories,
The spring birds pipe amid my garden trees,
And dense and green the new year's grass hath sprung:
Ay, though my light is dimmed and my heart wrung
By pitiless eld's unsparing cruelties.

Ah, for that shore beyond the unsailed seas!
Where burns the Fire of Life with equal flame:
Where never sigheth song nor bringeth breeze
One whisper of the pride of youth's surcease,
The faded years' inevitable shame.

And yet — and yet — most sweet it is to know
That though my meagre days be withering,
Still shall be wrought the miracle of Spring,
That deep May nights shall bloom, and love-lamps glow,
Still shall the town's bright rapids swirl and flow,
The meteor troop of passions come and go;
That men shall love, and hate, and laugh, and sing.

I see my imperfection perfected,
My hampered hopes by stronger hearts set free,
My halting plans by others crowned and sped,
Whose feet shall find the paths I might not tread,
Whose clearer eyes the things I loved shall see: —
The sunlight gold — the shadow of the dawn —
The autumn evening's amber sorcery,
When o'er my head the veil of death is drawn
And all the waves of Night go over me.

And so I cannot but be comforted
To think how fair my world will always be,
That Youth and Spring revive eternally,
That abler hands shall labour in my stead,
And gay new ventures dare the hazardous sea:

Thus shall I live again though I be dead;
And all my soul is glad unspeakably.

EPITAPH

Now lay thee down to sleep, and dream of me;
  Though thou art dead and I am living yet,
Though cool thy couch and sweet thy slumbers be,
  Dream, — do not quite forget.

Sleep all the autumn, all the winter long,
  With never a painted shadow from the past
To haunt thee; only, when the blackbird's song
  Wakens the woods at last,

When the young shoots grow lusty overhead,
  Here, where the spring sun smiles, the spring wind
    grieves,
When budding violets close above thee spread
  Their small, heart-shapen leaves,

Pass, O Belovèd, to dreams from slumber deep;
  Recount the store that mellowing time endears,
Thread, through the measureless mazes of thy sleep,
  Our old, unchangeful years.

Lie still and listen — while the sheltering tree
  Whispers of suns that rose, of suns that set —
For far-off echoes of the Spring and me.
  Dream — do not quite forget.

MICHAEL FIELD

ACROSS A GAUDY ROOM

Across a gaudy room
I looked and saw his face,
Beneath the sapless palm-trees, in the gloom
Of the distressing place,
Where everyone sat tired,
Where talk itself grew stale,
Where, as the day began to fail,
No guest had just the power required
To rise and go: I strove with my disgust;
But at the sight of him my eyes were fired
To give one glance, as though they must
Be sociable with what they found of fair
And free and simple in a chamber where
Life was so base.

As when a star is lit
In the dull evening sky,
Another soon leaps out to answer it,
Even so the bright reply
Came sudden from his eyes,
By all but me unseen;
Since then the distance that between
Our lives unalterably lies
Is but a darkness, intimate and still,
Which messages may traverse, where replies
May sparkle from afar, until
The night becomes a mystery made clear
Between two souls forbidden to draw near:
Creator, why?

THE TRAGIC MARY QUEEN OF SCOTS

I could wish to be dead!
Too quick with life were the tears I shed,
Too sweet for tears is the life I led;

And ah, too lonesome my marriage-bed!
I could wish to be dead.

I could wish to be dead,
For just a word that rings in my head;
Too dear, too dear are the words he said,
They must never be rememberèd.
I could wish to be dead.

I could wish to be dead:
The wish to be loved is all mis-read,
And to love, one learns when one is wed,
Is to suffer bitter shame; instead
I could wish to be dead.

METE ME OUT MY LONELINESS

Come, mete me out my loneliness, O wind,
For I would know
How far the living who must stay behind
Are from the dead who go.

Eternal Passer-by, I feel there is
In thee a stir,
A strength to span the yawning distances
From her gravestone to her.

MARY E. COLERIDGE

"HE KNOWETH NOT THAT THE DEAD ARE THINE"

The weapon that you fought with was a word,
And with that word you stabbed me to the heart.
Not once but twice you did it, for the sword
Made no blood start.

They have not tried you for your life. You go
Strong in such innocence as men will boast.
They have not buried me. They do not know
    Life from its ghost.

JEALOUSY

" The myrtle bush grew shady
  Down by the ford." —
" Is it even so? " said my lady.
  " Even so! " said my lord.
" The leaves are set too thick together
For the point of a sword."

" The arras in your room hangs close,
  No light between!
You wedded one of those
  That see unseen." —
" Is it even so? " said the King's Majesty.
  " Even so! " said the Queen.

SELF–QUESTION

Is this wide world not large enough to fill thee,
  Nor Nature, nor that deep man's Nature, Art?
Are they too thin, too weak and poor to still thee,
  Thou little heart?

Dust art thou, and to dust again returnest,
  A spark of fire within a beating clod.
Should that be infinite for which thou burnest?
  Must it be God?

UNWELCOME

We were young, we were merry, we were very very wise,
  And the door stood open at our feast,
When there passed us a woman with the West in her eyes,
  And a man with his back to the East.

O, still grew the hearts that were beating so fast,
　The loudest voice was still.
The jest died away on our lips as they passed,
　And the rays of July struck chill.

The cups of red wine turned pale on the board,
　The white bread black as soot.
The hound forgot the hand of her lord,
　She fell down at his foot.

Low let me lie, where the dead dog lies,
　Ere I sit me down again at a feast,
When there passes a woman with the West in her eyes,
　And a man with his back to the East.

MARGARET L. WOODS

GAUDEAMUS IGITUR

Come, no more of grief and dying!
Sing the time too swiftly flying.
　　Just an hour
　　Youth's in flow'r,
Give me roses to remember
In the shadow of December.

Fie on steeds with leaden paces!
Winds shall bear us on our races.
　　Speed, O speed,
　　Wind, my steed!
Beat the lightning for your master,
Yet my Fancy shall fly faster.

Give me music, give me rapture!
Youth that's fled can none recapture,
　　Not with thought
　　Wisdom's bought.
Out on pride and scorn and sadness!
Give me laughter, give me gladness.

Sweetest Earth, I love and love thee,
Seas about thee, skies above thee,
 Sun and storms,
 Hues and forms
Of the clouds with floating shadows
On thy mountains and thy meadows.

Earth, there's none that can enslave thee,
Not thy lords it is that have thee;
 Not for gold
 Art thou sold,
But thy lovers at their pleasure
Take thy beauty and thy treasure.

While sweet fancies meet me singing,
While the April blood is springing
 In my breast,
 While a jest
And my youth yet must leave me,
Fortune, 'tis not thou canst grieve me.

When at length the grasses cover
Me, the world's unwearied lover,
 If regret
 Haunt me yet,
It shall be for joys untasted,
Nature lent and folly wasted.

Youth and jests and summer weather,
Goods that kings and clowns together
 Waste or use
 As they choose,
These, the best, we miss pursuing
Sullen shades that mock our wooing.

Feigning Age will not delay it —
When the reckoning comes we'll pay it,
 Own our mirth
 Has been worth

All the forfeit light or heavy
Wintry Time and Fortune levy.

Feigning grief will not escape it,
What though ne'er so well you ape it —
    Age and care
    All must share,
All alike must pay hereafter,
Some for sighs and some for laughter.

Know, ye sons of Melancholy,
To be young and wise is folly.
    'Tis the weak
    Fear to wreak
On this day of life their fancies,
Shaping battles, shaping dances.

While ye scorn our names unspoken,
Roses dead and garlands broken,
    O ye wise,
    We arise,
Out of failures, dreams, disasters,
We arise to be your masters.

THE MARINERS

The mariners sleep by the sea.
The wild wind comes up from the sea,
It wails round the tower, and it blows through the grasses,
It scatters the sand o'er the graves where it passes
And the sound and the scent of the sea.

The white waves beat up from the shore,
They beat on the church by the shore,
They rush round the grave-stones aslant to the leeward,
And the wall and the mariners' graves lying seaward,
That are bank'd with the stones from the shore.

For the huge sea comes up in the storm,
Like a beast from the lair of the storm,
To claim with its ravenous leap and to mingle
The mariners' bones with the surf and the shingle
That it rolls round the shore in the storm.

There is nothing beyond but the sky,
But the sea and the slow-moving sky,
Where a cloud from the grey lifts the gleam of its edges,
Where the foam flashes white from the shouldering ridges,
As they crowd on the uttermost sky.

The mariners sleep by the sea.
Far away there's a shrine by the sea;
The pale women climb up the path to it slowly,
To pray to our Lady of Storms ere they wholly
Despair of their men from the sea.

The children at play on the sand,
Where once from the shell-broider'd sand
They would watch for the sails coming in from far places,
Are forgetting the ships and forgetting the faces
Lying here, hid in the sand.

When at night there's a seething of surf,
The grandames look out o'er the surf,
They reckon their dead and their long years of sadness,
And they shake their lean fists at the sea and its madness,
And curse the white fangs of the surf.

But the mariners sleep by the sea.
They hear not the sound of the sea,
Nor the hum from the church where the psalm is uplifted,
Nor the crying of birds, that above them are drifted.
The mariners sleep by the sea.

WILLIAM WATSON [1]

LACHRYMAE MUSARUM

(6th October, 1892)

Low, like another's, lies the laurelled head:
The life that seemed a perfect song is o'er:
Carry the last great bard to his last bed.
Land that he loved, thy noblest voice is mute.
Land that he loved, that loved him! nevermore
Meadow of thine, smooth lawn or wild sea-shore,
Gardens of odorous bloom and tremulous fruit,
Or woodlands old, like Druid couches spread,
The master's feet shall tread.
Death's little rift hath rent the faultless lute:
The singer of undying songs is dead.

Lo, in this season pensive-hued and grave,
While fades and falls the doomed, reluctant leaf
From withered Earth's fantastic coronal,
With wandering sighs of forest and of wave
Mingles the murmur of a people's grief
For him whose leaf shall fade not, neither fall.
He hath fared forth, beyond these suns and showers.
For us, the autumn glow, the autumn flame,
And soon the winter silence shall be ours:
Him the eternal spring of fadeless fame
Crowns with no mortal flowers.

What needs his laurel our ephemeral tears,
To save from visitation of decay?
Not in this temporal light alone, that bay
Blooms, nor to perishable mundane ears
Sings he with lips of transitory clay.
Rapt though he be from us,

[1] The poems of William Watson are reprinted by permission of Dodd, Mead & Co., New York.

Virgil salutes him, and Theocritus;
Catullus, mightiest-brained Lucretius, each
Greets him, their brother, on the Stygian beach;
Proudly a gaunt right hand doth Dante reach;
Milton and Wordsworth bid him welcome home;
Keats, on his lips the eternal rose of youth,
Doth in the name of Beauty that is Truth
A kinsman's love beseech;
Coleridge, his locks aspersed with fairy foam,
Calm Spenser, Chaucer suave,
His equal friendship crave:
And godlike spirits hail him guest, in speech
Of Athens, Florence, Weimar, Stratford, Rome.

He hath returned to regions whence he came.
Him doth the spirit divine
Of universal loveliness reclaim.
All nature is his shrine.
Seek him henceforward in the wind and sea,
In earth's and air's emotion or repose,
In every star's august serenity,
And in the rapture of the flaming rose.
There seek him if ye would not seek in vain,
There, in the rhythm and music of the Whole;
Yea, and for ever in the human soul
Made stronger and more beauteous by his strain.

For lo! creation's self is one great choir,
And what is nature's order but the rhyme
Whereto in holiest unanimity
All things with all things move unfalteringly,
Infolded and communal from their prime?
Who shall expound the mystery of the lyre?
In far retreats of elemental mind
Obscurely comes and goes
The imperative breath of song, that as the wind
Is trackless, and oblivious whence it blows.

Demand of lilies wherefore they are white,
Extort her crimson secret from the rose,
But ask not of the Muse that she disclose
The meaning of the riddle of her might:
Somewhat of all things sealed and recondite,
Save the enigma of herself, she knows.
The master could not tell, with all his lore,
Wherefore he sang, or whence the mandate sped:
Ev'n as the linnet sings, so I, he said; —
Ah, rather as the imperial nightingale,
That held in trance the ancient Attic shore,
And charms the ages with the notes that o'er
All woodland chants immortally prevail!
And now, from our vain plaudits greatly fled,
He with diviner silence dwells instead,
And on no earthly sea with transient roar,
Unto no earthly airs, he trims his sail,
But far beyond our vision and our hail
Is heard for ever and is seen no more.

No more, O never now,
Lord of the lofty and the tranquil brow
Whereon nor snows of time
Have fall'n, nor wintry rime,
Shall men behold thee, sage and mage sublime.
Once, in his youth obscure,
The maker of this verse, which shall endure
By splendor of its theme that cannot die,
Beheld thee eye to eye,
And touched through thee the hand
Of every hero of thy race divine,
Ev'n to the sire of all the laurelled line,
The sightless wanderer on the Ionian strand,
With soul as healthful as the poignant brine,
Wide as his skies and radiant as his seas,
Starry from haunts of his Familiars nine,
Glorious Maeonides.

Yea, I beheld thee, and behold thee yet:
Thou hast forgotten, but can I forget?
The accents of thy pure and sovereign tongue,
Are they not ever goldenly impressed
On memory's palimpsest?
I see the wizard locks like night that hung,
I tread the floor thy hallowing feet have trod;
I see the hands a nation's lyre that strung,
The eyes that looked through life and gazed on God.

The seasons change, the winds they shift and veer;
The grass of yesteryear
Is dead; the birds depart, the groves decay:
Empires dissolve and peoples disappear:
Song passes not away.
Captains and conquerors leave a little dust,
And kings a dubious legend of their reign;
The swords of Caesars, they are less than rust:
The poet doth remain.
Dead is Augustus, Maro is alive;
And thou, the Mantuan of our age and clime,
Like Virgil shalt thy race and tongue survive,
Bequeathing no less honeyed words to time,
Embalmed in amber of eternal rhyme,
And rich with sweets from every Muse's hive;
While to the measure of the cosmic rune
For purer ears thou shalt thy lyre attune,
And heed no more the hum of idle praise
In that great calm our tumults cannot reach,
Master who crown'st our immelodious days
With flower of perfect speech.

" THE THINGS THAT ARE MORE EXCELLENT "

As we wax older on this earth,
  Till many a toy that charmed us seems
Emptied of beauty, stripped of worth,
  And mean as dust and dead as dreams, —

For gauds that perished, shows that passed,
 Some recompense the Fates have sent:
Thrice lovelier shine the things that last,
 The things that are more excellent.

Tired of the Senate's barren brawl,
 An hour with silence we prefer,
Where statelier rise the woods than all
 Yon towers of talk at Westminster.
Let this man prate and that man plot,
 On fame or place or title bent:
The votes of veering crowds are not
 The things that are more excellent.

Shall we perturb and vex our soul
 For "wrongs" which no true freedom mar,
Which no man's upright walk control,
 And from no guiltless deed debar?
What odds though tonguesters heal, or leave
 Unhealed, the grievance they invent?
To things, not phantoms, let us cleave —
 The things that are more excellent.

Nought nobler is, than to be free:
 The stars of heaven are free because
In amplitude of liberty
 Their joy is to obey the laws.
From servitude to freedom's *name*
 Free thou thy mind in bondage pent;
Depose the fetich, and proclaim
 The things that are more excellent.

And in appropriate dust be hurled
 That dull, punctilious god, whom they
That call their tiny clan the world,
 Serve and obsequiously obey:

Who con their ritual of Routine,
  With minds to one dead likeness blent,
And never ev'n in dreams have seen
  The things that are more excellent.

To dress, to call, to dine, to break
  No canon of the social code,
The little laws that lacqueys make,
  The futile decalogue of Mode; —
How many a soul for these things lives,
  With pious passion, grave intent!
While Nature careless-handed gives
  The things that are more excellent.

To hug the wealth ye cannot use,
  And lack the riches all may gain, —
O blind and wanting wit to choose,
  Who house the chaff and burn the grain!
And still doth life with starry towers
  Lure to the bright, divine ascent! —
Be yours the things ye would: be ours
  The things that are more excellent.

The grace of friendship — mind and heart
  Linked with their fellow heart and mind
The gains of science, gifts of art;
  The sense of oneness with our kind;
The thirst to know and understand —
  A large and liberal discontent:
These are the goods in life's rich hand,
  The things that are more excellent.

In faultless rhythm the ocean rolls,
  A rapturous silence thrills the skies;
And on this earth are lovely souls,
  That softly look with aidful eyes.

Though dark, O God, Thy course and track,
    I think Thou must at least have meant
That nought which lives should wholly lack
    The things that are more excellent.

STEPHEN PHILLIPS

MARPESSA [1]

Marpessa, being given by Zeus her choice between the god
Apollo and Idas a mortal, chose Idas.

Wounded with beauty in the summer night
Young Idas tossed upon his couch, and cried
" Marpessa, O Marpessa! " From the dark
The floating smell of flowers invisible,
The mystic yearning of the garden wet,
The moonless-passing night — into his brain
Wandered, until he rose and outward leaned
In the dim summer: 'twas the moment deep
When we are conscious of the secret dawn,
Amid the darkness that we feel is green.
To Idas had Marpessa been revealed,
Roaming with morning thoughts amid the dew,
All fresh from sleeping; and upon her cheek
The bloom of pure repose; like perfect fruit
Even at the moment was her beauty ripe.
The god Apollo from the heaven of heavens
Her mortal sweetness through the air allured;
And on this very noon she shall decide
'Twixt Idas and the god, take to herself
A brief or an eternal lover. So
When the long day that glideth without cloud,
The summer day, was at her blue deep hour
Of lilies musical with busy bliss,
When very light trembled as with excess,

[1] Reprinted by premission of Dodd, Mead & Co., New York.

And heat was frail, and every bush and flower
Was drooping in the glory overcome;
They three together met; on the one side,
Fresh with diffusing light on all the world
Apollo; on the other without sleep
Idas, and in the midst Marpessa stood.
Just as a flower after drenching rain,
So from the falling of felicity
Her human beauty glowed, and it was new;
The bee too near her bosom drowsed and dropped.
But as the god sprang to embrace her, they
Heard thunder, and a little afterward
The far Paternal voice, " Let her decide."
And as a flame blown backward by a gust,
Burned to and fro in fury beautiful
The murmuring god; but at the last he spoke,
And smiled as on his favourite western isle.
" Marpessa, though no trouble, nor any pain,
So is it willed, can touch me; but I live
For ever in a deep deliberate bliss,
A spirit sliding through tranquillity;
Yet when I saw thee I imagined woe,
That thou who art so fair shouldst ever taste
Of the earth-sorrow: for thy life has been
The history of a flower in the air,
Liable but to breezes and to time,
As rich and purposeless as is the rose:
Thy simple doom is to be beautiful.
Thee God created but to grow, not strive,
And not to suffer, merely to be sweet,
The favourite of his rains; and thou indeed
Lately upon the summer wast disclosed.
Child, wilt thou taste of grief?　On thee the hours
Shall feed, and bring thy soul into the dusk:
Even now thy face is hasting to the dark!
For slowly thou shalt cool to all things great,
And wisely smile at love; and thou shalt see

Beautiful Faith surrendering to Time,
The fierce ingratitude of children loved,
Ah, sting of stings!   A mourner shalt thou stand
At Passion's funeral in decent garb.
The greenly silent and cool-growing night
Shall be the time when most thou art awake,
With dreary eyes of all illusion cured,
Beside that stranger that thy husband is.
But if thou'lt live with me, then shalt thou bide
In mere felicity above the world,
In peace alive and moving, where to stir
Is ecstasy, and thrilling is repose.
What is the love of men that women seek it?
In its beginning pale with cruelty,
But having sipped of beauty, negligent,
And full of languor and distaste: for they
Seeking that perfect face beyond the world
Approach in vision earthly semblances,
And touch, and at the shadows flee away.
Then wilt thou die?   Part with eternal thoughts,
Lie without any hope beneath the grass,
All thy imaginations in the dust?
And all that tint and melody and breath,
Which in their lovely unison are thou,
To be dispersed upon the whirling sands!
Thy soul blown seaward on nocturnal blast!
O brief and breathing creature, wilt thou cease
Once having been?   Thy doom doth make thee rich,
And the low grave doth make thee exquisite.
But if thou'lt live with me, then will I kiss
Warm immortality into thy lips;
And I will carry thee above the world,
To share my ecstasy of flinging beams,
And scattering without intermission joy.
And thou shalt know that first leap of the sea
Toward me; the grateful upward look of earth,
Emerging roseate from her bath of dew, —

We two in heaven dancing, — Babylon
Shall flash and murmur, and cry from under us,
And Nineveh catch fire, and at our feet
Be hurled with her inhabitants, and all
Adoring Asia kindle and hugely bloom; —
We two in heaven running, — continents
Shall lighten, ocean unto ocean flash,
And rapidly laugh till all this world is warm.
Or since thou art a woman, thou shalt have
More tender tasks; to steal upon the sea,
A long expected bliss to tossing men
Or build upon the evening sky some wished
And glorious metropolis of cloud.
Thou shalt persuade the harvest and bring on
The deeper green; or silently attend
The fiery funeral of foliage old,
Connive with Time serene and the good hours.
Or, — for I know thy heart, — a dearer toil, —
To lure into the air a face long sick,
To gild the brow that from its dead looks up,
To shine on the unforgiven of this world;
With slow sweet surgery restore the brain,
And to dispel shadows and shadowy fear."
When he had spoken, humbly Idas said:
" After such argument what can I plead?
Or what pale promise make? Yet since it is
In women to pity rather than to aspire,
A little will I speak. I love thee then
Not only for thy body packed with sweet
Of all this world, that cup of brimming June,
That jar of violet wine set in the air,
That palest rose sweet in the night of life;
Nor for that stirring bosom all besieged
By drowsing lovers, or thy perilous hair;
Nor for that face that might indeed provoke
Invasion of old cities; no, nor all
Thy freshness stealing on me like strange sleep.

Not for this only do I love thee, but
Because Infinity upon thee broods;
And thou art full of whispers and of shadows.
Thou meanest what the sea has striven to say
So long, and yearnéd up the cliffs to tell;
Thou art what all the winds have uttered not,
What the still night suggesteth to the heart.
Thy voice is like to music heard ere birth,
Some spirit lute touched on a spirit sea;
Thy face remembered is from other worlds,
It has been died for, though I know not when,
It has been sung of, though I know not where.
It has the strangeness of the luring West,
And of sad sea-horizons; beside thee
I am aware of other times and lands,
Of birth far-back, of lives in many stars.
O beauty lone and like a candle clear
In this dark country of the world! Thou art
My woe, my early light, my music dying."
As he was speaking, she with lips apart
Breathed, and with dimmer eyes leaned through the air
As one in dream, and now his human hand
Took in her own; and to Apollo spoke:
" O gradual rose of the dim universe!
Whose warmth steals through the grave unto the dead,
Soul of the early sky, the priest of bloom!
Who beautifully goest in the West,
Attracting as to an eternal home
The yearning soul. Male of the female earth!
O eager bridegroom springing in this world
As in thy bed prepared! Fain would I know
Yon heavenly wafting through the heaven wide,
And the large view of the subjected seas,
And famous cities, and the various toil
Of men: all Asia at my feet spread out
In indolent magnificence of bloom!
Africa in her matted hair obscured,

And India in meditation plunged!
Then the delight of flinging the sunbeams,
Diffusing silent bliss; and yet more sweet, —
To cherish fruit on the warm wall; to raise
Out of the tomb to glory the pale wheat,
Serene ascension by the rain prepared;
To work with the benignly falling hours,
And beautiful slow Time. But dearest, this,
To gild the face that from its dead looks up,
To shine on the rejected, and arrive
To women that remember in the night;
Or mend with sweetest surgery the mind.
And yet, forgive me if I can but speak
Most human words. Of immortality
Thou singest: thou would'st hold me from the ground,
And this just opening beauty from the grave.
As yet I have known no sorrow; all my days
Like perfect lilies under water stir,
And God has sheltered me from his own wind;
The darling of his breezes have I been.
Yet as to one inland, that dreameth lone,
Sea-faring men with their sea-weary eyes,
Round the inn-fire tell of some foreign land;
So agéd men, much tossed about in life,
Have told me of that country, Sorrow far.
How many goodly ships at anchor lie
Within her ports; even to me indeed
Hath a sea-rumour through the night been borne.
And I myself remember, and have heard,
Of men that did believe, women that loved
That were unhappy long and now are dead,
With wounds that no eternity can close,
Life had so marked them: or of others who
Panted toward their end, and fell on death
Even as sobbing runners breast the rope.
And most I remember of all human things
My mother; often as a child I pressed

My face against her cheek, and felt her tears;
Even as she smiled on me, her eyes would fill,
Until my own grew ignorantly wet;
And I in silence wondered at sorrow.
When I remember this, how shall I know
That I myself may not, by sorrow taught,
Accept the perfect stillness of the ground?
Where, though I lie still, and stir not at all,
Yet shall I irresistibly be kind,
Helplessly sweet, a wandering garden bliss.
My ashes shall console and make for peace;
This mind that injured, be an aimless balm.
Or if there be some other world, with no
Bloom, neither rippling sound, nor early smell,
Nor leaves, nor pleasant exchange of human speech;
Only a dreadful pacing to and fro
Of spirits meditating on the sun;
A land of baréd boughs and grieving wind;
Yet would I not forego the doom, the place,
Whither my poets and my heroes went
Before me; warriors that with deeds forlorn
Saddened my youth, yet made it great to live;
Lonely antagonists of Destiny,
That went down scornful before many spears,
Who soon as we are born, are straight our friends;
And live in simple music, country songs,
And mournful ballads by the winter fire.
Since they have died; their death is ever mine;
I would not lose it. Then thou speak'st of joy,
Of immortality without one sigh,
Existence without tears for evermore.
Thou would'st preserve me from the anguish, lest
This holy face into the dark return.
Yet I being human, human sorrow miss.
The half of music, I have heard men say,
Is to have grieved; when comes the lonely wail
Over the mind; old men have told it me

Subdued after long life by simple sounds.
The mourner is the favourite of the moon,
And the departing sun his glory owes
To the eternal thoughts 'of creatures brief,
Who think the thing that they shall never see.
Since we must die, how bright the starry track!
How wonderful in a bereavéd ear
The Northern wind; how strange the summer night,
The exhaling earth to those who vainly love.
Out of our sadness have we made this world
So beautiful; the sea sighs in our brain,
And in our heart that yearning of the moon.
To all this sorrow was I born, and since
Out of a human womb I came, I am
Not eager to forego it; I would scorn
To elude the heaviness and take the joy,
For pain came with the sap, pangs with the bloom:
This is the sting, the wonder. Yet should I
Linger beside thee in felicity,
Sliding with open eyes through liquid bliss
For ever; still I must grow old. Ah I
Should ail beside thee, Apollo, and should note
With eyes that would not be, but yet are dim,
Ever so slight a change from day to day
In thee my husband; watch thee 'nudge thyself
To little offices that once were sweet:
Slow where thou once wert swift, remembering
To kiss those lips which once thou couldst not leave.
I should expect thee by the Western bay,
Faded, not sure of thee, with desperate smiles,
And pitiful devices of my dress
Or fashion of my hair: thou wouldst grow kind;
Most bitter to a woman that was loved.
I must ensnare thee to my arms, and touch
Thy pity, to but hold thee to my heart.
But if I live with Idas, then we two
On the low earth shall prosper hand in hand

In odours of the open field, and live
In peaceful noises of the farm, and watch
The pastoral fields burned by the setting sun.
And he shall give me passionate children, not
Some radiant god that will despise me quite,
But clambering limbs and little hearts that err.
And I shall sleep beside him in the night,
And fearful from some dream shall touch his hand
Secure; or at some festival we two
Will wander through the lighted city streets;
And in the crowd I'll take his arm and feel
Him closer for the press. So shall we live.
And though the first sweet sting of love be past,
The sweet that almost venom is; though youth,
With tender and extravagant delight,
The first and secret kiss by twilight hedge,
The insane farewell repeated o'er and o'er,
Pass off; there shall succeed a faithful peace;
Beautiful friendship tried by sun and wind,
Durable from the daily dust of life.
And though with sadder, still with kinder eyes,
We shall behold all frailties, we shall haste
To pardon, and with mellowing minds to bless.
Then though we must grow old, we shall grow old
Together, and he shall not greatly miss
My bloom faded, and waning light of eyes,
Too deeply gazed in ever to seem dim;
Nor shall we murmur at, nor much regret
The years that gently bend us to the ground,
And gradually incline our face; that we
Leisurely stooping, and with each slow step,
May curiously inspect our lasting home.
But we shall sit with luminous holy smiles,
Endeared by many griefs, by many a jest,
And custom sweet of living side by side;
And full of memories not unkindly glance
Upon each other. Last, we shall descend

Into the natural ground — not without tears —
One must go first, ah god! one must go first;
After so long one blow for both were good;
Still like old friends, glad to have met, and leave
Behind a wholesome memory on the earth.
And thou, beautiful god, in that far time,
When in thy setting sweet thou gazest down
On this grey head, wilt thou remember then
That once I pleased thee, that I once was young? "
When she had spoken, Idas with one cry
Held her, and there was silence; while the god
In anger disappeared. Then slowly they,
He looking downward, and she gazing up,
Into the evening green wandered away.

CHRONOLOGY

Chronology of the more important works in drama, novel,
and poetry that appeared during the Nineties

1890

KATHARINE TYNAN HINKSON: Ballads and Lyrics
HENRY JAMES: The Tragic Muse
RUDYARD KIPLING: Life's Handicap
GEORGE MOORE: Impressions and Opinions
JAMES WHISTLER: The Gentle Art of Making Enemies

1891

JAMES BARRIE: The Little Minister
A. CONAN DOYLE: The Adventures of Sherlock Holmes
GEORGE GISSING: New Grub Street
THOMAS HARDY: Tess of the D'Urbervilles
KATHARINE TYNAN HINKSON: Ballads and Lyrics
RUDYARD KIPLING: The Light That Failed
GEORGE MOORE: Modern Painting
WILLIAM SHARP: Sospiri di Roma
G. B. SHAW: The Quintessence of Ibsenism
ROSAMUND MARRIOTT WATSON: A Summer Night and Other Poems
    J. T. Grein's Independent Theatre

1892

GEORGE GISSING: Born in Exile
W. E. HENLEY: London Voluntaries
RUDYARD KIPLING: Barrack Room Ballads and Other Verses
G. B. SHAW: Widowers' Houses
ARTHUR SYMONS: Silhouettes
WILLIAM WATSON: Lachrymae Musarum
OSCAR WILDE: Lady Windermere's Fan
W. B. YEATS: The Countess Cathleen
ISRAEL ZANGWILL: Children of the Ghetto

1893

HUBERT CRACKANTHORPE: Wreckage
JOHN DAVIDSON: Fleet Street Eclogues (first series)
GEORGE GISSING: The Odd Women
MICHAEL FIELD: Under the Bough
JOHN GRAY: Silverpoints
HENRY HARLAND: Mademoiselle Miss and Other Stories

RUDYARD KIPLING: Many Inventions
ARTHUR W. PINERO: The Second Mrs. Tanqueray
DORA SIGERSON SHORTER: Verses
FRANCIS THOMPSON: Poems
ROSAMUND MARRIOTT WATSON: Vespertilia and Other Verses
OSCAR WILDE: A Woman of No Importance
ISRAEL ZANGWILL: Ghetto Tragedies

1894

A. E.: Homeward Songs by the Way
ROBERT BRIDGES: Shorter Poems (collected edition)
JOHN DAVIDSON: Ballads and Songs
GEORGE EGERTON: Discords
THOMAS HARDY: Life's Little Ironies
ROBERT HICHENS: The Green Carnation
KATHARINE TYNAN HINKSON: Cuckoo Songs
ANTHONY HOPE: The Prisoner of Zenda
NORA HOPPER: Ballads in Prose
H. A. JONES: The Case of Rebellious Susan
RUDYARD KIPLING: The First Jungle Book
EUGENE LEE-HAMILTON: Sonnets of the Wingless Hours
GEORGE MOORE: Esther Waters
ARTHUR MORRISON: Tales of Mean Streets
G. B. SHAW: Arms and the Man
WILLIAM WATSON: Odes and Other Poems
OSCAR WILDE: Salome
W. B. YEATS: The Land of Heart's Desire
    The Yellow Book (established)

1895

GRANT ALLEN: The Woman Who Did
LAURENCE BINYON: London Visions, Book I.
JOSEPH CONRAD: Almayer's Folly
GEORGE DU MAURIER: Trilby
HENRY HARLAND: Grey Roses
LIONEL JOHNSON: Poems
RUDYARD KIPLING: The Second Jungle Book
ARTHUR W. PINERO: The Notorious Mrs. Ebbsmith
                The Benefit of the Doubt
G. B. SHAW: Candida
ARTHUR SYMONS: London Nights
FRANCIS THOMPSON: Sister Songs
OSCAR WILDE: An Ideal Husband
            The Importance of Being Earnest
W. B. YEATS: Poems

1896

JAMES BARRIE: Sentimental Tommy
MAX BEERBOHM: Works

MARY E. COLERIDGE: Fancy's Following
JOHN DAVIDSON: Fleet Street Eclogues (second series)
ERNEST DOWSON: Verses
THOMAS HARDY: Jude the Obscure
NORA HOPPER: Under Quicken Boughs
A. E. HOUSMAN: A Shropshire Lad
LAURENCE HOUSMAN: Green Arras
W. W. JACOBS: Many Cargoes
H. A. JONES: Michael and His Lost Angel
RUDYARD KIPLING: The Seven Seas
FIONA MACLEOD: From the Hills of Dream
GEORGE MOORE: Evelyn Innes
MARGARET WOODS: Aeromancy
    The Savoy

1897

A. E.: The Earth Breath
JOSEPH CONRAD: The Nigger of the Narcissus
GEORGE GISSING: The Whirlpool
HENRY JAMES: The Spoils of Poynton
          What Maisie Knew
LIONEL JOHNSON: Ireland and Other Poems
H. A. JONES: The Liars
HENRY NEWBOLT: Admirals All
STEPHEN PHILLIPS: Poems
G. B. SHAW: The Devil's Disciple
ARTHUR SYMONS: Amoris Victima
FRANCIS THOMPSON: New Poems

1898

LAURENCE BINYON: London Visions, Book II
JOSEPH CONRAD: Tales of Unrest
THOMAS HARDY: Wessex Poems and Other Verses
KATHARINE TYNAN HINKSON: The Wind in the Trees
LAURENCE HOUSMAN: Spikenard
RUDYARD KIPLING: The Day's Work
G. B. SHAW: Mrs. Warren's Profession (published)
          You Never Can Tell (published)
WILLIAM WATSON: Collected Poems
OSCAR WILDE: The Ballad of Reading Gaol

1899

JOHN DAVIDSON: The Last Ballad and Other Poems
ERNEST DOWSON: Decorations
HENRY JAMES: The Awkward Age
RUDYARD KIPLING: Stalky and Co.
STEPHEN PHILLIPS: Paolo and Francesca
ARTHUR W. PINERO: The Gay Lord Quex

BIOGRAPHICAL NOTICES

A. E. (G. W. Russell) was born in County Armagh, Ireland, in 1867. In 1874 he went to Dublin with his parents and attended school there, but did not go to the University. He began his career in business, but his real interests were art and mysticism. He soon became one of the most active and influential members of the Dublin Theosophical Society. Though A. E. has painted pictures and written poetry, the greater part of his activity has been devoted to the improvement, by means of coöperative societies, of the agricultural and economic conditions of Ireland. He has been editor, since 1904, of the *Irish Homestead,* and has written much on political and economic subjects.

There is a study of A. E., as economist rather than as mystic, by Darrell Figgs. A. E. is also one of the leading characters in George Moore's *Hail and Farewell.*

BEARDSLEY, AUBREY, was born at Brighton in 1872, and received his earliest education there, in a private school. When four years old he drew, and not long afterward he was playing the piano. In his twelfth year he played at public concerts. Between 1888 and 1890, having removed to London, he worked for brief periods in an architect's office and for a life insurance company. About 1890 he became known to a small group of friends for his very original drawings. He was encouraged to take up art as a profession. In that field he soon created a furore. Some of his best work was contributed to the *Yellow Book* and the *Savoy.* He worked with tremendous energy, driven on, perhaps, by the presentiment of premature death, for he always suffered from weak lungs. The condition of his health obliged him to spend the winter of 1896–97 at Bournemouth, and sent him, in the latter part of 1897, to southern France, where he died (at Mentone) in the spring of 1898. He was converted to Roman Catholicism about a year before his death. He wrote but little verse, but he always cherished an ambition in that direction and took great pains with what he did write.

There are memoirs by Arthur Symons (1905) and by Robert Ross (1908).

BINYON, LAURENCE, was born in 1869. He was educated at St. Paul's School and Oxford University. He is the assistant keeper of the Department of Prints and Drawings in the British Museum.

BRIDGES, ROBERT, was born in 1844. He was educated at Eton and Oxford. He then studied medicine at St. Bartholomew's Hospital, London, but retired from the profession in 1882. Since then he has devoted himself chiefly to literature. He was appointed Poet Laureate in 1913, to succeed Alfred Austin.

CHATTOPADHYAY, SAROJINI, contributed the poem entitled " Eastern Dancers " to the *Savoy*.

COLERIDGE, MARY E., was born at Hyde Park, London, in 1861. Her grandfather was the son of James Coleridge, elder brother of Samuel Taylor Coleridge, the poet. She was educated at home. The poems which she published during her lifetime — few in number — were either unsigned or signed with a pseudonym, as she feared to tarnish the name of her illustrious ancestor. She died in London, unmarried, in 1907. In the same year her published and unpublished poems were collected and edited by Henry Newbolt. In addition to writing verse, she wrote various articles and reviews for London newspapers and periodicals, and several novels.

DAVIDSON, JOHN, was born at Barrhead, Renfrewshire, Scotland, in 1857. His father was a minister of the Evangelical Union. His early education was very irregular, and his attendance at Edinburgh University was cut short by the necessity of teaching. After several years of teaching in various schools he was dismissed from his position for asking an increase in pay, and went up to London (1890) to make his way in literature. He found the way difficult, as many had done before. He had some success with his " Ballads " and " Fleet Street Eclogues," but his literary plays were not produced, and the foreign plays which he translated for the stage had slight success. He became embittered by his struggle against poverty, ill health, and neglect. In 1906 he was awarded a pension of £100 a year, and in 1908 he went to live in Penzance. But he was still unable to provide for his family or to reconcile himself to his fate. One day, in the spring of 1909, he left home and did not return. Several months later his body was found drowned. The circumstances indicated suicide.

DOUGLAS, LORD ALFRED, was born in 1870. He came into notoriety through his association with Oscar Wilde. He has published several volumes of verse.

DOWSON, ERNEST, was born in Kent in 1867. A large part of his early life was spent abroad, and he did not stay at Oxford long enough to take his degree. After leaving Oxford (1887) he lived a few years in London. He belonged to the Rhymers' Club, but was too reserved to form intimacies with his associates. He fell in love with the daughter of a humble restaurateur, and for two years paid her an eager though shy courtship, but she married a waiter. This was a blow to Dowson, whose affection for the girl had been profound. Lacking the moral and physical strength to combat his various misfortunes, he sank into dissipation and became increasingly morbid and reserved. He died in 1900, a convert to Roman Catholicism.

FIELD, MICHAEL, was the pseudonym of two ladies, Katharine Harris Bradley and her niece, Edith Emma Cooper. They lived together many years and published several volumes of verse. They died, both of cancer, within a year of one another, Miss Cooper in 1913, Miss Bradley in 1914. They had been received into the Roman Catholic Church. A study of Michael Field has been published, by Mary Sturgeon (1922).

GRAY, JOHN, lived in London in the early nineties, a friend of English æsthetes and decadents, and an admirer and imitator of French decadent poetry. He was one of the permanent guests of the Rhymers' Club. In the later nineties he entered the priesthood, and has spent his life in Liverpool.

GREENE, G. A., was born of Anglo-Irish stock in Florence in 1853. He was educated in Florence, and later at Dublin University. After spending several years as professor of English literature in the Alexandria College, Dublin, he went to London, and became one of the leaders of the Irish literary movement there. He contributed to the two volumes of the Rhymers' Club. He has translated a volume of modern Italian poetry, entitled *Italian Lyrists of Today*, and has published a collection of sonnets entitled *Dantesques, A Sonnet Companion to the Inferno*.

HARDY, THOMAS, was born in Dorsetshire in 1840. He was educated at local schools and by private tutors and attended King's College, London, for a time. He first chose architecture as a profession and won some distinction in his studies, but about 1868 literature began to get the better of architecture. He practised verse in his early years, but gave it up in his mid-career of prose, only to return to it in his later years. He has lived his life near Dorchester and is intimately acquainted with the region called Wessex in his novels. There are studies of Hardy by Lionel Johnson (1894), L. Abercrombie (1912), and E. Brennecke (1925).

HENLEY, WILLIAM ERNEST, was born in Gloucester in 1849. He was educated at local schools. A tubercular affection attacked him about the age of twelve. One foot had to be amputated, and the other leg was condemned. To prevent a second amputation, Henley went to the Edinburgh Infirmary, where Dr. Lister was coming into fame. Henley's instinctive faith in Lister was justified, for the leg was saved. It was while Henley was in the Infirmary that R. L. Stevenson was brought to meet him, and so began a famous literary friendship. In 1877 Henley went to London and entered journalism. He was editor, in the early nineties, of the *National Observer,* a journal which had a small circulation but a large and distinguished list of contributors. He dominated a group of younger writers who in turn were very loyal to him. His literary evenings were often the scene of brilliant conversation. In spite f his precarious health, Henley was vigorous and energetic; but his " indomitable soul " was at last broken by the death of his s t-year-old daughter Margaret, in 1894. He died in 1903.

HILLIER, A. C., contributed to the secor d volume of the Rhymers' Club but published no independen volume.

HINKSON, KATHARINE TYNAN, was born in Dublin in 1861. Her early education was received at the Dominican convent of Siena, Drogheda; but she left the convent at the age of fourteen, and received the rest of her education at home. In 1893 she married H. A. Hinkson, and since then she has lived in or near London. She has published several volumes of reminiscences and numerous volumes of poems and stories.

HOPPER, NORA, was born in Exeter in 1871. In 1901 she married W. H. Chesson. She died in 1906.

HOUSMAN, A. E., was born in 1859. He was educated at Oxford and has been professor of Latin, first at University College, London, later at Cambridge University.

HOUSMAN, LAURENCE, was born in 1867. He is a brother of
A. E. Housman. He is an illustrator as well as an author. He
has published numerous volumes of prose and verse.

JOHNSON, LIONEL, was born at Broadstairs, Kent, in 1867.
He was educated at Winchester and Oxford. He was one of
the three or four most influential members of the Rhymers'
Club, being a distinguished talker and a marvelous reader of
poetry. He was also active in the Irish literary movement in
London. In spite of these apparent activities he led an extremely secluded life, though he sometimes took long rambles in
the country. In 1891 he was received into the Church of Rome.
He died in 1902.

KIPLING, RUDYARD, was born in Bombay in 1865. He went
to England for his education, which he received at the United
Services College, in North Devon. At the age of seventeen he
returned to India, where he became sub-editor of the *Lahore
Civil and Military Gazette.* In that journal his earliest poems
and stories were published. With the beginnings of literary
success he again went to England, and has spent the most of
his life there.

LE GALLIENNE, RICHARD, was born in Liverpool in 1866. He
was educated at Liverpool College. After spending seven years
in business he abandoned it for literature and settled in London.
He came to the United States in the early nineteen-hundreds
and has lived in or near New York.

LEE-HAMILTON, EUGENE, was born in London in 1845. He
was educated in France and Germany and at Oxford University.
He entered the diplomatic service, but his career was cut short
in 1875 by an illness which rendered him incapable of any
physical exertion and continued for about twenty years. These
years were spent in Florence. He consoled himself by writing
verse ("Sonnets of the Wingless Hours" were written between
1880 and 1888) and by receiving company. In 1896 he recovered, and in 1898 he married. A daughter was born in 1903,
but died the following year. The father's depression culminated
in his death, in 1907.

MEYNELL, ALICE CHRISTINA THOMPSON, was born in 1850.
She was the daughter of Thomas J. Thompson, an intimate
friend of Charles Dickens. The Thompsons lived much abroad,
especially in Italy. While a girl Miss Thompson went over to

the Church of Rome and was followed by other members of the family. In 1877 she married Wilfrid Meynell, a well-known Catholic journalist. The Meynells rescued Francis Thompson from the streets and looked after him as long as' he lived. Mrs. Meynell died in 1922. A study of her by Anne Kimball Tuell (1925) is chiefly devoted to her prose.

O'NEILL, MOIRA. In the preface to the *Songs of the Glens of Antrim* it is stated that these songs " were written by a Glenswoman in the dialect of the Glens, and chiefly for the pleasure of other Glens-people."

PHILLIPS, STEPHEN, was born at Somertown, near Oxford, in 1868. He entered Queens College, Cambridge, but soon left it to join his cousin, F. R. Benson's company of Shakespearean players. He remained with this company six years. He then adopted literature as a profession and produced a succession of poems and poetic dramas which were much read in the nineties and early nineteen-hundreds. He died in 1915.

PLARR, VICTOR, was a member of the Rhymers' Club and published a volume of verse, but his life-work has been as librarian of the Royal College of Surgeons.

ROLLESTON, T. W., was born in King's County, Ireland, in 1857. He was educated at St. Columba's College, near Dublin, and at Dublin University. He has published some scholarly works besides some verse in the two volumes of the Rhymers' Club and in London periodicals.

SHARP, WILLIAM, was born in Paisley, Renfrewshire, Scotland, in 1856. His early life was spent chiefly in the west Highlands of Scotland. He attended Glasgow University and then went to Australia in search of health. He returned again to London (1879), but was obliged, on account of his health, to spend his winters abroad. Under his own name he published poems, criticisms, and biographies. Under the pseudonym of Fiona Macleod he expressed, from 1894 onward, the more romantic side of his nature. In that work he let his Celtic imagination roam in the regions of Celtic myth and Celtic mood. The secret of Fiona Macleod's identity was kept until the end (1905).

SHORTER, DORA SIGERSON, was the daughter of Dr. George Sigerson, one of the leaders of the Gaelic revival. She married Clement Shorter, a well-known journalist and biographer.

STEVENSON, ROBERT LOUIS, was born in Edinburgh in 1850. After an irregular preparation he entered Edinburgh University, which he attended from 1867 to 1873. He was expected to follow the family profession of engineering, but broke away to devote himself to literature. His health always being precarious, he sought relief in various climes, and spent his last years in Samoa. He died in 1894.

SYMONS, ARTHUR, was born of Cornish parentage in Wales in 1865. He attended several private schools. He has spent a great deal of time on the Continent, especially in Paris, where he became acquainted with many of the French poets. T. Earle Welby is the author of a study of Symons (1926).

THOMPSON, FRANCIS, was born at Preston, Lancashire, in 1859. His father was a physician. The boy was educated at Ushaw College, near Durham, and hoped to enter the priesthood but was advised against it. He then studied medicine at Owens College, Manchester, and was expected to adopt his father's profession; but he broke with his family over this matter and went up to London, where he lived for a time in dreadful poverty. The misery of his condition was deepened by the acquisition of the opium habit. He was discovered and rescued by Wilfrid and Alice Meynell. His health remained feeble, and he died of tuberculosis in 1907.

TODHUNTER, JOHN, was born in Dublin in 1839. His parents were Quakers, and he was educated at Quaker schools. At sixteen he was placed in a mercantile establishment, but got free of it and entered Dublin University, where he took the degrees of B.A. and M.D. He practised medicine for a few years but gave it up to devote himself to literature. His later years were spent in London. He died in 1916.

WATSON, ROSAMUND MARRIOTT, was the wife of H. B. Marriott Watson, a London journalist, novelist, and short-story writer. She was born in 1863 and died in 1911.

WATSON, WILLIAM, was born in Yorkshire in 1858. His early work won much praise. He was knighted in 1917.

WILDE, OSCAR, was born at Dublin in 1856. He attended Oxford University and won a great reputation there as an "æsthete," a reputation which was soon spread far and wide. His plays are his most important work. He spent two years in

Reading Gaol, out of which experience the " Ballad " came. He died in Paris in 1900.

Woods, Margaret L., was born at Rugby in 1856. Her father, an assistant master of Rugby from 1846 to 1858, was distinguished as a scholar and divine. She married H. G. Woods, who has been president of Trinity College, Oxford, and Master of the Temple, London.

Yeats, William Butler, was born at Sandymount, Dublin, in 1865. His father, John Butler Yeats, was an artist. The greater part of his childhood was spent in Sligo, in close touch with nature and fairy lore. This period of his life is the subject of his *Reveries over Childhood and Youth.* He was educated partly in Dublin, partly in London, and studied art as well as literature. His first ambition was to found a national poetry for Ireland. This failing, he worked with Lady Gregory and others toward the establishment of a national theatre, but this movement also failed. In 1917 he married. He now lives in Ireland. There is a study of Yeats by Forrest Reid (1915).

INDEX OF AUTHORS

INDEX OF POEMS